G. F. Scott (George Francis Scott) Elliot

A Naturalist in Mid-Africa

Being an Account of a Journey to the Mountains of the Moon and...

G. F. Scott (George Francis Scott) Elliot

A Naturalist in Mid-Africa

Being an Account of a Journey to the Mountains of the Moon and...

ISBN/EAN: 9783744799676

Printed in Europe, USA, Canada, Australia, Japan

Cover: Foto ©Andreas Hilbeck / pixelio.de

More available books at **www.hansebooks.com**

A NATURALIST

IN

MID-AFRICA

BEING AN ACCOUNT OF

*A JOURNEY TO THE MOUNTAINS OF THE
MOON AND TANGANYIKA*

BY

G. F. SCOTT ELLIOT, M.A., F.L.S., F.R.G.S.

LONDON
A. D. INNES & CO
BEDFORD STREET
1896

To

MY FORMER PRECEPTOR,

PROFESSOR PATRICK GEDDES,

THIS RESULT OF A MOST INCONVENIENT LOVE

OF BOTANY IS VERY RESPECTFULLY

DEDICATED.

PREFACE.

It is a pleasure as well as a duty to begin this work by an attempt to show the indebtedness of which I am fully conscious to the many who have assisted me directly and indirectly in the preparation of this work.

If it had not been for the care and hospitality of Captain Gibb, the French Fathers in Buddu and on Tanganyika, Mr. Law, Mr. Heard, and the late Dr. Scott in British Central Africa, I should certainly not have survived the expedition.

In the preparation of it, I must express my thanks first to Mr. A. D. Innes for the numerous suggestions and revisions that have shaped my rough-hewn manuscripts. Dr. Gregory should have the credit of much of the geological portion, and Mr. Butler and Mr. Murray have given me two lists which are now printed in the Appendix.

In the preparation of the illustrations, I have to thank first Mr. J. Thomson, to whose excellent teaching the photographs are really due; and I have also to thank the London Stereoscopic Company, Messrs. Gunn and Stuart, Mr. Percy B. Highley, and Mr. B. F. Anderson for the preparation of prints and drawings from materials so bad that the results are sufficiently astonishing to myself. The conditions under which my photographs were taken scarcely gave them a fair chance. The original negatives have not been in any way interfered with; although it would have in many cases been easy to make an infinitely more attractive picture by touching up and redrawing, it seemed to me preferable to reproduce the picture as it appeared.

Dr. Mill and Dr. Günther have most kindly permitted me to make use of the plates reproduced in Figs. 31 and 12, and I have to express my thanks to them, as well as to the publishers.

I have also to thank Mr. Coles for the instruction which has resulted in the map now produced for the first time. The Royal Geographical Society very kindly prepared a map from my materials for their October Journal. I could not utilise this map for my own work, as several inaccuracies were retained in deference to a more recognised authority than myself. I have therefore had a new map produced, in which some of these are corrected for the first time, though unfortunately in a very hurried manner.

G. F. SCOTT ELLIOT.

CONTENTS.

CHAPTER I.

MOMBASA TO KIKUYU.

Reason of expedition—Royal Society grant—At Mombasa—Imperial British East African Company—Thorn-tree desert—Mkuyuni—Difficulties with porters—Ukambani—Formation of forest and steppes—Wakamba customs—Products—Cultivation—Hartebeest—Kikuyu . . . . pp. 1-22

CHAPTER II.

KIKUYU TO THE VICTORIA.

Donkey caravan—Masai Elmoran, camps and travelling—Future of Masai and their country—A stampede of cattle—Wandarobbo—The firestick—The Mau forest—Valleys in the Nile drainage area—Jackson's hartebeest . . . . pp. 23-35

CHAPTER III.

THE VICTORIA REGION; INCLUDING UGANDA.

The Nandi hills—Kavirondo—Native rotation of crops—Villages—Samia iron mines—The area and characteristics of the Victoria region—Uganda—Sinking of the Nyanza level—Consequent character of valleys—Alluvium—Papyrus swamps—Ridges—Fertile places—Forests—Climate—Banana—Wheat—Rice—Coffee—Tobacco—Cotton—Cattle—Horses . . . pp. 36-51

CONTENTS.

CHAPTER IV.

THE WAGANDA AND TRAVELLING EXPERIENCES.

The Waganda—Their feudal system—Effects on labour—Currency—Customs—Origin of the race—Wahima—Demand for European goods—Number of Europeans required—Stations suggested—On the march—Crossing swamps—Forests—A day's work—Kampala—The Unyoro campaign—Taratibu . . . . . pp. 52–68

CHAPTER V.

ANKOLE AND KARAGWE.

The first view of Kagera river—Arabs—The geology, valleys, and inhabitants of Karagwe and Ankole—Lukala—Langheld's expedition—Suliman Msudi—Ruizi river—First view of Ruwenzori—The Albert Edward at sunset—Kuliafiri's . . . pp. 69–80

CHAPTER VI.

NORTH-EASTERN VALLEYS ON RUWENZORI.

Arrival—Mubuku valley—Leopards in camp—Elephants—The plains round the mountain—Butanuka—Kasagama—Lion hunting—Kivata Camp—Temperate plants—Makwenda—Forest formation—Bamboos—Heather region—Sunbirds—Yeria summit—Wimi valley . . . . pp. 81–103

CHAPTER VII.

WAHIMA, WAKONDJA, AND SUAHILIS.

Kasagama—Maosolia at the Salt Lake—Visit of Wanyuema—Congo ivory—Chiefs—Oppression exercised by them—Untruthfulness—Wakondja—Cultivation—Laws—Treatment of Women—Kabarega's raids—Future prospects of district—Communications—Cost of administration . . . . pp. 104–122

CHAPTER VIII.

THE SALT LAKE AND SEMLIKI VALLEY.

Plains of Eastern side—Drought—Thorn woods—Unpromising country—Animal life—Chukarongo—The Salt Lake—Formation

CONTENTS.

of salt—Unhealthiness—Mosquitoes—People on the Nyanza—
The Semliki—Butagu valley—Ascent—Attack by natives—
Vegetation and insects—Return to Salt Lake—Ascent by
Nyamwamba—Monkeys . . . . . . pp. 123-147

CHAPTER IX.

THE WAWAMBA.

Wawamba—Affinity—Language—Physical appearance—Character—
Raids from the West—German methods—Attack on my men—
Tengetenge and his chiefs' desire for Europeans . pp. 148-160

CHAPTER X.

GEOLOGY.

The Victoria region—Iron mines—Changes of level—Ruwenzori,
according to Stairs, Stuhlmann, and Gregory—Recent volcanoes—
Hot Springs—Glaciation—Geology of Central Watershed . pp. 161-177

CHAPTER XI.

METEOROLOGY AND CLIMATE.

Instruments—Oil-palm, coffee, colony zones, and cloud belt—Short
account of climates—Table—Rainfall and monsoons—Climates
of Mombasa and Taru, Masai Highlands, Victoria region,
Ruwenzori—Cloud phenomena and mountain breeze—Discovery
of mountain—Rainfall—Climate of Central Ridge, Tanganyika,
Stevenson Road, Shiré Highlands, Zambesi valley—Moist heat
—Malaria—Mosquitoes—Hints on position of stations . pp. 178-206

CHAPTER XII.

BOTANY.

Evolution and systematic botany—Differentiation of species by
flowering season—Westerly wet, Central Ridge dry, Easterly
wet floras and climate—Statistical method—North to south
migration—Origin of Victoria region plants—Origins of Tropical
African flora — Comparison with economic regions — South
America and Africa—Botanical mountain phenomena . pp. 207-226

CONTENTS.

CHAPTER XIII.
MPORORO AND EAST SHORE, ALBERT EDWARD.

Kwa Kaihura—Waruanda inroads—Raids—Eastern shore of the Albert Edward—Volcanic area—Lake shore—Characteristics of people—German enterprise—Rufue and Kakitombo rivers—Kagera river—Hippopotami—Hot springs . . . pp. 227–239

CHAPTER XIV.
KARAGWE.

Rumanika—Decline of country—Kajeti—Character of valleys—Water—Distances from Tanganyika to the Victoria—Rhinoceros hunting—Windermere—Kakaruka—Sunstroke—Buhimba—Ru-Vuvu . . . . pp. 240–254

CHAPTER XV.
BUGUFU AND URUNDI.

Absence of Alexandra Nyanza—Boundaries of Bugufu—Fertility—People—Dances—Ornaments—Urundi—The Central African mountains—Valleys—Cultivation—Attack by the natives—Dense population—Mwesi—Kiriba chain . . . . pp. 255–269

CHAPTER XVI.
THE TANGANYIKA BASIN.

Source of the Nile—Height of Kiriba chain—Alpine flora—Valley to north of Tanganyika—Kilimanyambi's country—Fertility—Tanganyika—Arab dhow—Ujiji music—Storm—Rumonge—Sefu bin Raschid—Ujiji—Karemi—Kala—Kituta—History of Tanganyika—Changes of level—Flora—Arab question—Rumaliza—Former slave raiding—Present distribution . . pp. 270–287

CHAPTER XVII.
BRITISH CENTRAL AFRICA.

Method of travel—Blindness—Stevenson Road plateau—Nyassa—Mlanje—Crossing rivers—Expenses of journey—Formation of colony—Buchanan—Prosperity of colony—Coffee planting—Area and natural state of coffee zone—Alternatives—Native labour—Locusts—Future native troubles—Requirements pp. 288–304

CONTENTS. xiii

CHAPTER XVIII.

TRANSPORT.

Suahilis unsatisfactory — Water transport — Bullock waggons and railways compared — Pack animals — The three railway routes — Kagera river — Central African Lakes Route — Comparison of country opened to commerce — Union of East and British Central Africa . . . . pp. 305-340

CHAPTER XIX.

THE SUAHILI.

Origin of name — Contradictory qualities — Life history — Approaching extinction — Slavery and Arabs — Missions — Roman Catholic and Protestant . . . . pp. 341-355

CHAPTER XX.

HINTS ON OUTFIT AND EXPENSES.

Packing and marching routine — Medicines — A month's supply — Packing — Bed — General list of outfit — Canteen — Tent — Mosquito curtain — Photography — Shooting — Botany — Mammalia — Insects — Trade goods . . . . . . pp. 356-382

APPENDIX.

A. Names of Native Chiefs about Ruwenzori   383
B. Altitudes   383
C. Scientific Collections . .   387
D. Articles of Export . .   391

ILLUSTRATIONS.

	PAGE
Frontispiece. "Snow Peaks of Ruwenzori" (*from a photograph*)	
Fig. 1. Mombasa Fort (*from a photograph*)	3
,, 2. Euphorbia Trees in Desert of Taru (*from a photograph*)	7
,, 3. The Thorn-tree Desert (*from a photograph*)	9
,, 4. Forest and Wind (*from a sketch*)	14
,, 5. View from Maungu Camp (*from a photograph*)	25
,, 6. Rock Pool at Taru (*from a photograph*)	27
,, 7. Wandarobbo Weapons (*from a drawing from nature*)	30
,, 8. Camp at Mkuyuni (*from a photograph*)	34
,, 9. Samia Hills, Geological Section (*from a sketch*)	38
,, 10. Kampala (*from a photograph*)	45
,, 11. Kinani Hill (*from a photograph*)	50
,, 12. New Reptiles (*from a drawing from nature*)	57
,, 13. Banana Grove (*from a photograph*)	72
,, 14. Scenery in the Central Watershed (*from a photograph*)	77
,, 15. A Papyrus Swamp (*from a photograph*)	79
,, 16. Kasagama (*from a photograph*)	87
,, 17. Bush and Forest (*from a sketch*)	94
,, 18. Botanical Section of Ruwenzori (*from a sketch*)	96
,, 19. Makwenda, a pure Mhima Chief (*from a photograph*)	115
,, 20. The Albert Edward Plains (*from a photograph*)	119
,, 21. Sabeido Mkondja Chief (*from a photograph*)	124
,, 22. Bamboos (*from a photograph*)	136
,, 23. The Wild Banana (*from a photograph*)	142
,, 24. Wawamba Articles (*from a sketch*)	151
,, 25. The Wimi Valley (*from a photograph*)	153
,, 26a. Geology of Ruwenzori (*diagrammatic*)	167
,, 26b. Section of Fig. 26a	170
,, 27. A Gorge in Wimi Valley (*from a photograph*)	173
,, 28. Glaciation Phenomena (*from a sketch*)	175
,, 29. A Dense Forest (*from a photograph*)	191

ILLUSTRATIONS.

		PAGE
Fig. 30.	The Bark Cloth Fig (*from a photograph*)	191
,, 31.	Sea Breeze (*after Dr. Mill*)	196
,, 32.	Waterfall on the Wimi River (*from a photograph*)	213
,, 33.	In the Victoria Region (*from a photograph*)	225
,, 34.	Hippopotamus Trap (*from a sketch*)	231
,, 35.	Euphorbias of the Albert Edward Plains (*from a photograph*)	243
,, 36.	Canoes on the Kagera River (*from a photograph*)	250
,, 37.	Karagwe Hills (*from a photograph*)	255
,, 38.	Bananas in Mubuku Valley (*from a photograph*)	268
,, 39.	Hillsides	271
,, 40.	Suahili Women (*from a photograph*)	283
,, 41.	Elevation of Three Railway Lines (*from a drawing*)	319
,, 42.	Acacia Typical of Thorn-tree Desert (*from a photograph*)	331
,, 43.	Maungu Waterhole (*from a photograph*)	333
,, 44.	The Originals—Wateita (*from a photograph*)	342
,, 45.	Wawamba	353
,, 46.	Camp at Mkuyuni (*from a photograph*)	359
,, 47.	An Askari (*from a photograph*)	360
,, 48.	Patent Bed (*from a sketch*)	366
,, 49.	Mosquito Curtain (*from a sketch*)	371

MAPS.

Headwaters of Msonje and Yeria Rivers	*to face* 112
Central East Africa	*folded at end*
Part of East Africa	,, ,,
Sketch Map of Ruwenzori	,, ,,

A NATURALIST IN MID-AFRICA.

CHAPTER I.

MOMBASA TO KIKUYU.

THE idea of going to Africa again suddenly occurred to me after a long conversation on African Floras. I came to the conclusion that if I entered the continent by the Zambesi and went up *viâ* Tanganyika to Ruwenzori and thence by Uganda to Mombasa, I should be able to solve the question of botanical areas which on this side of Africa had often puzzled me.

I sent in my application to the Royal Society, and to my great surprise it was granted. The accompanying proviso, that I should start from Mombasa, put me in a great difficulty, since it involved engaging Suahilis for the whole journey, and thereby at least doubling my expenses; but as the Committee were very kind in giving me the money (a grant of £700), without any limit of time, I determined to go.

I had everything except trade goods packed ready for starting on arrival in London, and reached Zanzibar on the 28th of October, 1893, and Mombasa on the 1st of November.

Here I found that Messrs. Smith, Mackenzie and Co., had engaged seventy-one men for me instead of thirty as I had requested them.

The manner in which porters were engaged at that time was as follows:—Anybody who felt inclined to carry a load went to one of the British East African Co.'s headmen and gave him a rupee. The headman then took him to the Transport Office and declared that he knew the man to be a good porter, who had often been to Uganda and would never run away. The porter was then enrolled, and received his three months' wages in advance, upon which he became, as a rule, incapably drunk for a fortnight.

When I saw the band that were to take my things up-country I was filled with despair. Many were boys not fully grown, and every kind of illness was represented amongst them. Certainly 20 per cent. would have been rejected on the most casual inspection. I knew nothing of the Suahili at that time, and was rather inclined to trust to the opinion of others, so I contented myself with refusing four of the most obviously unfit, thereby losing, of course, their advance pay and posho money.

I spent five days in arranging for the start,

during which time I experienced the very greatest kindness from every one in Mombasa, as well as the most generous hospitality. Mr. Younger very kindly put me up during my stay, which was partly occupied in botanising round Mombasa. The island seems to consist chiefly of coral rock, and is in most places covered by dense bush only

Fig. 1.—MOMBASA FORT.

two or three feet high. Here and there are clumps of bananas, graceful date-palms, and one may even see an occasional mango-tree, though the island distinctly gives a bad impression as far as its soil and general fertility is concerned. This may be due to the lack of a good rainfall (see chap. xi. p. 183), as the total for 1893 seems to have been only 64·17 inches.

The climate is, however, fairly good, showing, as I have often noticed in other parts of Africa, that a very rich and fertile soil which can of course only be formed in a hot and moist climate where vegetation is rapidly forced into being, and as rapidly decays, is almost always found in an unhealthy and enervating climate. The laziness of human beings in such places is counterbalanced by the abundance of food and the small amount of labour required to produce it.

The "network of tramways" and "narrow gauge railway" of which we have heard at Mombasa is in reality a single tramway about 18 inches wide, and is now used only to convey the acting Administrator from his bungalow at Kilindini to Mombasa and back. There are many other points with regard to the work of the I.B.E.A. Co., which were distinctly disappointing, but the Company is now completely dead, and it is best to say nothing except *requiescat in pace*.

The reason of the peculiar and thorough failure of this Company is to be sought not so much in their ideas or the schemes they set on foot as in the manner in which they were carried out. A deliberate attempt was made to direct and manage everything from London, and the manager on the spot was not allowed to carry out things on his own responsibility, with results that are only too disastrously obvious. It is necessary to mention this on account of the extreme probability of the same unfortunate policy being still continued. Individual energy and competition should always be encouraged and not crushed, for these have been the secret of our successful colonisation.

On the 9th of November, I at last got away in spite of curious difficulties owing to loads multiplying exceedingly and porters perpetually disappearing to say good-bye to their friends; my knowledge of Suahili (solely derived from a study of Steere's exercises) was not sufficient to express my feelings, but we did eventually get clear of the town, and camped at Changamvi that evening. Next day we reached Mazera, where the cocoa-nut palm district ends, and we entered what may be called the Thorn-tree desert of Taru, extending as far as Nzowi.

The district we were leaving is not by any means so fertile as is usual in tropical Africa. In fact the cocoa-nut palm and perhaps rubber (*Landolphia Kirkii*), which exists in profusion about Mombasa, are the only products which can be regarded as likely to prove very valuable in the future. I expect, however, that the Sabakhi and other river valleys which carry this cocoa-nut zone far into the interior are more fertile than the hillsides about Mazera.*

The Thorn-tree desert which stretches from

* The following products were noticed in the region:—manioc, pigeon pea (*Cajanus indicus*), millet, maize, bananas, oranges, henna, semsem, mangoes.

Mazera to Nzowi is a most curious district. Gnarled and twisted Acacias of all sorts and sizes, usually with bright white bark and a very thin and naked appearance, cover the whole country. Amongst these one finds the flat-topped Acacia, which, I noticed, prefers the lower slopes of the hills and usually places where game is more abundant and where the soil is a little better (if possible in so poor a country). Amongst these one finds curious trees of Euphorbia. The grasses and sedges in this part grow in little tufts at some distance from one another, leaving the general tint of the landscape that of the soil itself. No sward or turf is formed, and except immediately after the rains, all these grasses are dead, dry, and withered up.

Most of the plants are either thorny or fleshy, as is usual in all desert countries. The reason of this is not, I think, because there are antelopes and giraffes which must be kept at bay, although the foliage *is* undoubtedly protected by its thorns ; it is, more probably, a result of the intense heat of the sun which by transpiration (or evaporation) makes the walls of the cells very thick and hard, and thereby produces a cure for the evil which it itself brings about. A thorn is, of course, a hair, leaf, or branch, which has become thickened in this way.

Through this wilderness runs with almost painful and Roman straightness of aim the excellent road

Fig. 2.—Euphorbias in Taru Desert.

decorated by mile-posts and sign-boards, that has been recently finished to Kibwezi by Mr. George Wilson.

Game is abundant everywhere, a kind of small bustard and guinea-fowl being very common.

Fig. 3.—The Taru Desert.

Occasionally a tiny gazelle, " paa," with large ears, springs out of the thorns and vanishes down the path. I saw footprints of giraffe, and came across ostriches more than once. I also made a persevering attempt to kill a Clarke's gazelle—an animal with enormous ears and long thin neck, which lifts its head above the usual short thorny bush. All these long-necked creatures, such as Clarke's gazelle, ostrich, and giraffe, are usually found in countries where the bush is rather thick and short. Hence their height gives them a power of observation which makes them extremely difficult to approach; and this, not the ability to crop trees, is the main advantage of this structure. But the general impression of the country is very bad, and its commercial future probably means only the formation of perhaps twenty ostrich farms. One can only buy a chicken at four places between Mombasa and Kibwezi.

Another bad feature of the desert seems to be the absence of water over long stretches of the way. It is, I think, very probable that water exists under the stony grit soil, and might be obtained by boring wells, but at present one has to be contented with that found in the stagnant pools at Taru, Maungu, &c., which if not occupied by the decaying remains of a dead antelope are as a rule drinkable.

One of the most lovely spots on this journey is in a delightful little glen called Mkuyuni, under a magnificent fig-tree which hangs over one of the very few rivulets in the Teita hills. Here it is the custom to fire a gun twice, to induce the Wateita who inhabit this part of the country to descend with provisions.

The curious dress of these people, as well as the manner in which they carry loads by a band slung across the forehead, will be fairly obvious from the figure (chap. xix. fig. 44).

During all this part of my journey I had the most incessant and wearisome trouble with my caravan. Unfortunately the list of my men and loads was not given to me till the very moment of starting. On examining it, I made some curious discoveries. It is the custom for arrangements to be made that three rupees a month should be handed to a porter's representative while he is away on a caravan. Usually speaking this "family remittance" is taken by the man's master if he is a slave. I found, however, that my headman was having the *whole* of his wages paid in Mombasa. He was in debt to the I.B.E.A. Co., and this plan was adopted to obtain the money; his wages were also nearly double what he had ever received before! Of course, being an ordinary human being, his object was to spoil the expedition altogether, and to get money out of the porters in every possible way; consequently these porters were deserting daily.

At the Tsavo river I called a general meeting and asked the men why they were running away, as they had light loads, plenty of food, and were only being chastised very slightly when they stole things or disobeyed orders. One old fellow, Mabruki Sirkali, who subsequently became my right-hand man, told me that they all said that they were going to run away by twos and threes if the headman Chakulacho remained. I, therefore, sent him back, choosing the risk of having no headman at all. To add to my difficulties I had a Government caravan of about fifty men who were to go up with me, and their Government loads were mixed up with mine, and many wrongly numbered.

These first days were a terrible trial, as no one knew what he had to do, and in addition to the daily disappearance of my porters, I had myself no experience of camp routine. After a few days, however, when my supposed trustworthy leader had departed, things became more settled; every man knew exactly what he had to do on arriving in camp and leaving in the morning, and we usually started when there was enough light to see our road. I found it necessary to put about ten porters under an askari or soldier; these parties took it in turn to fetch wood and water, and the askari themselves had special days to watch and arrange other little matters. Once these details were settled the men quickly got into the way of things, and it was as a rule quite unnecessary to give an order at all.

I lost three more men and their loads, however, soon after leaving Kibwezi; one of these had a load of photographic plates and botanical paper to carry, and as I had foolishly told him the load was very valuable and that he was to be very careful, he ran away with it, to be, I expect, extremely disgusted when he found what the contents were. One of these runaways I found had been, according to the natives, attacked, when sleeping, by a hyena and very nearly killed. I told this to the others with great effect.

Masongoleni and Kibwezi are the first places on the road where one meets true forest and a fairly well-peopled district; there is also a little tsetse fly on this part of the journey. It struck me that Kibwezi was not well placed for a mission station, as the population is not nearly so dense as in Ukambani proper. There is a pleasant little river and a good amount of cultivation about the station.

The country begins to improve as one reaches the hilly districts of Ukambani, until at Nzowi one leaves finally behind the useless thorn-tree desert.

This difference in the fertility of the soil is largely due to a difference in height. The winds from the sea deposit much of their moisture on the hills immediately bordering the coast. They blow freely over the thorn-tree desert, and are again checked by the highlands of Ukambani, where they leave a good deal of rain and (as is perhaps more important for vegetation) keep the flanks of the hills and the branching valleys in a moist and humid condition. The fertility is perhaps due in part to the presence of the vast series of basaltic floes and volcanic material which one finds at various places along the Masai highlands.

The whole structure of the country is, in fact, a series of gigantic steps from the coast to the summit of the Nandi range, or one might say to Elgon.

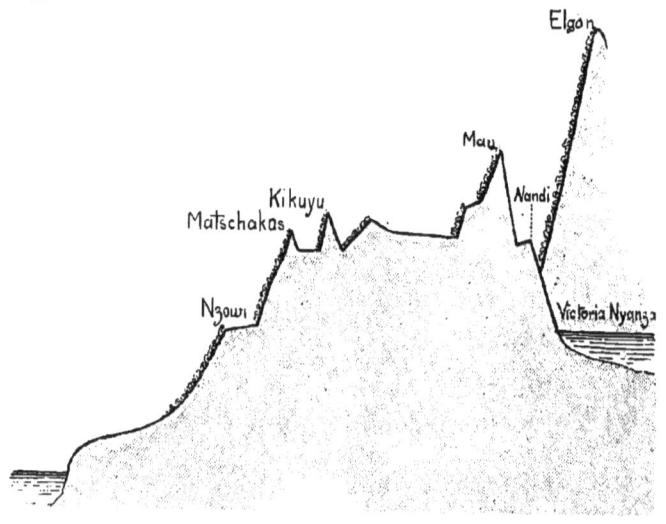

Fig. 4.—Forest and Wind.

There is first the ascent to Mazera village, which is fertile and densely wooded, then a much gentler gradual rise to Nzowi (about 3,650 feet), which is covered by the thorn-trees and succulents characteristic of a dry climate.

Nzowi, to the beginning of the Athi plains at Languru, forms another steep ascent, probably originally a dense jungle, but now largely cultivated and yielding abundant crops.

The wind then sweeps over the Athi plains, which are grassy steppes without trees, until it meets the steep ascent before Kikuyu; from this point a dense unbroken forest probably stretched to the second swamp beyond Kikuyu station, but a large part of this is now the endless cultivated *shambas* of the Wakikuyu.

From the second swamp at Kikuyu to the beginning of the further ascent at Raomi of the Mau hills, there is again a grassy steppe region. From Raomi (6,965 feet) to the Mau summit is another thick forest, after which the wind has free play, and a rolling grass country dotted with scattered trees reaches to the foot of Elgon, where there begins a fresh belt of forest at about 7,000 feet. Those curious in such matters will find that Darwin, in the "Voyage of the Beagle," has pointed out the essentials of the foregoing theory, viz., that an atmosphere kept constantly moist, *e.g.*, by a cloud, is essential to the formation of forest.

The little valley at Nzowi, with its running water and numerous affable, if lightly-clad, natives, is a great relief after the desolate thorns, and one soon finds oneself at the first European station, Machakos.

Mr. Ainsworth, who has been several years at this place and is very much at home amongst the Wakamba, gave me many interesting details about these curious people.

The government, I learned, is in the hands of the Wazee, or old men, one of whose privileges seems to be the right to get drunk on *tembu* as often and as thoroughly as they choose.

Every married man has his thorn boma or kraal, in which are the huts of his wives (naturally one hut to each). The bachelors are nobodies, and have no say in anything. Murder is looked upon as a theft merely, and the murderer has to pay the value of his victim to the latter's nearest relations. If any person approaches a kraal at night, it is the correct thing to shoot him at sight without inquiry. They have a curious, obstinate appearance, but they seem to have been very badly treated by one of Mr. Ainsworth's predecessors. Now, however, they are most friendly, and brought into the fort while I was there a ton of flour, and asked him to let them know when he wanted more! One can scarcely estimate the good that Mr. Ainsworth has done amongst these people. He has stopped intertribal fighting, kept off the Masai, and by a system of isolation prevented the cattle disease from entering the country. He has also induced them to carry the mail and loads and is training a kind of militia in view of the Masai.

Their country is full of little valleys with permanent running streams, and is well cultivated, the banana often growing up to the level of about 6,200 feet.

These Wakamba, who number probably a million, can make rough pottery and work native iron. They can also manufacture bags from Sanseviera fibre. Any number can be got to work for two rupees a week.

They grow during the rains two crops of maize, millet, and other cereals; and, in the same year after the rains are over, obtain two further crops of sweet potatoes.

Here I was, as usual, kindly treated by Mr. Ainsworth, and rested a few days for Mr. Watt's party, with whom I went on to Kikuyu. Mrs. Watt and her five little children were most plucky in coming to settle so far from any human habitation.

From Languru to the beginning of the Kikuyu bush is a very gradual ascent, and forms the well-known Athi plains. The abundance of game is still extraordinary, in spite of the amount of extermination which has been practised by certain persons. A tale of 380 head in three months fell to one "sportsman," which, considering that a little antelope meat is a great blessing to the caravans on this road, seems quite inexcusable.

A curious feature is the abundance of the *Kongoni*, or hartebeest, the most timid as well as the ugliest of them all. This Kongoni, like the gnus and the majority of antelopes which inhabit open grassy plains, has enormously developed fore-quarters and a very sloping shoulder. The hind-quarters are small and drooping (like the "wee droop-rumpled hunter cattle"). This build appears to enable it to attain great speed, just as occurs in horses, without stumbling. The bush-buck, which inhabits dense forest, has quite the reverse formation, for everything slopes backwards from the pointed nose and small fore-quarters to the relatively large hind-quarters. Hence the animal goes through bush like a wedge.

In the hartebeest it is the fore-quarters chiefly, and in the bush-buck the hind-quarters, which do the work.

In one day I saw rhinoceros, ostriches, hundreds of hartebeest, and a most beautiful little antelope (*Thomsonii*), besides wildebeest, a few sand-grouse, &c. Zebras and lions are also abundant, and we came across both. Such places are, of course, eminently suited to cattle ranches, and they are even now inhabited, or as one might say with almost equal truth, rendered desert by the Masai. Sand-grouse are pretty common, and herds of zebra may be seen trotting quietly away. I saw one rhinoceros, which winded our caravan at about half a mile away and immediately fled!

On entering the thick forest at the beginning of the steep ascent to Kikuyu one has still to be extremely careful. The Wakikuyu are thoroughly treacherous, and are only too anxious to spear a lagging porter. Mr. Hall at that time never went more than half a mile from the fort; one of his headmen had been attacked and lost a portion of his nose within 400 yards of the gate, and they had even attempted to take the fort itself.

One of these people described to Mr. Hall how they killed forty-nine out of fifty men of a Suahili or Arab trading caravan who had offended them. "We crept very closely round their camp at night and watched their sentinel. First he walked about, and we kept very quiet; then he sat down by the fire and his head began to nod; sometimes he would raise it and yawn; but at last he rolled himself in his rug and blanket and went to sleep. Then we told off four men to every tent and ran in and killed them all. We got lots of ivory and cloth and guns and beads."

These are the people amongst whom Mr. and Mrs. Watt and their five children (the eldest only, I think, ten years of age) proposed to settle down!

The entrances to their villages, usually built in very thick thorny bush, are carefully arranged in such a way that a visitor who does not know when to take a turn to the right or left will probably find himself in a pit and very likely impaled on a sharp-pointed pole—like Ben Battle of classic memory—which stands in the bottom of it.

The Kikuyu country, however, is a most fertile

one. After passing through the first fringe of forest at the end of the Athi plains (left as a protection against Masai), one enters on a densely cultivated district. Food is so cheap that a man can be rationed for about 1½ pice a day; and cattle, sheep, and goats seem to thrive exceedingly. Donkeys can be procured in large numbers from the Masai at a price of about six to twelve rupees a head, though I had to pay the I.B.E.A. Co. twenty-five rupees apiece.

Altogether the prospects of the country seem very bright in the future, particularly now that a colony of Masai and another of Sudanese are settled near the fort, forming a good "buffer-state" to the Wakikuyu.

All this country from Nzowi and beyond Kikuyu to the Nandi range is well suited to Europeans. The rainfall is sufficient, but not severe, and there is a good bracing cold at night, which is one of the chief requisites in the tropics. I am told that fever is quite unknown amongst Europeans unless they bring it with them from the coast or Uganda. Wheat and English vegetables can be easily grown, and probably in quantity, and the latter seem to have most abnormal developments.

Cabbages and cauliflowers become shrubs, and parsnips are almost as large as turnips at home; moreover, every conceivable kind of vegetable seems to have grown with great success. Rice has not, however, turned out well so far, though the Kikuyu wheat and barley were considered very good in London.

Though it is obvious from the preceding remarks that the essentials of European life exist in Kikuyu, this is not sufficient to induce settlers to come out to this country. I find it extremely difficult to see what they could do when they arrived. Cattle could certainly be raised in considerable quantities and driven to the coast for sale, but there is no plant, except perhaps tobacco, which can be recommended confidently as sufficiently profitable and promising for cultivation.

Sir John Kirk has recently pointed out that the only portions of tropical Africa in which true colonies are possible is that above 5,000 feet. It is only, in my opinion, the strip between this level and 7,000 feet, where the climate is far too wet and cold for residence, that Europeans can live in any degree of comfort.

One can distinguish below 5,000 feet in most places two distinct areas. That below 3,000 feet, which I have called in the preceding the cocoa-nut zone, but which might be better described as the oil-palm zone, and that between 3,000 and 5,000 feet, which may be named the coffee zone.

The former is always in a thoroughly bad and dangerous climate. The latter, though not colonisable, is quite suited for plantations, at which Europeans can reside for perhaps five years at a time. In this part of Africa it is probably too dry and of small extent. It would begin between Tsavo and Kibwezi and end shortly before Machakos.

CHAPTER II.

KIKUYU TO THE VICTORIA.

AFTER Kikuyu commences the uninhabited region which extends as far as the villages of Kavirondo.

I was obliged to buy twenty-two donkeys to carry food for my porters. These animals were quite unsubjugated and became a perfect nuisance. Their ingenuity in getting rid of their loads was extraordinary, and every morning each required some five men to load him.

After leaving the second swamp, one day out from Kikuyu forest, we crossed the watershed into the "meridional rift valley," along which lie the Lakes Elmenteita, Naivasha, and Nakuru. I was disagreeably surprised to see a large party of Masai passing down the valley just when I was about to descend into it. These were Elmoran on the war-path, probably five or six hundred warriors, all bachelors, and under thirty years of age. They are tall and well-built, and walk at a tremendous pace, with a curious long, lolloping step, and with the little bells on their legs tinkling as they go. I was at the time a little in front of my men, and brought forward my askari to be ready in case they were disposed to attack, but they took very little notice of us, and when the Lygonani appeared, I had the pleasure of shaking hands with him and some hundred stalwart young fellows who had attempted to heighten the ferocity of their appearance by enclosing their faces in a bush of feathers, often three feet across, and plastering their bodies with crimson or white clay. They were probably on their way to attack the more industrious, agricultural peoples, Wakikuyu or Wakamba, but we parted the best of friends.

At this point, to get down into the rift valley, a small precipice of rough dolerite has to be descended; and this being cleared, we found the land covered with herds of cattle and goats. We passed several of the little square camps of the married people, and until we arrived at our camp on the first Kidong river, our ears never rested from the strains of the various troops of donkeys.

At this camp the country had a most curious appearance. It was eaten down to the ground. Scarcely a blade of grass was an inch long. It is owing to the habit, very unusual with a pastoral people, of camping in large numbers, that the Masai are unable to remain more than a few days in one spot, and also that the cattle disease has been so deadly amongst these people, while the same fact is probably responsible for the formation of these bands of Elmoran, and for a morality

KIKUYU TO THE VICTORIA. 25

which is common in civilised cities, but most unusual amongst savage races.

Next morning when we started I saw to my disgust that their kraals were also on the march.

Fig. 5.—VIEW FROM MAUNGU CAMP.

The goats and cattle were collected into flocks and driven by the boys and slaves of their owners. Their huts, which are of a beehive shape formed of hides stretched over curved sticks, were rapidly taken to pieces. A donkey was caught and six of these long poles tied on each side of it; then the hides were folded and laid on its back.

Their caravan must have extended over nearly ten miles, and was, of course, in a most helpless condition. Some of the younger women had such masses of brass wire on their legs that they were almost unable to walk. The number of people suffering from frightful ulcers on the legs was almost incredible, and explains why the Masai are undoubtedly a diminishing and falling race. The Wanandi, Waleikipia, Wasuk, and other races are encroaching upon them, and I do not think they will ever again be the dangerous people which they were a few years ago.

The Germans about Kilimandjaro seem to have shot any Masai that they saw at sight, and it is those that have fled from German territory that are the worst. Yet they might become of great assistance to Europeans in the management of cattle and in waggon transport, and probably would make excellent soldiers. It is obvious that these enormous camps, and therefore the Elmoran which live upon them, could be very easily kept in order, but the best policy would be to try and induce them to settle in small parties at different spots.

After leaving these Masai we saw no human beings, save three Wandarobbo and Major Smith's caravan, till we reached Kavirondo.

It gives one a curious impression to march day after day over lovely grass plains covered with zebra, hartebeest, and other antelopes, past beautiful lakes where geese, ducks, and other water-fowl

Fig. 6.—TARU WATERHOLE.

almost cover the water, then perhaps through a dense virgin forest with magnificent timber, and all the time to see no human beings whatever. Yet the country is healthy and in every way suited for Europeans, while we have hundreds of people in England who do not know where to turn for employment.

I had bought twenty-two donkeys and four cattle at Kikuyu, and we were going on beautifully, with every one in the best of spirits, when I had a serious misfortune. Leaving Nakuru in the morning, I reached the Guaso Masai, a twenty-mile march, in good time. Having found that the natural pace of the porters was much faster than that of the donkeys, I had left six of my best men and two askaris in charge of the latter under Bakari ben Ali, the Government headman. After I got into camp Bakari sent to tell me that the donkeys had stampeded in the bush, and that he wanted me to send men to find them. I did not think it was a matter of much importance, but when Bakari came in without them, about six in the evening, I saw things were serious. The four men in special charge had not come in, and as we had passed Major Smith's caravan two days before, I jumped to the conclusion that these men had stolen them and driven them back to Nakuru. On hearing that there was no water anywhere to the east or west, I inferred that they must have returned to Nakuru. Accordingly I took six men and walked back that night. In the dusk, and having gone too fast for my men, I missed the way and wandered about till morning, when I reached my yesterday's camp. There was no trace of them, so I walked back, doing fifty miles in thirty hours. Next day both I and the men were knocked up, so I sent almost the whole caravan to go to various points which I marked out, and light fires (so that I could see that they had been there), and examine all the country on the way. Suahilis are absolutely useless for this work, and I was not surprised that nothing was found; so next day I went myself over the whole country, to try and find out some trace of the missing loads, but entirely without success. My supply of food was running too short for me to delay longer, and so I was obliged to go on.

This was a most severe loss to me as altogether seventeen loads, six cattle, and eighteen donkeys had disappeared. What tried me more than anything else was the fact that four were boxes of stores belonging to Government. I have never been able to find out who stole these things; either it was Suahilis from Major Smith's caravan, or Masai, or Wandarobbo. It would never have happened if I had had a satisfactory headman, or sufficient experience to know that no Suahili can be trusted; but one cannot be both in front and behind the caravan at the same moment.

After this I was obliged to press on as fast as possible to Kabrassie as these days' delay were seriously diminishing my food supply.

Just after the Guaso Masai or Maji-moto, where this happened, we passed through a series of grassy hills with patches of beautiful forest, until the deep Eldoma ravine was reached.

There are many Wandarobbo in this part, and three accompanied me during two days. Near Eldoma they had set an ambush for us, and one of my men who was straggling behind was fired at. After this, however, they ran away, and we were not attacked as I half expected.

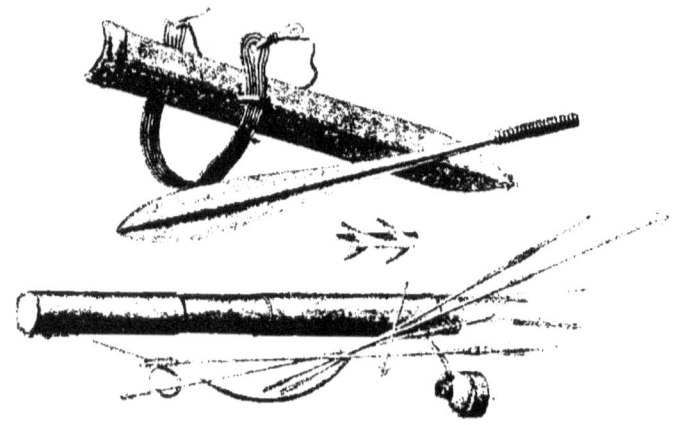

Fig. 7.—WANDAROBBO WEAPONS.

The weapons of these people consist of bows and arrows. The latter are of three quite different kinds. One is a simple lance-headed arrow which is used at close quarters. Another type is barbed, with a row of curious twisted back-pointed hooks, as shown in the figure. Another type is a simple sharp-pointed piece of wood covered with poison, which seemed to me identical with that of the Wakamba arrow poison "Acokantherin." A heavy sword is also worn. A band of leather ornamented with white beads is tied round the waist, and they appear to prefer blue beads as necklaces. In their quivers they always carry firesticks. One of these, which has a small hole in it about the middle, is put flat on the ground and held in position by the toes, while the second stick is held vertically between both palms, the point being in the hole of the other, and twisted very rapidly round and round. It is very hard work, and if the weather is at all damp it takes half an hour and two men to ignite the tinder. The Wandarobbo possess a few cattle and grow a little Wimbi (*Panicum exilum*) or *hungry rice*, but they seem to depend more on hunting than any other race I have seen.

From the deep gorge of Eldoma one enters on the Mau forest, an extremely steep ascent to about 8,000 feet. In the gorges and sheltered valleys the trees are often of large size, with trunks more than 18 inches in diameter, but on the more exposed ridges there seem to be usually a number of slender stems springing from the same root. The bamboo, which occurs in vast numbers towards the top of the Mau forest, has, of course, the same method of growth. I fancy it is due to any trunk that has become of very large size being blown down by the wind, in which case several suckers spring up from the root; as these slender stems are able to bend freely in a wind, they are not so liable to break, so that the plant has been induced to take on a habit fitted to resist strong wind by the direct action of the wind itself. The whole structure of the bamboo is also adapted to resist wind. The thin, wiry, flexible twigs on which every leaf is hung, bend freely in any direction. This mode of growth has become a settled character of several species in the Mau forest.

One very striking tree has the most beautiful silvery leaves, and was called by my Suahilis "Mau," but I rather fear that this was an effort of imagination on their part. I know of no other explanation of the name however.

After passing Mau I first came across locusts, and from this point to the Shiré highlands, they were abundant everywhere. This was on the 30th of December, 1893. It had been suggested that they came to the Shiré highlands and also north in consequence of fighting which took place in 1894 in the Congo region, but of course this cannot be the reason of their presence on Mau in 1893. Probably they were unusually favoured by the climate when hatching (see p. 300).

It was on this date, 30th of December, that I first came upon the watershed of the Nile, and I was at once struck by the curious appearance of the valleys, which are broad and flat and occupied frequently by marshes and weeds. Valleys of this nature are the typical ones through the whole drainage area of the Victoria Nyanza. I found them all through Karagwe and Urundi, and even close to the watershed of Tanganyika, and at a level of some 4,300 feet. (Above this latter altitude the valleys are usually narrow ravines.) In this part of the country the effect of grass fires is very curious indeed. Above 5,000 feet they are of no importance, but below this level they completely change the appearance of the country. One reason why the curious tree Euphorbias are so common lies in the fact that they are almost entirely unaffected by these fires. In places particularly subject to conflagration, there are only a very few trees which are able to grow, and these usually have a very thick, gummy bark, which seems to act as an insulator. These trees are of very different orders—a kind of Protea, an Eugenia, &c.

These African fires are not in the least like the American pictures, where one sees mustangs with their eyes protruding, and a happy family of jaguars, snakes, pronghorns, &c., all fleeing for their lives. It is a very insignificant line of blazing grass, which one can easily step across. It is sometimes stopped by a hard-trodden native path and almost always by a river, where the thick foliage of the trees keeps sufficient permanent moisture to save all except the outlying branches from being even singed. It has a curious effect on some of the smaller shrubs, which patiently put on every year a stem and branches which is annually burnt down. Sometimes a stem, apparently ten years old, may be seen supporting a trunk of only a few months' growth.

From the top of the Nandi range I sent back

Fig. 8.—Camp at Mkuyuni.

the head of my first buck, a Jackson's Hartebeest (*Bubalis Jacksoni*); this was a young and confiding animal, which allowed me to creep up to within 100 yards behind an ant-hill and kill it with a Winchester rifle. My ball hit just two inches below the spine, a little in front of the pelvis, and its hind-quarters were paralysed. I have found this since to be a very deadly shot, as the animal cannot move from the spot.

My previous experiences as a hunter had been maddening. They usually consisted of crawling in breathless and perspiring silence on my stomach for about 500 yards (always losing my pipe in the process), to be rewarded, on cautiously raising my head above the grass, by the view of a hartebeest shambling awkwardly away with a derisive and malevolent look in his eye—the characteristic expression of this, the most ugly of all the antelopes.

With the summit of the Nandi range the traveller leaves the high, healthy Masai highlands and descends to the great Victoria Nyanza region. Due west, stretching right across to the base of Ruwenzori, is a vast plateau which hardly seems to reach 5,000 feet, and is usually only from 3,900 to 4,100 feet in altitude. The whole of this mass of material, 1,000 feet thick and 400 miles broad, has been apparently gradually carried away by the Nile to form the vast alluvial of Lower Egypt. The plants from Abyssinia, which had crossed to the Masai highlands and taken refuge from the changed climate in Kilimandjaro and Kenia, were thus separated from their congeners. Those that remained were then obliged to change their habits, seasons of flowering, &c., and became the new species which now inhabit the Victoria region, the *Central Seen Gebiete* of German botanists.

CHAPTER III.

THE VICTORIA REGION, INCLUDING UGANDA.

IMMEDIATELY after passing the Nandi hills, the descent of the plateau of the Victoria region commences. The Nandi hills themselves are composed of a series of schists, which have been carefully described by Dr. Gregory from my specimens.*

The country rapidly sinks in level from this point to Mumia's and the proposed port on the Nyanza, at Berkeley Bay, and a marked difference in temperature is at once apparent. This is, in fact, the commencement of the coffee zone, below 5,000 feet, which extends to the base of Ruwenzori. It is on reaching Kabrassie that one again finds oneself amongst human beings. These are the Wakavirondo, who brought us welcome quantities of sweet potatoes, "podjo" (a kind of bean), fowls, eggs, quails in small baskets, &c.

These people are dressed chiefly in air, and, as one always finds in scantily clothed native races,

* The paper has been handed in to the Geological Society.

are peculiarly moral as compared with the decently attired Waganda and other races. In Madagascar, West Africa, and the Cape, I have always found the same rule. Chastity varies inversely as the amount of covering.

The natives, when first clearing a plantation or "shamba" from the original bush, plant, as soon as the rains begin, "wimbi," or *hungry rice*, which springs up and yields a crop almost immediately; then they put in Indian corn and millet; sweet potatoes are taken from it during the third and fourth year, and after planting beans during the fifth and sixth year, the land is allowed to revert to bush again, in which state it usually remains at least five years. The cattle disease, apparently a liver complaint, has destroyed most of their cattle, but they seem to have plenty of fowls, goats, sheep, &c. There appears to be no ivory or rubber in Kavirondo now, and the country is very much under Uganda, and would not give the slightest trouble if administered from there.

The villages are usually surrounded by a deep ditch and mud wall, and contain quantities of little circular huts with walls under 4 feet high. As a rule the roofs are of grass, and the walls chiefly made of the "elephant grass" or *Mateitei*.

After passing Munia's, where I rested for a day to allow my men to feed thoroughly, we went on to the shore of the Victoria Nyanza, where we arrived on the 11th of January, 1894.

I visited some very curious iron mines close to the proposed station at Berkeley Bay.

On reaching the foot of the low hills which border the Victoria Nyanza at this spot, I could see no sign of workings; but suddenly an extremely dirty native emerged from what, in my ignorance, I had supposed to be the burrow of an animal. There were four or five of these holes in a space of about 40 yards in diameter. They are only about 15 yards deep, and have been apparently scraped out by hand. The man (or woman) lies on his back and scrapes the iron ore

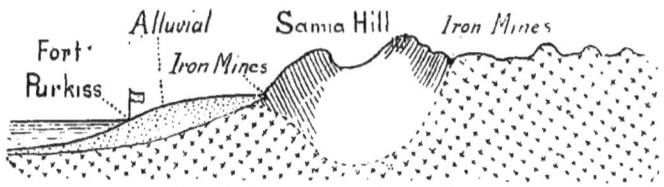

Fig. 9.—SECTION OF SAMIA HILLS.

with his fingers from the roof and sides of the burrow. This is then carried in baskets to the neighbouring villages, where it is smelted by means of goatskin bellows and charcoal. Sometimes it is carried as far as the frontiers of Usoga, where I passed a market in which it was being exchanged for bananas and fowls.

The beds containing it appear to be about 200 feet thick, and are probably a late and local deposit round the lake. The iron is found at two or three spots close to the lake a little further south, and it is also extracted from the other side of the Samia hills. A similar deposit occurs in Uganda, near the Sekibobo's village, also along the lake shore, and I fancy the same beds also occur in Usoga, near the Kavirondo border, and possibly in Buddu. It would be a very easy matter to work this iron, as it would only be necessary to run it by a tramway down a gentle descent of two to three miles to the lake, and thence ship it by canoes to one of the numerous places where wood is abundant. It appears to be of fairly good constitution. I found two varieties; one of these is yellow when ground to powder, and contains appreciable quantities of sulphur and phosphorus with only a trace of titanium. The percentage of iron is 61·69. The other, dark red when powdered, contains appreciable quantities of phosphorus and silica with no sulphur or titanium. The iron is only 41·08 per cent. For these analyses I have to thank Mr. W. Tate, F.C.S.

It is not my intention to write at great length about Uganda, since others who have had much better opportunities than myself are probably industriously doing so at the present moment.

But from this position on the shore of the Victoria Nyanza, round which lie Usoga, Uganda proper, and Buddu, it is easy to give a general idea of the region.

The lake has had a curious history. At one period it must have been 100 feet higher than its present level.* Hence at this time most of these countries would have been a series of islands something like the present Sesse archipelago. During the time that it remained at this level, the rain washing down the sides of the hills filled the hollows between them with a flat deposit of alluvial matter, giving the characteristic long, broad, flat valley bottoms found on all the present rivers which enter the Nyanza.

Then, either by the cutting away of a rock barrier at the present Ripon falls, or by the formation of the Somerset Nile itself (for I fancy that some authorities suppose that the original outlet of the Victoria Nyanza was towards the north-east), the lake began gradually to sink. It appears to have remained stationary about 40 feet above its present level for a considerable time; at least there is at Tsimbande hill, near the Kagera, a very marked terrace which makes me think so. After this, it continued gradually to sink, and is still falling.

The effect of this process is curiously visible all along the course of the Kagera, and even as far as Urundi. One finds at fully 200 miles distance from the Nyanza those long, flat, and dry valleys, filled with the rich neutral-tinted alluvium that is common in Lower Egypt. As such a valley gradually dries up, the Papyrus swamps which

* This I give from my observations of the height of the alluvial deposit in Usoga and Kavirondo.

occupy all the shallower reaches and river courses of the Nyanza gradually proceed lakewards, leaving behind a dry alluvial soil, under which such little water as still finds its way down the valley proceeds to the lake.

In the course of the Kagera, and in all places where irrigation could be carried on by means even of the primitive shadouf and sakkieh, this means the possibility of enormous crops of cotton, sugar, rice, and wheat, for the alluvium is often 30 feet deep.

Thus the whole of Uganda, Usoga, and much of Karagwe consists of an infinity of hills and ridges 4,110 feet, on an average, above the sea; their flat valleys are usually occupied by swamp-rivers, often half a mile wide, such as the Nabajisu, the Nakaiba, and Katonga. These curve and twist about in an extraordinary fashion and have numerous minor swamps connected with them. It is thus immediately obvious that railways are impossible and roads extremely difficult. In the course of 20 miles one may have to cross eight swamps from a quarter to three-quarters of a mile wide, and mount and descend twelve hills each 300 feet high and also steep.

Transport in future will probably be carried on by utilising these swamp-rivers, now a barrier to locomotion, as means of transport.* Either canals will be cut and barges kept to proceed up and

* This has already been suggested by Captain Lugard.

down, or a corduroy road of palmstems will be made along them.

The formation of canals will probably be the best method. If a channel is cut through the centre of the marsh, and if the material (chiefly papyrus roots) be piled upon either side, the current, although sluggish, will probably keep it clear; and with suitable rough machinery, I do not think there would be very much difficulty in cutting it.

The papyrus has a very curious growth. The knotted roots crawl horizontally over the surface, and these are so close together that dead leaves and mud soon begin to form a soil. A number of marsh-loving plants, chiefly Convolvulus (*Ipomœa*), and grass grow on this, and soon turn it into nearly dry ground, on which, in uncultivated districts, fine forests spring rapidly into existence. Thus in such places one passes out of the dismal papyrus, first over a narrow strip of grass and then into a magnificent shady forest which usually covers the level bottom of the valley and climbs a little way up the hill. The trees are unable to resist fires after a short distance from the water, and become scattered or altogether absent, so that the tops of the hills are covered with grass. The hills themselves are usually granite, and the summits are often covered with a curious hard reddish-brown crust of rock—"laterite"—which appears to be a product of the intense sun-heat and carbonic acid of the rain water acting on iron and other minerals.

In a cultivated place the forest will have been cut down and replaced by banana plantations and fields of maize and millet.

Usually this cultivation extends from the end of the flat alluvium, the old marsh (which is liable to drought if not irrigated), two-thirds of the way up the hills, but in Uganda the population has been so much diminished that only a small proportion is under cultivation. Probably wherever a loose dark soil is found without pebbles of laterite, the land is good, and this is also the case wherever the "elephant grass" grows abundantly.

So far as has been ascertained at present, the natural productions of Uganda are not of very great value. Minerals, except iron, are not known to occur. Ivory certainly exists, but of course only in the most inaccessible places. In valuable medicines and fibre plants, as also in dyes and gums, the Victoria region is extraordinarily poor. There are certainly a very few products of considerable value (*e.g.*, beeswax and hippopotamus teeth), but the Victoria region can only yield any considerable export trade from the results of plantation.

Forests exist in almost every valley, and also on the immediate shore of the Victoria everywhere.

In the south of Buddu there seem to be enormous tracts of fine large timber. Sometimes on the march—which of course avoids forests as much as possible—one passes through a mile of forest in every fifteen miles' walking. But in most parts of the region the trees, though quite able to yield as much fuel as may be required for many years to come, are not on the whole large or of any specially valuable kinds. The most important are *Lusambia*, which seems a very ordinary useful wood, and *Nzo*, which takes a remarkably fine polish. Anywhere near a native village the forest is being continually cleared of timber to supply native fires and materials for building, and goats prevent any young trees from growing up to replace it. The effect of grass fires is to destroy annually a very large amount of forest. It would be very simple for the Government to arrange that only a certain proportion of the now existing forests should be touched in any one year, and thus allow the natural forest growth to afford a permanent source of timber. This is very important in view of the tremendous requirements of the steamers which every one hopes soon to see plying on the Victoria, and also in view of the rainfall.

The climate of Uganda is not really unhealthy. Europeans can easily walk about and superintend natives before noon; but at present the physical strain involved in walking 750 miles, the extraordinary and dirty productions of a Suahili cook, the miserable mud houses and the absence of any

Fig. 10.—Kampala.

good servants, are quite sufficient in themselves to produce ill-health. The rainfall is not very high.

	Jan.	Feb.	Mar.	April	May	June	July	Aug.
Inches.	2.37	4.38	4.47	7.66	5.30	3.00	3.17	2.89
Rainy days.	6	8	9	10	11	9	6	8

	Sept.	Oct.	Nov.	Dec.	Total.
Inches.	3.90	5.24	3.89	1.34	47.61
Rainy days.	12	12	14	8	113

These are the mean of eight years' observations at the Missionary Station of Natete, Mengo, by Mackay.

The most important plant is of course the banana. The French Jesuit fathers, who have attempted in many ways to make themselves real friends of the natives, manufacture the following from the fruit:—beer, brandy, champagne, vinegar, bread, jam, and puddings. This is a fairly varied dietary from one plant! The leaves are used to build the houses, and particularly for roofs. All kinds of plates, spoons, bottles, &c., are replaced by fragments of banana leaves. I have also seen a very voluminous though short skirt, like that of a pantomime artiste, constructed of these leaves. A single leaf is used as an umbrella. I have seen a native, during rain, take off his waistcloth (all the clothes he possessed), fold it carefully up, and carry it under his arm while he went happy and dry, to a certain extent, under the shade of a large banana leaf. The missionaries also told me that babies are usually brought to be christened enwrapped in one.

All kinds of rope, twine, &c., are made from the stem, and the fibre is undoubtedly of most excellent quality.

Wheat has been for some time grown in the district. One of the large native chiefs has cultivated quantities to sell to Europeans—one of those little facts that explains why one has a belief in the future of the Waganda. It has also been successfully grown by the French missionaries. The time of sowing must, however, be carefully judged. If sown in the very first showers of the rainy season, it is liable to be destroyed by a week's drought, which not infrequently occurs at that period; if sown in the middle of the rains it will not ripen; on the other hand, if sown too late it is liable to be injured by the dry season. In spite of this, however, the prospects of its cultivation are distinctly favourable.

Indian corn, and particularly millet, are the most commonly grown cereals, and seem to do fairly well. The swamps and alluvium of the valleys appears to be naturally well suited for rice, but, apparently through want of experience, it has not so far succeeded.

Coffee probably affords the most favourable prospect of all. The Uganda coffee is grown without any care whatever, and is neither pruned nor looked after in any way. Yet a sample which I obtained from M. L. Decle has been very highly spoken of in London, and is valued by Messrs. Patry and Pasteur, 38, Mincing Lane, as worth 75s. to 77s. per cwt. (*vide* Appendix). At present it is grown chiefly in Buddu and the islands, but if any encouragement were given I have no doubt that it could be produced almost anywhere round the Victoria. Probably the natives could be induced to grow it themselves, and bring the berries to Europeans for sale.

Tobacco is another possible article of export from the Victoria region. Wherever there are natives in Africa they seem to produce tobacco. It is, of course, grown and cured in a very haphazard way. The French missionaries have manufactured cigars from it, but naturally it would be necessary to import and test really good kinds before one could form any definite idea as to its prospects.

Cotton grows very well indeed wherever I have seen it. A sample which I brought back has been valued at 1d. per lb. (or if cleaned perhaps 4d. a lb.), but it would require a great deal of arrangement before this price would pay for export.

Such things as sugar, indigo, and perhaps cocoa, might be grown in various parts of the country. Tea would, I think, scarcely find sufficient rainfall (*vide* p. 116 on "Ruwenzori").

As far as I have been able to judge, a very large amount of the country is suited to cattle. In Usoga cattle are both plentiful and cheap, and, as I can say from experience, stand travelling well, and yield, for Africa, a fair supply of milk. Goats and sheep do well everywhere.

A very unfortunate fact seems to be that horses do not thrive in Uganda. The reason I cannot find out, but none seem to be in a really healthy condition anywhere in the country. The humble

Fig. 11.—Kisani Hill.

but useful donkey, on the other hand, seems to get on very well.

That English vegetables almost without exception thrive in Uganda, proves that at the lowest estimate the essentials of European food can be obtained. In my own opinion, however, it would not be going too far to say that, with proper transport, the Victoria region may become one of the greatest food-producing centres in the world.

The preceding remarks, which are necessarily

brief, may be taken solely as applicable to the question of products of which something can be learned at present. But in a country like this, one ought to assume a very large percentage of export from those products and plantations which can only arise when Europeans seriously begin to develop the country. A Roman scientific traveller reporting on London in the time of Julius Cæsar would probably have been able to point out that the Thames was a navigable river and full of salmon, that the natives were energetic, and so on, but most of his report would be occupied by such questions as whether woad could replace the expensive Tyrian purple; and the modern African explorer is in the same question. It appears to me that the few products on which one has enough data to speak are extremely favourable, but it is only when one turns to the question of imports that one sees how very full of promise the future of the country seems to be.

CHAPTER IV.

THE WAGANDA AND TRAVELLING EXPERIENCES.

THE Waganda are a very curious race, and have, for an African people, most unusual intelligence. This is shown by the existence amongst them of a most complicated feudal system. It is far more developed than that of the Zulus or any other African race which I have seen.

Theoretically, the king owns the land everywhere, and, in consideration for the use of the *shambas* (plantations), the people who occupy them are bound to render any service, military or other, which the king may require.

A certain proportion of the fruits (practically all, if the feudal superior requires it) are also at the king's disposal. Sometimes a man may hold his shamba direct from the king, but usually there are a large number (sometimes twenty) intermediaries, all of whom exact from those below them whatever in the way of produce or civil and military service they require.

The effect of this system is both bad and good. Through this perfect organisation the Waganda have been enabled to control Ankole, Unyoro, Usoga, and Kavirondo, a stretch of territory perhaps 300 miles broad.

The evil effects, on the other hand, are numerous. There is first the extremely unsatisfactory condition of labour. When a man works for nothing, he will do as little as he possibly can, and that only when it suits his own convenience. There is no security for him to enjoy the fruits of his own labour, and without this no human being will trouble himself to work for more than his bare living.

In Uganda, where the work of one woman will support ten men, and the area required for a single family is so very small (half an acre according to the French Fathers in Buddu), the result is to check all industry. The effect of this will be in the future to place grave difficulties in the way of Europeans.

The chiefs will undoubtedly oppose their people if they wish to work for the white man, and will take from them part of their wages. At present Europeans practically pay the chiefs, who tell their men to do the work, but although this seems to be at first sight a very cheap way of getting labour (from the European's point of view), it is a most pernicious and dangerous system. It is only the Government that should have the power of obtaining labour in this way, and neither missionaries nor traders should be permitted to get workers without directly paying them instead of the chiefs.

In fact, the policy which should be steadily kept in view is to replace this indefinite payment of rent in produce and labour by a fixed amount of money paid annually: for which a currency is urgently required.

There is already a kind of currency in cowries, but it is not yet sufficiently understood by the people. Just at present the Zanzibar currency is in a peculiarly hopeless state. There are Indian rupees, German rupees, Portuguese rupees stamped and not stamped, Imperial British East African rupees, Maria Theresa dollars and pice. All these coins vary in value partly conjointly from the value of silver and copper, and partly quite independently from the amount of each particular kind available. They should be replaced by a single standard coin, which should be current everywhere in British Africa—probably shillings, sixpences and pence.

If carefully done, neither the Sultan of Uganda nor his subordinates would object, because the present system has very grave disadvantages even from their point of view.

A chief, or an ordinary occupier, may be kept at the capital for months and his plantations may be quite destroyed through being neglected at a critical moment. Moreover, a chief is judged chiefly by the number of adherents which follow him, and hence a quantity of useless loafers have to be supported who do no definite work and always require feeding, and their work when given is half-hearted and bad. The chiefs are afraid to get full value from any person, for, if he considers himself ill-used, he will go and attach himself to some other master. The moral effect is still more serious, for without there being definite laws on the subject, all women and children are completely at the disposal of the feudal superior in practice, and the result can be easily understood.

Along with this fundamental ownership of land by the sovereign, there are many curious customs which in part counteract its effect. The chief, besides being landlord, is family solicitor, trustee, judge, jury, and field marshal of his people. There is even a kind of tenant-right, and unless there is some reason against it, a man's son will probably succeed to his father's shamba. All this shows, I think, a very high level of general intelligence in the people.

This is due probably to the dominant race, corresponding to the Normans in early England, being of a type far superior to the average negro. This race came from the north, probably the Soudan side of Abyssinia.* They are called in most works Wahima or Wahuma, and are probably seen in their least mixed condition in Karagwe,

* Certain authorities do not agree in my theory that the Wahima blood is the cause of the Waganda superiority.

particularly Buhimba and Kakaruka (see p. 252). They are mentally superior to, though morally far below, the average black man. In the Victoria region, they are much mixed with the aboriginal races, whose women have been brought as slaves from all directions, and the mixture produces a particularly promising type. They may be almost called the Japanese of Africa, from the manner in which they seem inclined to adopt and assimilate European ways and products. One Mganda, in Kampala, is a really good gunsmith; there are some who have begun to grow corn to sell to Europeans; and they are extremely anxious to get books, paper, pens, ink, crockery, European clothes, and, in fact, all articles which they see Europeans employ.

On entering the country I was much impressed by the way in which the first man I met begged me to give him a book. The only one I could spare was Coventry Patmore's "Angel of the House," with which he was entirely delighted. Probably, as he did not know a word of English, it really cultivated him as much as a Bible would have done.

It is this industrial development which should be fostered and encouraged by every possible means, and it is to my mind a great pity that the Church Missionary Society seem to have entirely dropped this part of their work which was most brilliantly inaugurated by Mackay. The French

Fig. 12.—A. CHAMÆLEON ELLIOTII GÜNTH.; B. CHAMÆSAURA TENUIOR GUNTH.; C. ELAPSOIDEA GUENTHERI JUN.

Fathers do far more service in prosaic commonplace ways to the Waganda on industrial lines.

It will thus be seen that there is an almost unlimited demand for our manufactures in the Victoria region. Every European in the country contributes, even if unintentionally, to produce this demand, and the following seemed to my mind the main objects to keep in view.

Countries which have been brought under our control by our own exertions should be settled by Waganda, with a fixed rent paid directly to ourselves, and a currency should be introduced for this purpose. This would not be difficult; the food they bring to us should be paid for in coin, and their tribute or rent for the lands on which they have been settled should also be paid in coin at a regular office in the station to the English administrator. Labour should be paid for in the same manner as food.

Every effort should be made to introduce gradually a currency payment in those parts of the country which have been long under the power of the native chiefs. These latter should be turned into paid Government officials in the process.

Europeans should be encouraged in every possible way. Means of transport should immediately be improved and rendered as cheap as possible. Another great requisite is a written codified law which could probably be extracted from the mass of customs and rules which exist now in the memories of the older chiefs.

When this is, even in a slight degree, attained, the coffee, tobacco, wheat, cattle, &c., of the Waganda will be paid for by our cloths, knives, and other articles, and both ourselves and the Waganda will be enormously benefited.

A very small number of Europeans—provided they are of the right class—would be sufficient to attain this end in some degree. One at Berkeley Bay, another in Kavirondo, one at Elgon, another in Usoga in a central position—not at Lubwas, which is a rather inconvenient place—two or three in Unyoro, one in Buddu, two about Ruwenzori, and perhaps three at Kampala; or say twelve Europeans in all, provided they knew the language and had a definite prospect of a career, if they proved capable, would entirely change the country, and in some degree produce a new British possession.

I was specially asked to look out in Buddu for a good station, and the arrangement of the swamps made this an easy matter. There is an isolated summit, Kiromanyi, so high that neither mosquitoes nor fever can do any harm: there are springs of good water and plenty of timber and cultivation in the immediate neighbourhood. It is only two hours from the Victoria, from which one could probably reach Ntebbi in two days and Changu in one day; this latter being rather an important spot, isolated from Kampala on the one side by the difficult Karungi swamps and from Buddu by the Katonga and Kurumbutu swamp-rivers, which are even worse.

On the other hand, from Kiromanji one could reach Villa Maria in one day and Bikira, the other important Roman Catholic mission station, in a long day's march. It also commands the one ford of the Nabajisu swamp, between which and the sea lies the most important part of Buddu.

If it were possible to have two stations in Buddu, a good site exists at Tiasimbe, not far from the Kagera river, and from this the various fords of the Kagera river could probably be controlled.

Marching in the Victoria region cannot be considered purely pleasure. The nights are long and hot, only varied by the constantly recurring buzz of a mosquito. Immediately one is killed another takes his place, for this insect never seems to learn by experience. Just as the morning grows comparatively cool and you are sinking luxuriously into sleep, the drowsy and shaky crow of the first cock rouses you. Then the boy enters the tent and begins to pack, so that there is no choice but to rise. The cold bath freshens one's spirits wonderfully, and two cups of cocoa and milk, a herring or sardine and two or three biscuits ornamented with jam, are rapidly swallowed, while things are disappearing into their proper boxes and the tent is taken down and packed. The way at first will lead through the curious hedges made of Euphorbia, then passing through a few little plots of maize and millet, it enters on a breezy, grassy plateau. After one or two hours of this, there comes into view a deep valley filled by a broad green swamp, bounded by strips of forest. Far too soon the morass is reached.

Now there are many ways of crossing a swamp. You may sit upon the shoulders of a stalwart Suahili and crook your legs under his armpits. The advantage of this method depends upon the efficiency of the Suahili and your own weight, but it is not pleasant at the best of times, as it is more than usual for your steed to subside, and you will emerge from the quagmire with mud in your eyes, rage in your heart, and improper words on your tongue.

Not at all a bad plan is to divest yourself of unnecessary clothing and march right through, but in this case your condition is appalling at the other end.

Another method is to scramble along the sides of the path, getting a precarious and slippery footing on the roots of the papyrus, and occasionally taking agile leaps over a hopelessly creamy piece. Only this almost always involves a false step, and one leg sinks into unknown depths of black and loathsome putrefaction.

Even twenty minutes of this sort of thing is exciting, but after half an hour one begins to look anxiously forward through the papyrus stems, which rise on either side to a height of 10 to 15 feet, for some sign of solid ground. Eventually, utterly tired out, wet and hot, and indescribably dirty, one reaches the bank, and perhaps immediately enters a dark, cool forest. The long tapering trunks seem to rise to an indefinite height, where, far overhead, the leaves, and perhaps a mass of blossom, can barely be distinguished. Sometimes a tangled mass of creepers hangs downwards, with gorgeous flowers scattered over it. Usually, the trunks are clothed with the broad, dark green leaves of climbing Aroids, and delicate feathery mosses cover every branch and twig. Over the muddy path, broken by gnarled, knotty tree roots, there are hundreds of little blue butterflies perpetually flitting to and fro, or sometimes stopping to suck, with apparently great enjoyment, the black and slimy soil. Occasionally a ghostly, pure white Papilio will swoop across the path, inviting wild plunges with the net. Often there are quantities of Acraeas, with transparent wings, dotted with bright crimson spots. These flap leisurely by, knowing that they are safe and inedible. Sometimes one comes across a flock of a large bright blue kind, which seems to be of a very sociable disposition.

After perhaps twenty minutes of this, the leader

emerges on the grass before the next ridge, and stops to rest. The porters come up one by one, throw down their loads with a bang, stretch their necks, and then carefully scrape off the caked filth from their legs. After a few minutes they begin to laugh and chaff the stragglers. When all have appeared, one has to start the caravan, climb the next ridge, and perhaps push on through the sweltering heat, possibly through another swamp, till two or three in the afternoon. About twelve the weary spirit begins to long for the sight of camp, and the happiest moment of the day is, undoubtedly, when, though tired and hungry, thirsty and footsore, you realise that, after an interval, a cold bath and food will be ready. To complete the experience of an average day, some Mabruki, or Khamis, will have been stealing from the Washinsi (*i.e.* savages), on whom the Suahili looks down with immeasurable contempt; and a long trial is carried on chiefly in a language of which your interpreter knows little, and which he translates into Suahili, of which very possibly you may know rather less. Then Mahamadi Wadi Musa will come up with the whole of a toe-nail torn away by a thorn, and you have to doctor him. You discover one of your boxes has been immersed during the day, and all the clothes will have a border of black. Another box will have been smashed against a tree, and you have to hammer and nail it together. All this is in

TRAVELLING EXPERIENCES.

addition to the day's work of drying and labelling your plants, putting animals into spirit, breaking rock specimens, packing up insects, plotting your day's march, taking the temperature, and perhaps a boiling observation for altitude, and writing your notes. Usually, one is busy from morning to night, and it is not till half an hour before bed-time that you close the day by half an hour of Shakespeare or Browning. (I cannot recommend anything else for daily and incessant reading.)

I notice that people always ask one when one returns home, "Did you enjoy yourself?"

A curious feature of some parts of the country is a gigantic grass, the "bamboo or elephant grass" of some travellers. This grows to a height of 10, 15, or even 20 feet, and the stems are usually scarcely 6 inches apart.

Sometimes I had to pass through this for 8 or 10 miles, and it was not pleasant. These stems, which overhang the path (only 18 inches wide), always begin to branch, and succeed in completely roofing it over. The way has to be forced under and through the haulms, which perpetually fly back and hit one across the face. The air is hot and stifling, and nothing is visible but this endless *matvitei*. The plant is, however, a sure sign of good and fertile soil, and the stems are extremely valuable for building houses. When young, the cattle are very fond of it, though it grows so quickly that it forms far too dense a thicket for them to graze in it. Probably, in the future, some means will be devised of cutting and storing these enormous supplies of green fodder for use in the dry season.

My own personal experiences in the Victoria region may be very shortly dismissed. After a rest at Mumia's and Lubwa's, where long lines of huts were rapidly springing up under the supervision of my host, Mr. Grant, I finally reached Kampala, the capital of Uganda. I found that Colonel Colville was engaged at the time in fighting Kabbarega, and that both the country to the east on the road to Elgon, as well as the direct route to Ruwenzori, were quite impracticable with the small number of men at my disposal.

Kabbarega was, as should be well known in this country, completely crushed by this expedition of Colonel Colville. The effect has been to free the whole of the country, from the Albert Edward and Albert Nyanzas to Kavirondo, from a constant standing danger. Kabbarega's people were one of those raiding, murderous races, whose very existence depends on theft and continual enslaving and destruction of the more peaceful and industrious peoples. Ruffians of this kind always obtain the sympathy of Mr. Labouchere and a certain section of fanatics in England, but those who know the cruelty and incessant destruction which the maintenance of Kabbarega's hordes involved, can only heartily congratulate Colonel

Colville on having brought peace and prosperity to this enormous country.

At Kampala, then, I had to spend a month waiting for news; and probably this was the pleasantest period of my journey, through the kindness and hospitality of Captain Gibb, who was in charge.

Finding that there was still no immediate prospect of the roads becoming clear, and being also very desirous of seeing the Kagera river, whose course seemed scarcely known in places, I decided to go down through Buddu to this river, coast along it for a certain distance, and then strike across Ankole to Ruwenzori. I hoped to return by a different route, and, in fact, did so, catching the Kagera at the bend of Latoma. I despatched some men with an old tweed suit and sundries to Antari, the sovereign of Ankole, with a request for a guide to show me across his country. One of these men, an Askari, Taratibu, was a most curious character. He was very plucky, very lazy, and seemed to have few redeeming qualities. In fact, I had had to degrade him to the condition of an ordinary porter for gross carelessness. I was struck by the fact that when this happened, and he refused to carry a load and made a disturbance, the others were afraid to tackle him, and I gave him therefore a chance to distinguish himself on this embassy. He managed it extremely well; made Antari believe I was a most important personage, and displayed such an amount of diplomacy and power of wheedling the natives that I made him eventually my headman, and he turned out the best I ever had. This is an instance of the advantage of watching carefully the disposition of one's men, without appearing to do so.

On leaving Kampala, Captain Gibb was most kind, giving me everything I could require, and particularly a valuable cow and calf, which kept me in fresh milk all the rest of my journey.

On the way I stopped a few days at the two French Catholic stations, Villa Maria and Bikira, where, as usual, I received the very greatest hospitality. It is the usual thing in a book of travels to write a chapter on Missions and Missionaries, but I have denied myself this pleasure (see chap. xx.), which would have involved a very high compliment to all the Roman Catholic Fathers, except their very diplomatic superior.

CHAPTER V.

ANKOLE AND KARAGWE.

AFTER traversing Buddu, I reached the Kagera river at the large village Musonje, and crossed it on the 11th of March. There were only two canoes available, and it took a great deal of time to pass over. I found at the crossing an Arab settlement. These Arabs were not in a happy frame of mind; one of them had been recently put in chains by the Government for slave dealing, and all complained that there was no ivory left. The German station, Kitangule, is considerably higher up the river, and there is another canoe there. I sent a letter of introduction, received from Professor Engler at Berlin, to the officer in command at Bukoba, and informed him that I had a pass, but this individual did not even reply.

I was able to understand Arab methods from the account of an unfortunate Munyamwesi porter, who had been engaged by an Arab to go to this place and return to Unyamwesi for seven doti of cloth : the poor wretch had been kept there half-starving for eighteen months!

After I had waited two days, my ambassador, Taratibu, appeared with the news that Antari was sending me a big chief, Lukala, to guide me through the country.

I went on past Kitangule, over the vast alluvial deposits of the Kagera river, which I kept in view till I crossed it at Kitoboka's on the 16th of March. I had reached the Karagwe hills on the 14th, and left the Victoria plateau. These hills, which extend over most of Karagwe and Ankole, are of a distinctly younger age than the granite of the Nyanza region. They consist of a series of clay slates, schists and quartzites, which appeared to me to be folded over and over again, and to overlie unconformably the granite and gneisses of which Uganda and the other countries in the Victoria region are composed.

They appear to be part of a series of rocks which are much developed in the basin of the Upper Congo, and probably extend south as far as the south end of Tanganyika. I call this the Central Watershed, for they separate the drainage area of the Nile from that of Tanganyika and the Congo.

These hills extend over most of Karagwe and Ankole; the Ruampala mountains, marked on most maps, are not easily distinguishable from the rest. Their general level is from 5,000 to 6,000

Fig. 13.—A Banana Grove on Ruwenzori.

feet (that of the Victoria plateau being usually from 4,000 to 4,100 feet); they are cut up by twisting and meandering valleys (often 1,000 feet deep) into a most curious meshwork. Travelling amongst these hills is not at all pleasant.

As a rule the road follows the watershed, keeping on the short grass which covers the summit; thus sometimes one may have to walk round a circle, perhaps 8 or 10 miles, to reach a point, separated by a deep valley, only some 4 miles off. These valleys are curiously steep-sided. Away down in the bottom one sees Euphorbia trees and isolated bushes or masses of bananas, and little grass huts, out of which the more active inhabitants come flying up the hill to stare on the European.

Usually speaking, they contain no running water, and the natives trust to springs which exist at isolated spots on the sides of the valleys, often about 4,700 feet up. This is an effect of the drying-up of the Victoria Nyanza, as already explained. Sometimes these valleys have only a narrow outlet, and are occupied by an immense papyrus swamp; some even appear to have no outlet at all.

The country appears to be very poor; there are only a few miserable huts, with scanty patches of sweet potatoes or beans, scattered about on the hills at long distances.

The best and most prosperous settlements are

along the sides of one of the few streams at the bottom of a valley, where there are often great plantations of banana, and a sufficiently strong population to keep off visitors.

The inhabitants of Karagwe and Ankole are very much the same. In both cases the present population is a mingling of an original Bantu race with Wahuma or Wahima people coming from Abyssinia. Of the two, the Wakaragwe ("Wa" means everywhere "people of") are much the best, and as is also the case everywhere, it is the Bantu section, usually the poorest and most hardworked labourers, who are good-natured and ready to assist.

A mere passing traveller like myself could not hope to unravel the mysteries of native races. There are some who obtain, by means of Suahili interpreters, curious and varied information as to native customs. One German scientist, in the course of a journey across Karagwe and Urundi which occupied less than two months, seems to have detected a "nordsudlicher Wandertendenz" in one-half of the country, a "sudnordlicher Wandertendenz" in the other, besides "closed colonies" of Zulus and others of unknown origin, and also "Watussi" and "Wassui."

He does not mention the Wahima or Wahuma. These to my mind are the dominant race, under whom live the remnants of the aboriginal (and quite distinct) Bantus. These latter are crossed

ANKOLE AND KARAGWE.

with slaves brought from all parts of Africa. Watussi seemed to me simply "herdsmen," not a national name, though, as stated above, they are usually of distinct origin.

The truth is that, unless one has resided for years in a country and knows both the language and people well, it is very difficult indeed to draw more than very general conclusions.

The WaAnkole are not at all a pleasant people. They are curiously sulky and obstinate. They are probably more inhospitable, without being simply warriors, than any other East African race. One effect of their quarrelsome nature is to isolate each little village from its neighbours, and the result is that every little collection of huts has a moral tone and character depending on that of the leading spirit in the community. Most of these little hamlets levy taxes on passers-by for water and wood or showing the way; and my small party (then only fifty men) would never have passed at all had I not been under the conduct of a well-known chief of Antari's.

We were supplied with provisions everywhere, and though I took care always to pay for them, it was only with much trouble that I prevented my chief, "Lukala," from annexing everything. The men usually wear a goatskin hung in an airy manner across one shoulder, and very often nothing else except amulets and ornaments. Some of the former seem to be charms written in bad Arabic characters; sometimes they are necklaces of leopard's or lion's teeth. They are fond of necklaces, bracelets, and leglets of beads or wire, and occasionally wear a thick ring of hippopotamus-skin round the wrist.

Both men and women seem to smoke as much as they possibly can, even while on the march. Nobody ever goes unarmed or lays aside his spear for a moment.

Lukala, the king's deputy, gave me a great deal of trouble; he was always begging and delaying our march as long as possible. He used to take it as a personal insult if I gave anything to the natives who had to bring us food by the king's orders, and occasionally stalked off in a huff, leaving us quite alone. Usually Taratibu managed to keep him in good humour, but I was very pleased indeed to get rid of him.

A German expedition, under Captain Langheld, had, for purposes which I do not understand, passed through Ankole a short time before my arrival. The leader wished, contrary to the expressed desire of Antari, to proceed to the latter's capital, and was in consequence attacked (though the natives say he fired upon them first). Langheld in a few minutes killed a pretty large number. The result was to make the people both bitter against and much afraid of Europeans.

A wretched porter of mine, at a spot near the route of this German caravan, who had only one

ANKOLE AND KARAGWE. 77

hand and neither spear nor gun, was foolish enough to go off by himself one night, and I never saw him again. Next morning I went all round the place and found every one had fled except one chief, who was too ill to move. I was in a terrible state of mind, but I did not think I was justified in punishing this man for a crime which he had apparently not committed, and we could not remain. The incident shows the utter

Fig. 11.—Scenery in the Central Watershed.

folly of the Suahili, who can never be taught caution, though he is not brave; and it greatly affected the spirits of every one.

Shortly after this we descended into the valley of the Ruizi river, which here flows through a broad alluvial plain and interrupts the mountains. This river rises in the Katara, a deep swamp valley in the hills, along which we passed later on, then emerging from a narrow pass into the plain, forms the broad and difficult Wamaganga swamp. From this point it flows to the Victoria Nyanza, broadening on the way into four or five large lakes, which have not been noticed, so far as I know, by any other observer.* It does *not* join the Kagera river, though it is represented as doing so on most maps—an error which appears to be due to Rumanika's information.

At last, on the 28th of March, after toiling up one of the stoniest and steepest of the Ankoli hills, I saw an enormous mountain mass, which could be nothing but Ruwenzori, the end and object of about 1,300 weary miles of marching. It was a very curious spot.

Looking south-east, my eye travelled along the edge of the Ruampalas; before me lay part of the Victoria plateau, here of a very broken, lumpy character, with occasional isolated hills, of which one, Ibanda, had much the appearance of a volcano. Except for these the plateau was seen to stretch right to the base of Ruwenzori.

This was one of the most agreeable periods of the trip, but it was soon overclouded, and all owing to the loss of an umbrella! I foolishly gave mine to Antari as a parting present, and in consequence got a slight touch of the sun which led to fever, from which I suffered at frequent intervals from that time till I turned the Cape of Good Hope on my way home.

* I have everywhere carefully abstained from giving names to any place, so that these lakes remain nameless.

ANKOLE AND KARAGWE. 79

It was a very bitter reflection to me when I was carried down to the shore of the Albert Edward Nyanza (two days afterwards) that a single act of folly had so greatly spoilt the value of my expedition.

That camp is one which I shall never forget. Just a little after sundown the dense white clouds

Fig. 15.—A Papyrus Swamp.

rolled away from the top of Ruwenzori, only leaving a white fleecy band across the dark blue hills. Every sharp indentation and jagged peak of the ridge for a distance of 50 to 60 miles was clearly outlined against the brilliant sunset sky, and over the main ridge the glittering snow peaks could be seen in every detail. Between us lay the silvery waters of Lake Ruisamba.

The scene after dusk was very different. The air was thick with mosquitoes; vast clouds of the males, with their feathery antennæ, were hovering round the fire, and soon afterwards the females began to dine. Sleep was impossible, and I had to listen all night to the frog-chorus. An old bass begins, Talk! talk! then the whole orchestra join in, keeping perfect time, till an ambitious youngster tries to lead himself, when some follow him and some the original leader, and all is discord for a minute or two. Then they stop and rest till the original majestic Talk! talk! begins, and so on.

Next morning we were carried over in canoes to a chief's town, called Kuliafiri, and on the very inauspicious date, April 1, 1894, I was carried, more dead than alive, to the base of Ruwenzori.

CHAPTER VI.

NORTH-EASTERN VALLEYS ON RUWENZORI.

OUR first camp on Ruwenzori was at the Lukojia river, just after its issue from the hills. From here we went on to Fort Edward (Captain Lugard's fort). This place lies between the Sebwe and Mubuku rivers; the latter had been mentioned to me by Lugard as being probably the best way to reach the snow. I therefore went up its valley, which took us about five hours. It has a curiously flat alluvial and stony bed, covered with Acacia, from which the hills rise abruptly on either side. Those near the fort are low and rather detached from the main range. About 8 miles up the valley I crossed a small spur to cut off a corner of the Mubuku, and entered another flat alluvial portion covered with long elephant grass, soon finding myself in a little village protected by a tall hedge, which belongs to Korohoro. This chief owns all the country on the left bank of the Mubuku river, and is a very decent person. I passed his village, and crossed the Mubuku at a very difficult ford, to establish my camp on a small buttress of the mountain, whence there was a most lovely view up the river. It is a steep, forest-clad valley, in which one sees here and there the silver streak of a waterfall. About sundown the clouds began to roll away with most aggravating hesitation, and a series of huge mountains with shining strips of snow on their precipitous sides began to appear one after the other. One I called Mount Premolar, from its shape; it seems to be the one which I reached from the Nyamwamba valley afterwards. I had one or two attacks of fever, and was waiting to enable me to get sufficient strength back, when several ominous facts began to appear.

Unfortunately there was no food to be had, and the people were shy and much afraid of Kasagama, the Sultan of Toru, who sent to say he wished to see me. I thought it best to go and see him first, intending to return after investigating the nature of the other valleys, for it seemed from my maps that near Butanuka I ought to be very close to the central chain.

This part of the mountain was a very bad place for leopards. One very dark night a porter went outside the camp and was seized by one. On hearing the noise I rushed out, and, after some trouble and much expenditure of powder, found the man with part of his cheek bitten out and severe wounds on the neck. As soon as I had attended to him the leopard leaped into the camp amongst the fires and seized another man. When I got to him I found a bad cut in his breast and blood spurting from a wound in the neck; he was breathing through the breast and part of the lung was visible. With much trouble we got his wounds sewn up by means of an ordinary needle and thread. I spent the rest of the night in a chair, with a rifle across my knee, and though the animal tried twice to get into the camp, we saw it in time.

These creatures never used to prey on man, according to native report; but since all the goats and fowls had been driven off by Kabbarega they had become a great nuisance. The natives build high fences of branches and elephant grass and retire within them at 3 p.m. every day. Leopards in this part hunt in perfect silence, never coughing as they do in West Africa. I am glad to say both these men reached the coast safely, in spite of my surgery.

Coming down the Mubuku valley, I had a magnificent view of eight elephants, who marched past us. When walking about they usually go in single file, forming a broad, well-trodden path. Usually their tails are stuck out at an angle of 45 degrees. One young bull tried to push in front of an older one, who simply turned and looked at him, on which the young one fell back, promptly curling up his trunk, shaking his ears, and looking very vicious. They deploy into line to graze.

Although we must have been only 100 yards off, they did not seem to notice us. I had already found that my ·577 rifle was too heavy for me, and did not attempt to shoot them.

Retracing our steps to Fort Edward, we started next day for Kasagama's. I managed to get a waterbuck near the fort, which I suspect is a new species not unlike the Singsing. Just after the curious isolated hill Kobokera, one has to cross the Mubuku which here forms about seven rivers, whose channels are constantly altering.

The way lies across the old bed of the Ruisamba lake, consisting of sand, shingle, and clay, covered with grass and a few thorn-trees. On my way to Kasagama's the young grass was springing up, and I saw quantities of antelope and several small herds of elephants.

On returning, the grass had sprung up to two or three feet and was partly withered, and no game was to be seen. It consists in this part of spear grass and several species of Andropogon, and is too dense when mature for the smaller antelopes to traverse it easily.

This is the general character of the plateau near the mountain (probably 200 feet above the level of the lake) from the Wimi river to near the Salt lake. On coming close to the lake shore thin woods of thorn-trees and Euphorbias appear. There is no cultivation on these plains worth mentioning, probably because, except on the rivers, there is no water and the natives cannot dig wells or irrigate. Cattle could probably be kept in large numbers, but would require to shift their feeding ground, though if the grass was burnt in portions regularly, probably a continual supply of fodder could be obtained.

At the Winni ford, which is a beautiful ravine full of fine timber, we entered on the lower outlying hills which before Butanuka give place to a richly cultivated area, extending all over the country to Kasagama's and even beyond this towards the Albert Nyanza.

Kyatwa hill, near Butanuka, is the remains of an old volcanic cone. Its top overlooks a vast plain stretching to the forest about Kivari; just under the hill is a beautiful little crater lake, and a few other volcanic cones, all of small size, are visible in the neighbourhood.

The cultivated country towards Kasagama's lies entirely upon gneiss and another rock "epidiorite," and though of considerable elevation is intersected by the usual broad swamp-rivers of the Victoria region. The abundance of elephant grass and a profusion of the flowering shrubs of Uganda clearly separates it from the grassy alluvial plains.

I had to spend three days of fever at Butanuka, which were rendered hideous by the lamentations of a "black Ibis," a bird with a long beak (8 inches) which frequents swamps, cannot be killed by Suahilis, and never stops screaming in a very raucous voice.

I found Kasagama to be a tall, rather stout young man, about thirty-five years of age. He was set on his throne by Lugard, and when driven from it by Kabbarega was reinstated by Major Owen.

On the way I had the pleasure of meeting his mother, who was going down to the Salt lake on some mysterious mission, accompanied by a most truculent-looking set of warriors. Both are of nearly pure Wahima race, and from my experience of them, both are cowardly and untrustworthy, though not lacking in cleverness.

A considerable amount of state is observed by both. They are constantly followed about by a crowd of dissipated courtiers, chiefly boys and young men. It is very funny to see the manner in which these hangers-on pretend to be desperately fond of the king and his mother, nestling up to their feet with little cries of joy and seizing their hands; but I fancy it is not a perfect love that is without fear.

I had the excitement of a lion hunt at Kasagama's. These animals hide near the native plantations and pounce on any woman who is working by herself. One morning a great crowd came rushing to me to say that one had seized a woman. I rushed, with some of my men, to the spot and found her remains in some long

Fig. 16.—Kasagama, Sultan of Toru.

elephant grass. It was a nasty place, and while going slowly through it, I just caught a glimpse of a lioness and four cubs disappearing. It was far too much of a snapshot to fire, and I got some natives to track, and spent four hours marching through a swamp by the road they were said to have gone. We were supposed to have chased them into a dense place at the end, and took our places in perfect silence and intense excitement while this was being driven out, but nothing appeared except a particularly vocal "black Ibis"!

From Kasagama's I also visited the charming little lakes of Vijongo. One of these is a perfect cone with a beautiful blue crater lake inside, and there is a row of four or five similar cones beside it.

I had another attack of fever, and told Kasagama I would die if I did not get up to the hills, so I at last started and set up my camp at Kivata, at about 6,615 feet, just above the Msonje river.

In two days we built a nice little fort of stick and elephant grass, thatched with banana leaves, which ran round two sides of a triangle; and though the chief, Makwenda, told me that if a lion or leopard felt the desire to jump in, he would have no difficulty in doing so, this gave a feeling of security to my men. As soon as this was ready, I had another fever attack.

It rained every day, turning the floor of my hut

to a black morass; and I had to remain for four or five days, too weak to move, and wondering what on earth had induced me ever to come.

Then at last I struggled up to the forest and managed to get to about 7,000 feet, where I found myself in a new world. There was the common English Sanicle, a beautiful Meadow Rue, a Cerastium, and many other plants which induced me to believe that I should really bring back something of interest.

The presence of forms like these almost on the equator involves certain facts that are rarely realised; perhaps less clearly by systematic botanists than by quite unscientific people. How did they get there?

It is not hard to see why they were able to live at this altitude, even on the equator, provided they were once introduced, because even at 7,000 feet the temperature is not very different from that of England. There is, moreover, no lack of moisture, which would produce the desert type of plant, especially when combined with heat; nor is there the excess of it and the steaminess found, for instance, in the Wimi valley (see p. 190), by which the characteristic tropical forest would be formed. In essentials, in short, the climate is fairly moist, not unlike Southern Europe in July; and I found these plants flowering in the same month as their cousins far away in Dumfriesshire.

The difficulty is to understand *how they got there.* I have never seen birds either swallowing or carrying about on their feet the seeds of the three plants named (I could also mention the Forget-me-not, the Willow herb, the St. John's Wort, &c.), so that one must hold it as proved that there was once a continuous European climate from the original birthplace of most of our genera (the Garden of Eden—vegetable department) to Ruwenzori, Kenia, and Kilimandjaro on the one side, and Ireland on the other. My own beliefs on this subject will be found in Chapter XII.

As my strength returned I managed to get to know the forest fairly well, and at last, greatly to my disgust, found myself at the top, which was only 10,544 feet, showing, of course, that I was much too far to the north and only on the ridge of the mountain.

It perhaps will give a good idea of the character of Ruwenzori to describe the position of my camp at Kivata.

It was on a sort of buttress. On one side there was a very steep descent, leading to a small stream about 1,000 feet below, which curved round the prolongation of my ridge to join the Msonje river; to which latter there was an almost equally steep descent on the north.

Below me lay a few rounded hills clustering near the foot of the mountain, and on them lay

Makwenda's little round camp and green masses of banana plantations. Away to the south-east stretched the grassy plain, with two little bright lakes and a corner of Lake Ruisamba in the distance. To the east this ended in the dark forest and distant and confused hills of Kivari. All round my camp were grassy hills and knolls covered with a few fields of beans, and (in the barer and drier parts) supporting quantities of beautiful orchids and flowering shrubs. Just above me lay the dark forest, and the ascent was so steep (nearly 70 degrees) that I could only see the bamboos on the extreme summit of the ridge, and had to imagine the snow peaks behind.

This chief Makwenda I found to be a most entertaining person. He had tried to prevent my reaching the mountain, but as I would not stop, though I listened gravely to his arguments, which lasted all day when he got the chance, we began to be friends. He had not the most rudimentary idea of the truth, but grew to respect me when he found that I always appeared interested in his stories, though it was obvious I did not believe a word of them. He also realised that the cloth and beads which I gave for my food were a good institution, and we really began to appreciate one another. He offered me everything he had (when he knew I did not want it), and was very anxious to marry me, which showed a good feeling.

It will be seen from his photograph (see Fig. 19, chap. vii.) that one would not be very surprised to see a similar face (in white) in Europe. This is a characteristic of the Wahima, of which he was a very pure specimen.

Thence I moved on to the Yeria valley, where I stopped several days in a new camp in a somewhat similar position, though here I was within a curious outer ridge of hill running parallel to the mountain through which the Wimi forces its way by a deep narrow gorge towards the south. The situation will be more clearly seen from the small map.

It will be noticed that a series of buttresses project outwards towards the deep and narrow valley, part of which is occupied by the Yeria and part by a small tributary of the Wimi.

All these ridges and the hill forming the barrier are covered with short grass or plantations of beans, &c. In sunny places on steep slopes from which the rain flows rapidly downwards, there is a kind of dry and sunny climate, leading to a profusion of orchids and of vivid-coloured flowering plants. I have noticed everywhere that in places like this, where there is plenty of sunlight and not enough humidity to form a large amount of branches and leafage, the surplus nourishment is usually disposed of in bright colouring. A curious instance of this effect carried to extremes is an orchid (*Disa erubescens* Rendle) which is all over the curious red colour which one often sees on the leaves and stems, *e.g.*, of our common Herb-Robert in England.

Other instances of this sort of flora may be seen, *e.g.*, on the limestone hillocks about Alexandria, and on Table Mountain summit.

Shortly before entering the forest proper, one is sensibly impressed by the extremely dense nature of the bush bordering it, which can be best described as a hedge of indefinite thickness through which the way had to be regularly bored.

Fig. 17. Bush and Forest.

This can be easily shown by a figure. It is practically a bush, and very much as if one tried to walk through the tops of the trees in a particularly dense forest. The wind on the orchid and grass ridges has free scope and prevents permanent humidity, and the formation of tall, straight trunks, which do not occur till one has definitely entered the dark cool aisles of the forest proper.

The hand of man even on Ruwenzori is not

entirely without influence. The natives are perpetually chopping at any branch large enough for firewood, and hence, on the border of the forest, assist in maintaining this dense hedgy bush.

If we suppose the explorer in the figure to have entered the forest and to be walking at ease by the enormous trunks where the ground is covered by ferns or scanty, long-branched bushes, he would, after three hours' climbing, reach a much gentler ascent at about 8,600 feet. Here the wind has no steep slope behind it, and big trunks are unable to resist its force. Hence, in a similar way to that noticed for the Mau forest, numerous slender, flexible trunks replace one enormous rigid one, though these are often found in the more sheltered ravines, and very soon the bamboos, which are exactly suited to these conditions, replace them and occupy the whole of the upper ridges. This elevated ascent, though gently sloped and exposed to wind, is not in the least dry; on the contrary, these ridges are in almost as moist a climate as one could find anywhere. The daily cloud which envelopes the mountain invests them all night and scarcely leaves them for an hour or so at sunset. Moreover, I do not think that in the early morning they are above the clouds like those parts of the chain above 10,000 feet.

Hence they are in a rather cold, very humid,

climate with, so far as I could judge, an average temperature of 50 to 60 degrees.

It will be noticed (by those who care to do so) that the grass order to which these bamboos belong is typically one suited to open plateaux and

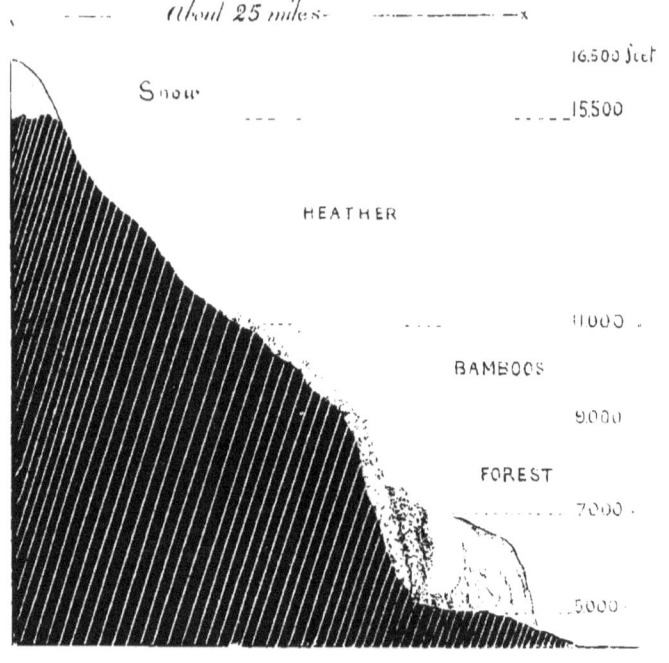

Fig. 18. VEGETATIVE SECTION OF RUWENZORI.

gentle mountain slopes, while the typical forest fills sheltered hollows and ravines, river valleys and steep ascents.

This brings me to another curious feature of Ruwenzori. The daily cloud does not hang exactly at the same height across the mountain side. In the valleys it is much lower, descending often to below 6,000 feet, while on the buttress-ridges it is usually 7,000 feet (on the eastern side). Moreover, towards the north end of the chain, it sinks and at the same time becomes narrower.

All these features can be readily perceived as wind-effects. The mist clings to the steep mountain sides and in the shelter of the valleys, and would of course be blown over the projecting ridges and the lower parts of the chain.

As the explorer pursues his way upwards, he suddenly finds the bamboos stop and a most curious difference in everything. The ground is a peat moss, covered with Sphagnums often to a depth of 18 inches. In this grow bushes and trees of heather, small trees of Hypericum and curious gigantic Lobelias, more like Echiums than anything else. Numerous forms belonging to such genera as Senecio (groundsel) take on the characteristic primeval branching of the Dragon-tree (*Dracæna Draco*) of the Canaries. That is to say, they branch six or seven times in their lives and all together, and leaves grow in a cluster at the ends of the branches.

In its curious ingenuous simplicity this form of vegetation irresistibly reminds one of Pterodactyls and Plesiosauri.

I was immediately struck with the extraordinary resemblance of the Flora to that of the peak of Teneriffe at a somewhat lower level. This resemblance is not an effect of fancy, but is really borne out by a variety of botanical details not suited to a book of travels. A curious difference lies in the absence of Conifers (except Podocarpus), which are replaced by bamboos, but with this exception the parallel is very curious.

From the various facts given in Chapter XII., it will be seen that Teneriffe would at one time have lain at the extreme end of the Sahara sea, which may have extended to the Abyssinian mountains, with which latter Ruwenzori is certainly closely related florally.

In some of the narrow corries about 11,000 feet, one finds an extraordinary development of heather trees. Some were certainly nearly 2 feet in diameter, and I estimated their height as 80 feet!

On emerging from the bamboos in a very tired and hot and wet condition, I always used to sit down beside the violets (*Viola Abyssinica*) and watch the myriads of small bees, butterflies, and long-tongued buzzing flies (*Bombylidæ*) which were always busy upon it. One of these butterflies appears to be a new species, *Amauris Elliotii*. All were quite different from those seen in the lower slopes; but it is one of the peculiarities of Ruwenzori that butterflies are not by any means common, whereas they seem to swarm in the low-level forests of the Victoria region.

On the other hand, sunbirds are common on the mountain. One of these, *Nectarinia Kilimense* (also found on Kilimandjaro and Mlanje), is frequent at low levels up to perhaps 7,000 feet, feeding on the banana flowers. In one spot there were numbers living on a flaming red Combretum. This is a beautiful little creature with a pink and bronze shot over the whole body.

Another Nectarinia (apparently *N. Johnstoni*) I have seen up to 11,000 feet. It feeds chiefly on long-tubed flowers of the Labiate and Acanthus families. In order to save it too much trouble in honey gathering, those flowers which it specially frequents are almost all collected in masses at the end of a branch.

I mention this because one of the most general rules of flowering is that a condensed rosette or umbel of flowers at the end of the stalk is characteristic of a dry and exposed climate.

During a pretty long stay between the Yeria and Kivata camps, I had plenty of opportunity for investigating the flora thoroughly. On days (far too frequent) when I was unable to walk far, I used to get up to the moistiest part of the forest and hunt for fungi. On the rotting sticks and leaves in this rainy and hot climate, these were curiously abundant. I have gathered perhaps seventy, all different, in as many minutes. One form has the most curious distribution I have ever heard of. It is only known from three places—Texas, Japan, and Ruwenzori! This is also a feature of the bamboo zone. Every old fragment has eruptions of delicate little white mushrooms, or red or yellow forms, besides slimy Myxomycetes and black dots of Perisporiaceæ. It is, of course, the moisture and rapid decay of everything that produce this effect.

Once in the forest I came across a swarm of locusts. Driven upwards by a strong east wind, they had arrived at about 7,000 feet and were covering every branch in heaps, unable to rise higher on account of the wet which clogged their wings.

At last, after I had refused to have any more guides, I discovered the two paths which lead over the mountain in this part to the Wawamba country and reached the summit at two places. That at the Yeria, which the natives had kept very dark, is a very fair path during the lower portion, as the natives constantly bring down bamboos for their houses. These are tied in bundles and hauled down. This is the only way in which the forest can ever be utilised, and it would not be at all difficult to slide the trunks down to one of the larger rivers, by which they might possibly be floated down to a navigable part of the Wimi or Durro, and even perhaps to the Ruisamba.

From this summit of the Yeria I could just catch a glimpse of the Semliki valley, on the west, before the clouds again shrouded everything in mist. Probably, however, it is by the Wimi valley that the best pass could be obtained.

I went on to this valley after satisfying myself

that the snow peaks were still a long way to the south-west, and from what I saw there I came to the conclusion that there was probably a deep depression in the chain. I tried to find a path along the valley several times, but came to the conclusion that there was none except those I followed, which always turned up into the bamboos after a considerable distance.

This valley is very different to any other which I saw. Its most objectionable feature is the rain. The natives said that it always rained every day; but this was injudicious, for during a fortnight's stay I had two moderately fine days (this was the dry season). In consequence probably of this, there is extremely little cultivation in the valley, and hence no paths.

It is also in consequence of this that the whole valley is covered with an extremely dense virgin forest of a type much more like those in the Congo basin than any others on the eastern side of Africa. I have been extremely interested to find that many of the forms I gathered there are species that occur all down the Congo river and along the West Coast of Africa, from Banana Point to Sierra Leone and Senegal.

There is a most exquisite waterfall just above my camp (see Fig. 32, chap. xii.). A turbulent mountain stream, the Wimi, springs down a precipice of black schist. The photograph I took does not, however, at all represent the extreme beauty of this gorge. I went a considerable distance up the river and found it one of the most interesting of all. There are probably 15 miles at least of virgin forest, and the valley is usually 3 miles wide. About two hours from my camp I was much astonished to find myself in a glade of tree ferns (*Cyathea sp. nov.*). Some of these were 20 feet high; all were covered with soft green moss and quantities of Peperomias, Begonias, and ferns of all possible different shapes. The wetness of everything was indescribable. One can form a fairly good idea of this valley by entering a conservatory, *e.g.*, the Fernhouse at Kew Gardens. So far as I could gather, the conditions are very much those of the Carboniferous age. They may be roughly described as a "dim hot steaminess." Although it is apparently fanciful, it is none the less literally true, that there has been a continuity of climate and physical conditions from that ancient date to the present, though the climate and conditions may have migrated over a whole continent in the interval. I have seen such places in West Africa and Madagascar, and also—though scarcely so marked —in the lowest and most sheltered spots of the Perie bush in South Africa, and everywhere one finds something of the same kind, an abundance of cryptogams of all kinds, Peperomias and a few other plants. Amongst the latter is a very delicate, slender orchid, which always lives on wet leaf mould and has been named *Disperis nemorosa* by Mr. Rendle.

In such a place vegetation of a low type can multiply indefinitely, because there is no check either by drought or cold. There is a want of sunlight and of the higher insects or sunbirds, so that there are very few brilliant flowers except on the very tops of the trees and high-climbers. Such flowers as do exist are usually pale coloured and occasionally large, and thereby gain an advantage in being more conspicuous; though the cause is simply the dim diffused light and the want of check to increase in the size of the petals. Leaves usually become large, flaccid, and drooping in such places, and this is an effect of the same thing, which once more exemplifies the way in which environment directly produces such variations as are distinctly advantageous under the circumstances.

After trying all the paths around the Wimi (which were very bad, as the ascents were usually precipitous and almost always slippery with wet mud and choked by branches), I determined to proceed down to Katwe, the Salt lake, and try the western side of the chain. I therefore started down the valley to Butanuka, passing on the way a hot spring, which joins the left bank of the Wimi just before it emerges from the hills.

CHAPTER VII.

WAHIMA, WAKONDJA, AND SUAHILIS.

I HAVE already alluded to Kasagama, who was found by Captain Lugard in Uganda, and was by him instated as the sovereign of Toru. When Kabbarega invaded Toru, of course Kasagama and his people fled to islands in the Albert Edward Nyanza. Neither he nor any of his chiefs had the pluck to attempt any resistance whatsoever. Major Owen and Mr. Grant reinstated Kasagama in his possessions when they had driven out Kabbarega's people, and also made him sovereign of a country called Usongora, which extends from the Semliki to the Salt lake, thus giving him a supremacy (which he, of course, looked upon as absolute authority) over the Wawamba on the western side of Ruwenzori. Immediately the Europeans had departed, Kasagama sent an expedition to assert his authority over various of the chiefs settled to the south-west of Ruwenzori. This expedition performed its duty by seizing the cattle of anybody who possessed such. At one village called Karimi they killed one woman and carried off twenty-one others. They also seized all the ivory which they could find and returned in triumph. This appears to be a strenuous policy, but it is only what every African potentate considers as his due; a chieftaincy simply consisting in their eyes of the right to screw as much of the three articles of value, cattle, ivory, and women, out of their subordinates as they possibly can. As an integral part of his treaty consisted in a promise to put down slavery, this was not exactly fair; but the real failure of Kasagama lies in the fact that he does not and never can carry out the supposed duty corresponding to the rights of the chieftain, which is to protect every one of his people from outside attacks and plundering from any source. The importance of protection against raids is so great that it counterbalances a very large amount of tyranny.

Kasagama is a tall, strong, and rather stout man, much bigger and finer to look at than any of his people, and he is not by any means wanting in the characteristic Wahima shrewdness and power of driving a hard bargain. His court consists of a large following of vicious and dissipated boys and youths, who enjoy a very bad reputation in the country. When he is in a bad humour, they receive knocks all round; and when he is good-natured, drinking, singing, and dancing go on all night long. His mother, Maosolia, enjoys a good deal of his confidence, and has a certain amount of authority on her own account. When proceeding to Kasagama's, I met her and an army of most villainous scoundrels on their way down to the Salt lake. She must have been once good-looking, and is a most affable and gracious lady, but I was not satisfied with her account of the expedition. It was really intended to turn out three minor chiefs, Kasuiri, Kuliafiri, and another, who had refused to fight Kabbarega, which was, of course, exceedingly wrong. They had probably added a crowning touch to their iniquity by sending ivory and provisions to the Suahili garrison at the Salt lake instead of to Kasagama himself.

The history of this expedition was peculiar. When the first two people of her advanced guard arrived, the erring Kasuiri and his friends fled with all their men. The Queen Mother then asked the Suahili headmen to hand over these two chiefs, as she wanted to kill them. This request was very properly refused. Mukwia, the headman of the Suahilis, then heard (or invented a rumour) that a party of Wanynema were coming to the Salt lake, and very pluckily (if it was really true that they came at all) went to see them and find out what they wanted. It was said thirty Wanynema did come simply to buy salt, and they are also said to have wished to settle there and send their ivory to the sea by Uganda.

This was a very important commercial proposal

if true. The news of these Wanyuema having been reported to the Queen Mother and her warriors, probably in a revised Suahili version, these and Maosolia at once fled precipitately to a safe island. While this was going on I had frequent and agonised messages from both sides, asking for advice and assistance; and this was the juncture at which I appeared upon the scene.

Now there were certain very suspicious charges of stealing women against Mukwia; but I considered he had shown, for a Suahili, such extraordinary qualities either of pluck or of ingenuity that I did not care to send him to the capital, as Colonel Colville in a way authorised me to do if necessary. I half suspected the Wanyuema were a Suahili invention; but if this was so, Mukwia was far too good a man to send away, so I had a long, weary talk, and arranged that Kasuiri and his two friends were to send their ivory and cattle only to the Government at the Salt lake and not to Kasagama. They were, however, to call Kasagama their father. As to the charges against Kasagama, they appeared to me to show that he did not put down slavery, but actually made slaves himself; and yet in the circumstances, without a resident European with proper authority, there was no use in doing anything for the Suahilis, if too much encouraged, would probably have behaved in a far worse manner. I therefore contended myself with asking Colonel Colville to send an officer to administer the country, and explaining things as well as I could.

In the light of recent information, it is obvious that this story of a wish to send ivory through our territory is an effect of the Belgian fighting in the north-west Congo region. Sefu, who was probably killed soon after sending this message, was hemmed in by the Ruanda on the east and Belgians on the west and south, and probably thought he could find an outlet to the north-east. If a European had been there at the time, it might have been possible to open up a new commercial road.

So far as I can gather, the nobility of Kasagama are the remnants of the great Wahima invasion which apparently travelled up the Nile from Abyssinia *via* Ankole and Karagwe to the borders of Uhha, Unyamwesi, and Urundi. This raid appears to have been definitely checked at Buhimba and Kakaruka, where small colonies, probably the nearest approximation to the pure descendants of these invaders, may now be found. They left in Toru a very considerable number of headmen, who have been placed as chiefs over the various Wakondja villages along the east and south-east.

In the Appendix I have given a list of the more important chiefs, which does not, however, pretend to be complete. The more important of these are small kings, with an almost unlimited power in their own district, as can be realised by the following story :—

At the Wimi, an old man came to me to say that Virungo had taken his two boys, one a son and the other his slave, and would not give them up. I told him to wait four days; and he waited, nearly dying of starvation in the interval. Then I sent an askari over to Virungo and told him to give up the boys. Greatly to my disgust the man and two boys came back and begged me to take them to the Salt lake, where they could join themselves to some other chief. Virungo came to see me on my way there, and tried every means of inducing me to give them up or send them to Kasagama. The man turned pale at the bare idea of this and fell down and seized my knee, saying they would kill him on the road. As I had no doubt whatever that this was true, and as Makwenda was obliged to admit that the man if he wished to join another chief had legally the right to take both his sons and slaves with him, I simply took them to Katwe, where they joined on to Kasuiri.

It is not too much to say that the chief has absolute power in his own district. He can take anybody's son or wife, or as much of his property as he likes and, unless the man is able to over-bribe Kasagama, there is no appeal. Unless he is also a man of great pluck and determination, he would never reach the supreme chief at all. In fact, the sole resource for a man in bad odour with his chief, is to fly to some one else and leave everything behind him. If burdened with property and children, he would be overtaken and speared on the road.

These Wahima seem on the whole to be an extremely shrewd, clever people, with plenty of obstinacy and a certain amount of dogged perseverance. They are very cowardly, and seem to be peculiarly immoral even according to African and Arab points of view. Of course they have no idea of the truth, and their answers are solely dictated by a desire to please.

As an instance of minor difficulties in work, and the value of native geographical testimony, I received the following three opinions as to the course of two rivers.

1. The Msonje river joins the Mpango.
2. The Msonje river joins the Yeria.
3. It goes quite by itself to the Albert Edward Nyanza.

Of course there was no fourth alternative possible, or else there would probably have been a fourth answer.

The number of chiefs is not very large and they appear to belong to particular families. I found that the chiefs of fairly important sub-districts were often boys of ten to fourteen years of age. Most of these boys were on property belonging to the Queen Mother, and they were usually called her sons. Sometimes also a very old man may be found as chief.

These little points mark very clearly the unwarlike character of the Watoru, for in a warlike and active people like the Waruanda the chief is almost always a young man in the prime of life, and able to lead the war-parties.

The Wakondja have a very different expression and build; they are rather thick-set, with the appearance of greater strength. They have more hair on the face, and particularly a much more negroid jaw than the Wahima. They are not by any means intelligent, and in spite of the oppression of their chiefs, exhibit a degree of obstinacy and determination which one would not expect. Once they realise that you wish to be fair and just to them, they will trust you and be very friendly. With a Suahili caravan, it is quite impossible to prevent a great deal of small larceny and oppression being exercised by your own people without your knowledge, and hence one is at a great disadvantage in dealing with the natives of the country, but I think a perfectly fair and just European would be simply worshipped by them, and be in no danger whatever.

The heavier work of clearing the land is done by the men, who are extremely expert at this business, and they also assist the women in the ordinary work of cultivation. They usually begin work about 7.30 a.m. and keep on pretty steadily till midday. I do not think they often work in the afternoon.

Bananas are usually planted in the more

sheltered valleys and gentle slopes, up to 6,600 feet. In the Wimi, and elsewhere, they are greatly plundered by a kind of baboon, which comes down in bands with sentinels posted on a prominent place to give notice of danger. The elephants in the Nyamwamba valley also do a great deal of damage, and if a flock of locusts should happen to alight on a plantation, nothing is left but the midribs of the leaves—this damage, however, is not permanent, as the plants soon recover.

Usually speaking these banana plantations are covered by a dense jungle of weeds curiously distinct from those found in uncultivated places. Many of these plantation plants are of American origin, and I fancy most have accompanied the banana wherever it has been carried by man. Sometimes, however, a good deal of care is taken, and in one place I have seen a very considerable amount of irrigation carried on.

On the bare slopes, and high up the valleys to nearly 7,200 feet, the cultivation usually consists of beans, wimbi, "hungry rice," and sweet potatoes; there are also in the higher valleys quantities of the edible Arum. Fresh cleared land is planted in May with beans, which are said to yield a crop three or four months afterwards, and along with them pumpkins and gourds of various sorts. It is afterwards planted with "hungry rice," and then left to the bush, and a fresh

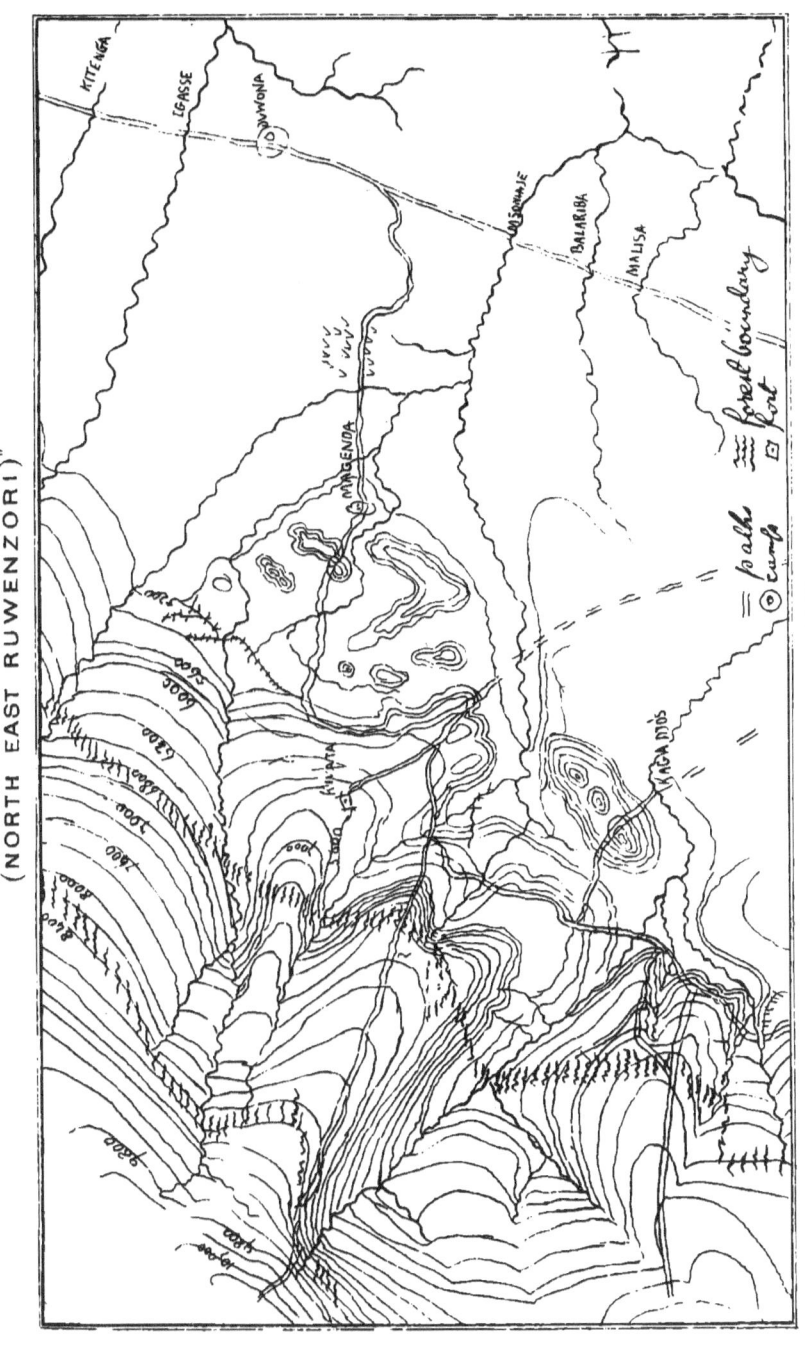

clearing is made. The houses are built of a framework of sticks and chiefly covered by banana leaves or elephant grass.

The people seem to have no amusements whatever. They are very much afraid of appearing too well off, so that I fancy they are much more industrious than they appear to be.

The ownership of every plantation is entirely with the chief of the district; if there happens to be an abundance of food then every one gets as much as he wants, but in a state of famine or scarcity there is absolutely no kind of communal property; everybody looks most strictly after his own farm, and is quite justified in killing any one who takes food from it.

When a man dies, the plantations are usually carried on by his grown-up sons, one of whom is appointed by his immediate superior to succeed him.

If he dies leaving only young children, the chief acts theoretically as the trustee for these children, and keeps things going till the sons grow up and succeed. I fancy, however, the trustee is usually a fraudulent one, and he can certainly very easily get rid of the children if he wishes to put somebody else in the farm. Women have no rights of succession at all (at least so far as I could gather), and a man's daughters are simply part of his estate and enrich the chief who owns it. Each is worth three cows or thirty goats.

It is said that the woman is always asked by her *fiancé* before the latter goes to her father to make his bargain about buying her. Prince Krapotkine's idea that savages adhere to their unwritten marriage laws quite as closely as civilised people to their written ones is in a sense true. This is because the law is so very indefinite. A chief can obtain as a wife anybody in the district that he wishes, and as a rule there is no difficulty for an ordinary man in obtaining any woman as a wife, provided he can pay her father the amount required of cloth and cattle. If the woman is badly treated and runs away, she is brought back to her husband and thoroughly beaten. In rare cases I fancy she can remain with her father provided he gives back to her husband the amount received for her.

If a man is tired of his wife, he simply tells her to go, but this does not often happen, because women are useful as field hands; and seeing that a man can have as many wives as his means allow, one can realise how simple it is to keep such an unwritten marriage law! In fact, the idea of unfaithfulness in the sense in which it is understood by Europeans never, I think, enters the heads of natives. They are really fond of their children, but I do not think their affection for their wives is at all obvious.

Theft is punished by beating, and a man is usually tied up till he returns what he stole, or he may be sold as a slave.

When I asked Makwenda how they punished a man who had killed somebody, he replied, "They never did anything bad now they knew Europeans"; a delicious piece of humbug.

Everywhere I found the people most anxious for Europeans to come and settle amongst them,

Fig. 19.—MHIMA CHIEF.

and Kasagama himself was very pleased with the idea. The benefit to the natives would be incalculable, chiefly as a protection against the standing danger of invasion. During the recent raid of Kabbarega, for instance, the unfortunate Wakondja took refuge on the higher parts of the mountain, and in the deepest parts of the forest.

I have seen the little shelters they put up at about 11,000 feet, where the temperature at the hottest time of the day is only from 50 to 60 degrees. They told me thirty-seven people had died there of cold and starvation. They could watch the Wanyoro destroying their plantations below, and could only steal forth at night, in peril of their lives, to get some of their own food. The effect of these raids reaches far, for each means the loss of perhaps half the population killed or enslaved, and damage to the plantations which it may require years to set right. Moreover, it is the very greatest hindrance to all industry, for riches and prosperity are simply inducements to the robbers to return. Besides the great advantage which would come from European protection from these raids, a very large amount of suffering, and of oppression exercised by their own chiefs, could be palliated.

Unfortunately, it must be admitted that on the European side the advantages are not so obvious, because the difficulty of appraising an undeveloped country is almost inconceivable. Still, let us take for example the Shiré highlands and compare it with Ruwenzori. During practically eleven years the Shiré highlands have become a colony which now affords employment to some four hundred Europeans, and in the year 1894 showed a total export of £22,300 value besides imports of £13,800. Yet the Shiré highlands cannot possibly be compared with the Ruwenzori district in promise, natural fertility, or climate. The amount of alluvial deposits (corresponding to those of the Shiré river banks) is very much greater about Ruwenzori because most of the shore of the Albert Edward Nyanza and Lake Ruisamba as well as the Semliki valley, consists of this kind of soil. The rainfall round Ruwenzori is, I think, much greater than that of the Shiré highlands, and I believe that the Wimi valley alone probably contains more and better land adapted to coffee than the whole of the present cultivated area of the Shiré highlands. There is, moreover, a strong probability, in my opinion, of tea being a great success in these wet mountain valleys.

Again, the native population here is certainly small, and quite unaccustomed to European labour, but they are naturally more industrious than those of British Central Africa. There is also a considerable amount of ivory available for preliminary expenses.

But all the preceding advantages are at present nullified, because there is no means of exporting produce, nor any kind of transport.

My pet scheme for the development of Africa is explained at full length in Chapter XVIII., so that I shall simply try to show how this district could be connected with it. A good cart track or light railway from Latoma to the nearest point on the Albert Edward Nyanza would unite the latter to the main road. On the Albert Edward, communication by water (preferably steam launches or small steamers and barges) could convey goods to any point on the lake or Ruisamba, and probably up the Durro, and perhaps the Yeria, to some spot not 40 miles away from the more important valleys.

This is an extremely important point for many reasons. First, the rich and valuable valleys on the east side of Ruwenzori (speaking from personal knowledge only) are the Nyamwamba, the Mubuku, the Wimi, and the Yeria. The way to the latter lies through the very valuable Butanuka district which is only distant 30 miles from the Albert Edward. The rich district about Butindi and Kasagama's is about a day's march farther on from Butanuka, but I should consider the best road would probably lie along the Msonje river, leaving Butanuka on the left. It is possible that goods could be conveyed by the Mpango to a point not far from Kasagama's, but this is a matter on which I cannot speak. By the route I suggest, one could convey a large body of men, *even Europeans*, from the Albert Edward to the Albert without much difficulty. Embarking on the Albert Edward, they could probably reach Kaihura's in one day, where a large depôt of beans, cattle, and poultry could be got together; from there they could proceed on to the highest navigable point of the Durro and Yeria, where a similar depôt could be established

Fig. 20.—THE ALBERT EDWARD PLAINS.

from Butanuka, Wimi, and Yeria. From this a day's march would bring them to within measurable distance, at any rate, of Butindi, and from this point it is probably only 50 miles to the Albert Nyanza, the route lying through well-cultivated and fertile country. Thus to reach by this route the north end of the Albert Nyanza is about seven days' march from the Albert Edward Nyanza, and probably only fourteen days' march from the Kagera river.

Cattle appear to be very easily kept over the whole country around the Albert and Albert Edward Nyanzas; those which I saw being all in the very best condition.

To administer the whole district of Ruwenzori would neither be expensive nor difficult. It will be seen from the preceding remarks that the fertile and most promising part of the country is within the hills. It is also advisable that there should be a station within easy distance of, but not too near, Kasagama's capital, and it is above all things essential that it should be in a healthy position near running water and timber. Some of the ridges between the Yeria and Wimi rivers, nearly fulfil all these conditions; or it might be better to choose a spot on one of the outer hills from which it would be possible to overlook the plain to the north, or that of Ruisamba.

The cost of such a station would not be great. A competent European would probably require about £400 a year. It would be absolutely necessary for him *not* to employ Suahilis if he wishes to get the confidence of the natives. He would probably require a Maxim gun and a small body of Soudanese, and such labour as is required for station purposes could easily be obtained from the Watoru and Wakondja.

Probably the total cost of such a station might be £1,000 a year. With a currency and export trade this amount could very easily be raised, but until there is a cheap means of communication, there cannot, of course, be either plantation or export of any kind.

Of course the most obvious policy is simply to depose the paramount chief and put an European in his place. Such a Resident ought to use the labour-strength and produce of the district. He could do this without one-tenth part of the oppression now exercised, and at the same time afford real protection to the natives and recoup much of his expenditure.

CHAPTER VIII.

THE SALT LAKE AND SEMLIKI VALLEY.

ON the 13th of June I determined to go down to Katwe, and, after settling matters, proceed round to the west side of Ruwenzori and try to get higher up the mountain. On reaching Butanuka I had a long debate about a slave girl who had apparently been captured and ill-treated by the Suahilis. I had the satisfaction of handing her over to her family; but the incident shows the ill effect of placing natives in responsible posts.

Butanuka is just on the edge of the Victoria plateau, and one descends to the alluvials of the old Albert Edward Nyanza shortly afterwards. The change is very curious; short grass and a level, apparently endless, road replaces the elephant grass and numerous small hills and valleys of the plateau. From this point, until one reaches the Salt lake, there are only two insignificant plantations and one little stretch of thorn-tree forest. Hour after hour has to be spent toiling over this monotonous road in a temperature of 88 to 90 degrees in the shade. The grass is usually burnt, and sometimes one passes for miles over charcoal and blackened ground: while the dust of burnt cinders fills the nose and eyes; there is nothing to see or notice except the hills covered with their usual monotonous roofing of heavy cloud.

Fig. 21. Sabeido Mkondja Chief.

Just before reaching the Muhokia river, we passed over a small stream, Ntsora, which is very distinctly salt. This is the first sign of recent volcanic action since leaving Kyatwa hill, at Butanuka; the area of recent volcanic rock extends from here past the Salt lake to the Nyamgassa river (see chapter x.).

The cause of the desolate and barren character

of these alluvials is not at all difficult to understand. It is simply the absence of water; the soil is either a mixture of sand and gravel, brought down by the river and unable to retain water, or the clayey mud due to an old swamp. Where there is any kind of protection against wind, as along the Nyamwamba river in its lower alluvial part, it is covered by a wood, not exactly a forest, of Acacias and other, chiefly thorny, shrubs and trees. A similar wood also exists near the lake itself, where there is a constant supply of moisture in the air; but these are as different as possible from either the mountain forests or the low-level jungle of the Victoria region.

The one mentioned above, where the road touches the shore of Lake Ruisamba, between the Muhokia river and Chukarongo, is characteristic. The tree trunks are quite distant from one another without either moss, ferns, or fungi. The ground is covered by yellow, burnt-up grass, and a few other plants all equally dry and withered, and so low that it is easy to see over the tops of everything. There is, in fact, no protection against the drying winds which pass through the trees and rapidly scorch up all those plants which require ground moisture.

The future of these grassy monotonous plains is extremely hard to estimate. There is probably plenty of moisture underground, and in many places irrigation is possible. On the whole I think that in the *alluvial* parts we may expect enormous crops and a dense population in some future day when there will be so many people that every one must work.

This really unpromising country may be said to extend all round Ruwenzori, from the Dumei river on the west to Butanuka on the east. There are, however, considerable patches of alluvium every here and there, and immediately one reaches the outlying hills one finds a good country. The land between the Dumei river and Tengetenge's on the west is very rich, probably because it is so close to the mountain.

Occasionally, when passing along these plains, a large rat or bandicoot may be seen scurrying through the path, and antelopes are often visible wherever the old grass has been burnt and is again springing up in a green and tender condition. Usually my terrier, Bobby, saw them at a long distance and impetuously pursued. No experience or chastisement ever taught him the futility of this predilection, and though, after such an escapade, he was made to walk solemnly in a string for several hours, I always let him loose again, partly because he was so inexpressibly miserable, and partly because my special boys had so much to carry that he was a nuisance. When I did get the chance of a shot, by crawling painfully 400 or 500 yards, I usually missed the animal altogether.

Birds are very common over all the country. In

the woods there are quantities of pigeons, magpies, &c. On the plains there are several pretty common kinds; one of the most abundant is a wagtail; another is a black and white bird, about the size and shape of a starling. This has a curious habit of taking little flights in the air for amusement during which it gives four or five little chirps of joy.

Chukarongo Lake is the first place calling for special mention. Usually its banks are lined by squadrons of pelicans, marabout storks or flamingoes, and quantities of geese, ducks, plovers, &c. It is an old volcanic crater, and curiously enough a small stream is *always falling into it*, though I cannot guess where the water disappears, for there is no visible outlet whatever. It may possibly make its way underground to the deep craters further along the road, but that does not explain the question. The rough lines of stratification, dipping slightly away from the lip of the old crater edge, are clearly visible.

After leaving this place comes a long and extremely trying march to the Salt lake itself. The first interesting point is reached in about two hours, when one passes first on the right an extremely deep, steep crater, with water at the bottom, and very shortly afterwards a similar deep lake on the left. In both these the level of the water seemed to me lower than that of the Nyanza, but I did not take observations (having quite enough to do to manage the day's march). After passing these two curious hollows, there is a long ridge to mount, and shortly afterwards another lake comes in view, above which, on a slight eminence, are the rough buildings constituting the settlement of Katwe, or the Salt lake.

A long gentle slope dotted with quantities of Euphorbia, in the shade of which are hundreds of hungry mosquitoes, leads to the broken tuff edges of the crater of this lake, in which, as usual, a row of solemn flamingoes watch the caravan from a safe distance.

After climbing the broken lip of the crater, we find ourselves in the collection of houses and unbuilt fort where there was at that time a small garrison of Suahilis. The fort is probably exactly in the state in which it was left by Lugard. A good description will be found in his work (vol. ii. p. 168). It is in a very strong position, for the Salt lake is separated from an arm of the Nyanza, probably also an ancient crater which has been broken down, by a narrow ridge which must be about 400 feet high.

It is so obviously a volcanic crater, with tuff arranged in well-marked stratification round it, that I cannot understand how this explanation was not given before.

A very curious instance of the danger of writing an account of a country which one has not personally visited, may be seen in the "Handbook of

British East Africa" (p. 78), where the Salt lake is called "evidently a pool left by the receding waters of Lake Albert Edward." It is rather unfortunate that the compiler of this book was quite unacquainted with the country, except by second-hand accounts; so that he mentions a country "Ukonju" (see p. 79) which has no existence whatever, and no one ever speaks as he does of "Awamba," which would be equivalent to saying that "Jones" is the name of a district in Wales, or "Campbell" that of another in Scotland.

Both these are generalisations from the fact that the northern part of the Semliki valley is inhabited by Wawamba, and the southern by Wakondja, which latter, however, extend from Karimi right round the east side of the mountain, as far as the Wimi valley. It is, moreover, the *Wanynema* who raid this country, not the pygmies, and the country of the Awamba, as far as I went, has no forest whatever except on the river, but is covered by long elephant grass, or short spear grass which is never long. One more criticism is demanded—the Wakondja's heads are not rounder than those of either the Wawamba or the "superior light race" by whom, apparently, the Wahima are meant.

Statements of this kind involve most dangerous errors; yet those which I have here controverted are comprised in the space of one half-page.

That the Government should have deliberately chosen an officer who knew nothing whatever of the country to draw up a report at the very time when Captain Lugard was at home, is only another instance of the extremely hard treatment which that gallant and energetic officer has (I am glad to say only in the past) received.

I have carefully abstained during this work from criticising either Mr. Stanley's, Captain Lugard's, or the above-mentioned work, partly because I wished to give simply my impression, but chiefly because of the utter futility of doing so in view of the detailed knowledge of the country which will probably deluge us in the next few years. One remark in the handbook, however (p. 53), cannot be allowed to pass. "They," *Waganda*, "are one of the strongest of the negroid races, and will carry loads of 100 or 120 lbs. for 20 miles a day with ease." Any person reading this in an authoritative Government work (and the work in question is very authoritative) would suppose that he could obtain as many porters as he chose in Uganda, and would be surprised on reaching Uganda to find that he could not get the Waganda to carry loads at all! A bunch of bananas would be quite as much as they could be induced to take. Such a misleading statement might mean the destruction of a carefully thought out expedition.

To return to the Salt lake, I quite agree with

Captain Lugard's opinion of its value. I have found the salt from it carried right across Mpororo and Karagwe to the Unyamwesi country. The whole of Ankole and the Wanyuema are dependent on it for a necessary of life, and it will most certainly be a very important item in the future development of the country.

The salt is produced apparently by precipitation from the water of two springs, entering the lake underground, and seems to be deposited regularly every day. Saline incrustations in the soil and in most of the crater lakes appears to be very common about the Salt lake, though I cannot profess to understand the reason. Even the water of the Albert Edward is slightly salt (at any rate bad) in the immediate neighbourhood of the ridge referred to above. It is, however, so far as I could find, only the Salt lake proper which yields a really useful kind. Some of the others are even said to be poisonous.

This situation is a most unfavourable place for Europeans to occupy permanently. One reason being the absence of any plantations anywhere near the fort. The whole country is of alluvial and recent volcanic origin, and it is only when one either crosses the lake to the borders of the Victoria plateau, or penetrates the outer border of the hills, that any cultivation worth mentioning can be found.

Of course this difficulty is not insurmountable,

because boats could bring all kinds of supplies from any part of the Albert Edward.

The other disadvantage is more serious. Life is almost insupportable on account of the mosquitoes. These creatures sting at all hours of the day, and are quite active in shady places during the very hottest part of it. It is only by keeping to paths which are vigorously patrolled by brilliant blue and red dragonflies that one can avoid them. Sleep is almost impossible, and even the pachydermatous Suahili used to come and complain to me that he could get no rest at all. The only manner in which I could obtain any relief was by arranging a fire and counter attraction of sleeping porters in front of the sole entrance to my hut; and even then, some always got inside my net.

I think it is chiefly on account of this that the few villages on the lake are inhabited by such a miserable, puny and unhealthy set; because at night their houses are kept constantly full of choking smoke from fires of green wood, which is almost worse than the evil itself. I am not sure that this is the true explanation, for I have noticed on Tanganyika and on the Shiré river, a similar wretched condition in those families which spend their lives in canoes and live chiefly on fish: a practice that certainly always produces a very weak development of the lower limbs, while of course a constantly moist and humid atmosphere is always unhealthy in a tropical climate.

Food has a very great deal to do with character in savage races.

Now, it is above all things essential that a resident European should be in the best possible condition, both of body and temper, and therefore the Salt lake should not be chosen as a permanent post.

On leaving to proceed round the western side of the mountain, one first crosses a broad cold river, the Nyamgassu, and then over a grassy alluvial plain to one of the outlying hills, Ambambe. The young chief was here most princely, and I had the pleasure of a good night's sleep.

Passing over a hilly and well-watered and cultivated district, we climbed a ridge or spur, on which Karimi is situated. This spot commands a lovely view up the Semliki valley and back over the plains to the Salt lake, which is within two days' easy marching. Looking south, the remains of an old volcano are seen, close to which is the shore of the Albert Edward Nyanza. The natives told me they could see a flaming mountain from this point, and by looking at the map it will be seen that this must be obviously Kissigali, belonging to the Mfumbiro chain.

Towards the mountain there seem to be many villages and banana plantations which are, however, carefully concealed from the view of passing strangers.

From here the descent passes by some steep hills and ravines to the Semliki valley, and thence over a monotonous grassy, almost uninhabited, country, intersected by numerous small tributaries of the Semliki. One of these, the Meronyi, marks the commencement of a rich and fertile area, full of running streams, but now rendered very unsafe by the constant raids of Karakwanzi and the Wanyuema from across the river.

In consequence of this, much of the best land is overgrown with interminable elephant grass, through which one has to burrow for hours.

I at last found that I was approaching Karewia, a German camp, and when the supposed site was shown me, decided on ascending the hills and forming a camp. The people were peculiarly shy, and I had great difficulty in finding any one to act as guide, but after some trouble, I found a fairly good spot on the left bank of the Butagu river. This was a most curious valley; the shape of it can be best understood by the drawing and the section (given on p. 175, chap. x.). Opposite me was a curious needle-like detached pinnacle of rock, and far up the valley I used to see at sunset the clouds gradually vanish away from the sharp snowy peaks which Dr. Franz Stuhlmann has christened after such well-known people as Weissmann, Moebius, &c.

I made a trial walk up the valley, and, after passing four or five precipitous ravines, I found

Fig. 22.—The Bamboo Zone on Ruwenzori.

myself near the head where there are two magnificent waterfalls and a considerable cultivated area. I returned on the other side by a much better path, most of which was covered by forest, in which were tree heather and other Alpine plants at a very low altitude.

There is a curious difference in the level of the forest on the western side. So far as I could judge, for even here, in one of the most unget-at-able places in the world, the hand of man has very much altered the aspect of nature, the forest begins at about 6,600 feet, but it does not seem to occupy more than from this level to 7,600 feet. At 8,000 feet the bamboos stop and one enters on the heather region. The reason of this can probably be best explained as an effect of the extremely sudden rise of the mountain and the manner in which the ridges jut out from the main mass, so that there is a sheer precipitous ascent to about 9,000 feet, from which long, narrow, gently sloping ridges lead up to the main chain.

At my camp at 9,800 feet I was a long way above the bamboos, which on the eastern side extended to between 10,000 and 11,000 feet. Apparently something of the same nature occurs both on Kenia and Kilimandjaro, where the snow and the levels of the bamboo and forest zones are said to be much lower on the west than on the east.

I thought my best chance of getting up the mountain would be to return by this path with a few men and a small supply of food, and try to establish a camp at about 10,000 feet, and afterwards another at about 13,000, from which I might possibly reach the snow. I therefore started with ten men, but was unfortunate from the beginning. The first day, after toiling up the valley in pouring rain, we were obliged to camp at 7,000 feet, amongst some miserable huts, with a very suspicious and unfriendly set of natives. Next day we got up through the forest and bamboos to 9,800 feet, where we camped on a peatmoss, compared to which my old friend Lochar moss was a pleasant and convenient situation.

We had no water till I thought of squeezing the damp Sphagnum, but the tea made from this peat extract had a horrible taste and colour. Next day I picked out three strong men and started, full of enthusiasm, under the guidance of two naked Wawamba.

It was an awful ascent. Sometimes over deep moss, where jagged root-ends of heather seemed to spring out and stab ankles and knees at every step: sometimes through a dense wood of gnarled and twisted heather-trees, fifteen to twenty feet high, and covered with grey lichens, then down a steep little ravine and dense jungle; and things soon became very hopeless. Everything was shrouded in a cold chilling mist, and first one man and then another, became knocked up, until about 10 a.m. I was left alone. I went on by myself till 2 p.m. The effect of mountain sickness was most trying; I could not walk more than 50 yards without stopping to get breath, and by 2 p.m. I was utterly exhausted, and without food or anything to sleep in. This was at about 12,500 feet. I determined to return and make another attempt later on, and came back to my camp, where everybody was numb and miserable to a degree. Two of my men never got over the effect of this little expedition, and I had to leave one of them at the Salt lake on my return. In fact, for any work of this kind, Suahilis are hopelessly unfit.

On my return to the Butagu camp, I was at once prostrated by an attack of fever, which made me useless for about five days, and then I had a difficulty with the natives. I had every intention of returning, but under the circumstances, all that I could have done would have been to ascend the valley again and leave my camp for a space of a week at least without protection. I only had forty-two men, and I was not disposed to risk losing even one; whereas, during my absence, I might have had twenty seriously wounded or killed, and could not have brought home the results of my expedition. It is in a case like this that a large expedition, well armed and carried out regardless of expense, or of native life, has such an enormous advantage over a small one-man party. On the other hand, provided the leader has good health and strength, and a small body of well-chosen men, a great deal more can be done with it; for the difficulty of supplies is very much diminished, and one has no responsibility with regard to the lives and wishes of other white men.

In the Emin Pasha expedition, Dr. Stuhlmann encamped on the left bank of the Butagu, apparently almost exactly on the spot where the attack was made on my people. He ascended the mountain, so far as I could learn, at once, and then proceeded along the high ridge which bounds the Butagu valley on the left, until he came, apparently, to within sight of a deep minor cross-valley, with a lake at the bottom, which separated him from the snow. This was a most wonderful performance, and he certainly did far better than myself. I fancy, however, if he had not been before me, I should have had no trouble with the people.

One of the most curious features of the valley is the deep precipitous trench (see Fig. 28) which the river has cut out for itself. This is probably in most places a hundred feet deep, and covered with an extraordinary profusion of climbing plants and shrubs. The wild banana, of which the photograph was taken, grew close to the river.

Fig. 23.—THE WILD BANANA.

This plant seems to thrive everywhere in the mountain, and I have seen it at 8,000 feet.

Portions of the valley are very beautiful, particularly where a gigantic shrubby balsam with a large white flower and spur four or five inches long enlivens the darkness of the forest. Probably this is visited by moths.

Another kind of balsam common in the banana groves is one of the main food stores of the hive bee.

A large carpenter bee is common in this valley, usually on some of the large yellow Crotalaria shrubs or numerous Melastomaceæ. It has very vivid yellow and black bands—that is to say the female. The male is yellow all over, and never seems to collect any food. Usually ten or twelve of the latter may be seen flying about near the tree from which they emerged in youth, and shining like golden jewels in the sunlight.

The natives often brought me the burrows. These are made by a female in an old, half rotten stick, or sometimes in a piece of elephant grass. The tunnel is just about the size of the bee, probably half an inch in diameter, and divided into little compartments by neat wads of sawdust plastered together. One finds the young bees in all stages of development, but usually those in one burrow are fairly alike. I think a large store of pollen is enclosed in each compartment beside the egg. There is a common form at the Cape

Colony which is at any rate very like this species.

After interviewing the Sultan of the Wawamba, and getting back my stolen gun, we retraced our steps to the Salt lake, where I left most of my porters to recruit, and decided to try the Nyamwamba valley farther back along the east side. On entering this valley with twelve men, I found the natives to be Wakondja and friendly and willing to assist. We got as far up as we could through dense elephant grass and made a camp. Next day I took two men and started up the valley. I found I had miscalculated the length of it, and did not reach the steep ascent till about 10 a.m. I decided, however, to go on that day, and got two men, carrying a tarpaulin bag and edibles, up to about 10,000 feet, when, to their great delight, I sent them back to their village. I slept in the bag, but could not manage well, as the fire, when lighted, always went out, and the cold woke me up.

Next morning I started and climbed steadily up through the bamboos till I emerged on the heather zone. The scenery here was most weird and unearthly. Huge trees of Erica (or rather Ericinella) and gigantic Lobelias were mixed with many very familiar-looking European plants. Enormous red and black brambles stretched out their branches over the track. At about 12 p.m., after climbing from about 6 a.m., I rested for half an hour, and then down came a heavy thunder-shower. I remained in the shade of a damp rock for nearly an hour and then decided to go on, but I was wet to the skin in a few minutes. I went on as well as I could for some time, but had got out of the forest into a most difficult place. Before me rose a huge precipitous cliff. The boulders from this were lying in confusion all round its base, and the crevices and crannies were half concealed and shrouded by masses of green moss and creepers. Amongst these were growing quantities of beautiful Alchemilla (*A. Stuhlmanni*) with shining silvery leaves. It was still raining, my khakee clothes were stiff, and I was shivering and half numb. After one or two tumbles, in which I nearly broke my leg, I decided that it would be useless to go further. I had got to the central core of the range, just at the back of the "Premolar" mountain, which I had seen from the Mubuku valley. I had, as I thought, then ascended far above anybody else (it turned out to be only 13,000 feet), and it was physically impossible to get up to the top that day and return to my provisions and bag within twenty-four hours. So I came down again and soon found that I was in the cold stage of fever. It was still raining, and the rest of that night was a sort of horrible dream.

When I got to my bag, I swallowed some Kola chocolate: I could not light a match, and was shaking from head to foot, so I had to climb down through the bamboos and forest till at last, in the middle of the night, I got to the village, and found my two men in great anxiety. I went into the hut and remember nothing till next morning, about 10 a.m., when the natives gave me a chicken and Arum roots to satisfy a raging hunger.

That day I crawled a few hundred yards into the jungle while my men were seeking the things left up the hill, and sat down on a fallen log to watch the forest. Such moments can be but rarely permitted to a conscientious naturalist, whose whole time should be spent in feverishly grabbing things not seen before and wild chases after flighty and restless insects; but they are very pleasant when one can allow oneself a rest. A beautiful bird, which I believe to be a touracoo, ran up and down a branch, using its broad expanded tail as a balance. A troop of monkeys were feeding not far off, and seeing me perfectly still, came quite close. They were probably a species of Cercopithecus, with brown fur and white eyebrows and imperial. Their expression is very melancholy and depressed. Eight or nine of the older males came within five or ten yards, and regarded me severely; then they would slowly produce an enormous smile with an extremely comic effect. This is intended to frighten the observer, and is quite a common habit of monkeys. I have seen, *e.g.*, the Colobus monkey doing the same thing.

THE SALT LAKE AND SEMLIKI VALLEY. 147

These things only happen when one has no gun and is in a very patient condition. To those who are not, by nature, naturalists, it is a useful hint to remember that if one wishes to observe the habits of any living creature, from a bumble bee to an antelope, the essential is to remain absolutely still. The very slightest movement directs the attention of any wild thing to the place, and it at once becomes suspicious. When quite still, they do not in most cases distinguish the difference in colour. It is just as hard for us to see an insect when it is quite quiet, but the slightest movement reveals it if one watches patiently.

I remember the first time I saw a monkey on Ruwenzori was after I had been trying hard to get a specimen all day, and had in rather a depressed mood wandered off by myself to rest underneath a tree. A monkey leisurely strolled on to a branch not 10 feet above my head, and began performing his toilet, while absently regarding the sky. It never saw me till I, in rage, threw a stone at it, when there was the usual flop-crash of the bushes and no monkey.

Next day I crawled back to my camp and had to take a full day's rest to get back sufficient strength to return to the Salt lake.

CHAPTER IX.

THE WAWAMBA.

THE Wawamba people seem to begin about the Meronji river on the west side of Ruwenzori. From this point they extend along the Semliki valley as far north, at any rate, as a point opposite Kasagama's, and not as far as the point where Captain Lugard crossed the Semliki.

They are certainly a very mixed race. Those who inhabit the hills are not very easily distinguished from the Wakondja, but those on the lower slopes and in the Semliki valley are different, and to my mind more closely related to the Wanyuema than any other tribe. Their language was at first quite incomprehensible to any one in my caravan, but one or two men who knew that of the Wanyeuma, soon got to know enough to converse pretty easily with them. The manner in which some natives have the power of picking up a language is most astonishing. Probably it is for the same reason that children learn so quickly, viz., an absence of distracting ideas about other things. My small boy "Tommy" learnt every language in every country through which we went, sufficiently to ask questions, in four or five days' time (viz., Kikuyu, Kiganda, KiAnkole, Kitoru, Kikondja, Kiwamba, Kikaragwe, Kinyoro, and Manganja, not to speak of English and my own idea of Suahili). I have only heard of one European who has anything approaching this facility. He is a missionary, who preached a sermon in Mombasa three days after landing, to which the people listened.

The language of the Wawamba has quite a different sound to the Victoria plateau group, containing, apparently, much more guttural and harsh combinations. The people are shorter and more squarely and stumpily built than the Wahuma or Wakondja, who are frequently tall and rather graceful and athletic-looking. A few have broad high foreheads and small lips. They file their teeth, which is a habit that seems frequently to go with cannibalism. They dress almost always in bark cloth—at least, if their clothing can be called dress. The women, whom one very rarely sees, seem to prefer cloth when they can obtain it, but usually are dressed in a short band of bark.

The fig producing this cloth is very widely cultivated all through the Victoria region, and up to 6,000 feet on Ruwenzori. On one of the rare occasions in which I managed to arrive unexpectedly in a Wawamba valley, we heard from every hamlet the knocking of the heavy wooden mallet with which they beat out the strip of bark which is taken from the tree. They usually cut away a nearly complete cylinder from as high as they can reach to the ground. This is spread upon the trunk of a tree and every portion is gently and regularly hammered till it becomes almost twice as wide as before. The cloth so formed is rather coarse in texture but of a very nice brownish terra-cotta colour. It is very easily torn, and becomes often completely spoiled by a single shower of rain.

Their houses are very neat and built with some care. The foundation is composed of burnt clay, and carefully raised at the edge to prevent water coming in; over this is mud beaten hard, and apparently carefully swept every day. The general shape of the hut is circular, or, rather, dome-shaped, and it is composed of arched sticks, on which is a thick roof of banana leaves; the outer part is covered by a close matting of old banana leaf stalks, carefully tied down. In the hills all the houses have a neat little porch about 3 feet long. Inside, the houses are very warm and quite watertight, and they are cut up into rooms by palisades of mateitei.

The Wawamba seem to sleep on long flat boards made of a single piece of wood, and they have little stools, also cut from a single piece of wood, which must have taken an enormous time to make with the extremely rough tools which they possess. They usually attach some kind of charm to the top of the roof. On my way back I noticed with some pride a bottle bearing the legend "Lennox, Dumfries," attached to a chief's house! Their hair is worn very short, and usually in tiny curls a quarter of an inch long. They often leave bare places amongst these curls, so as to shave a pattern on the scalp. They all wear a necklace, from which hang leopards' teeth, carved bits of wood, and other extraordinary articles. The men often have bangles, frequently arranged as shown in the figure, and almost always anklets. The women wear rings on the legs.

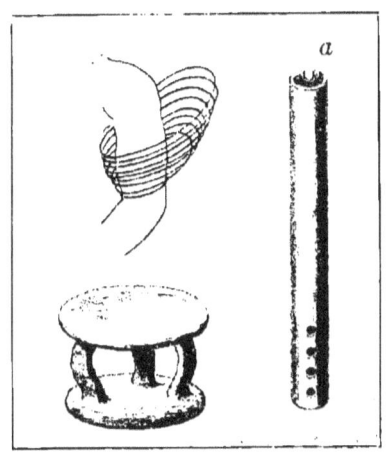

Fig. 21.— WAWAMBA ARTICLES.

They seem fond of music, and manage to produce really melodious little tunes out of extremely primitive instruments. One of these is a kind of harp, made with a sounding box of gourd. Another is a very primitive flute, which is simply a hollow tube of wood with three or four holes bored at one end, and a mouthpiece with a small semicircular cut in the rim at the other. The lower lip is placed at this ("a" in figure) and the fingers over the holes, and they thus extract an agreeable little tune.

They have the curious posture dance, very common in West Africa, which consists of wriggling the body and arms while keeping time to the music with the feet.

The spears are of two kinds, one with a long and heavy blade, while that of the other is quite short. I only saw bows and arrows in the plains, and these were of a very weak and feeble description. They use calabashes and also rough earthenware.

In the low grounds of the Semliki valley there is plenty of maize, millet and sweet potatoes, as well as numerous patches of bananas. A large proportion of the mountain valleys are covered with plantations of bananas and the bark-cloth fig, but the main food seems to be Arum and beans of various kinds, which may be seen even at 7,000 feet.

They are certainly industrious so far as one can judge, but it is very difficult to get to know much about them. This is on account of their extreme fear of strangers. They had been raided about three or four times in the five months preceding my visit by Kabbarega, Karakwanzi and Kasagama.

The effect of this constant marauding has been to develop a natural instinct in the race to fly to

THE WAWAMBA. 153

the hills on the very first appearance of an enemy; and in their eyes every stranger is an enemy.

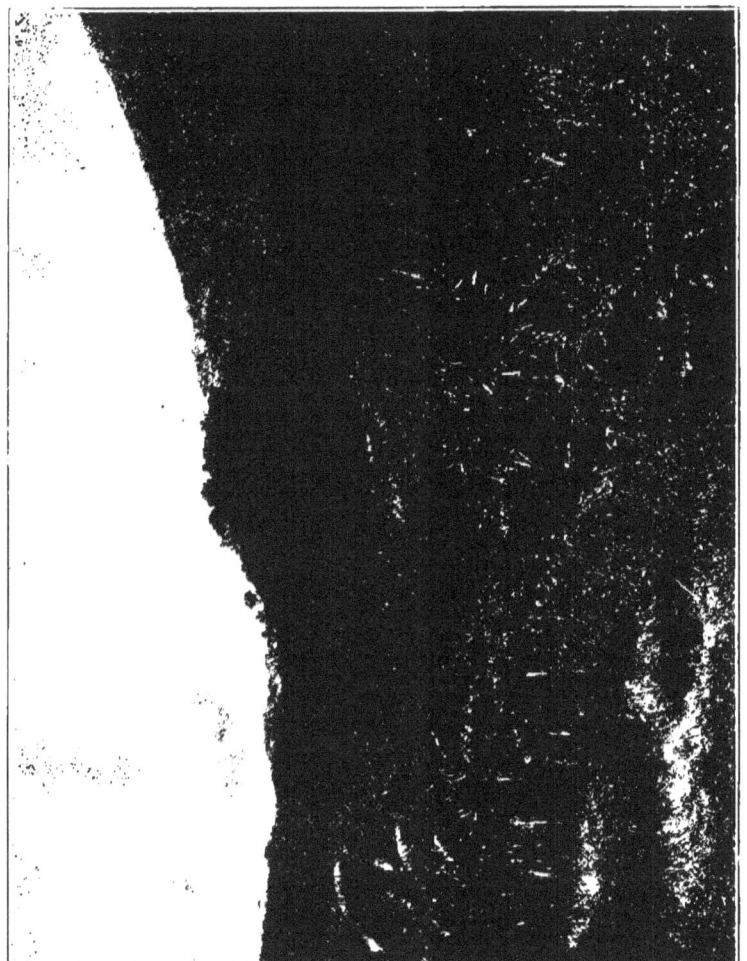

Fig. 25.—Upper Part of the Wimi Valley.

They are cowardly, suspicious and superstitious to an extraordinary degree. In fact, they are so accustomed to being ill-treated that they cannot understand a stranger behaving kindly. Whenever I entered a village every one promptly fled, and I shall never forget the amount of coaxing and wooing I had to go through in order to get the chief I first met to make friends. At first he stood amongst his bananas about 100 yards off, and my interpreter had to shout courtesies at this distance. Whenever I approached he ran, and it was only after I advanced alone to within speaking distance and had assured him over and over again that I only wanted to buy food, that he could be induced to wait for me. After he came to camp, it was about half an hour before he could be induced to come near enough to receive a present of beads.

This timidity is not confined to strangers. I am afraid all the Wawamba have a thoroughly bad character. When the king Tengetenge sent me a deputation with food, there was not a soul left in any village within three miles.

In the Butagu valley, the people on the left bank never cross to the right unless when raiding, and neither ever ascend the valley to the clearing at the head.

Possibly this habit has arisen because the valleys are so steep and precipitous. To cross from one ridge to the next involves at least three hours. There is first a steep descent composed of slippery black mud, and then a worse ascent, where the steepness and mud together form a combination impossible to describe.

It is only women that appear to carry on any kind of communication between the different villages. They had an impression that all Europeans were robbers. One man whom I induced after great trouble to go with me as a guide to the head of the valley gave me a good idea of their character. On arriving there, he at once began to steal bananas, supposing he could do anything he liked under my protection. On the way home, we passed a poor starved woman with a baby and a big basket of the edible Arum *leaves*. He was going to steal these; and finally, when we reached the settlement at the foot of the camp, he was going to plunder a hut of its most valuable contents; but by that time I had had enough and sent him home.

I promised two or three of those at the head of the valley a present of beads, but they dared not face the return journey by themselves.

These people are extremely superstitious; in every stretch of cultivation one finds curious little houses two or three feet high, in which are suspended little bits of bark cloth or banana, or occasionally some little grisly thing or other. These are to keep the spirits in good humour. They are also firm believers in charms and amulets, of which they have a very large variety.

All these little traits constantly reminded me of West Africa, and led me to believe that I was, at

Ruwenzori, on a borderline of peoples as well as of plants and animals.

I had not left my bed for four days when one of three men, whom I had sent to catch butterflies, came in to say that they had all three been attacked by the natives, and that he had seen one man killed. I immediately rushed off with ten men to the place, which was about three hours' off —a walk that tried me more than any I have ever undertaken. On arriving we found the spot covered with blood, and I ordered my men to attack the neighbouring huts. Of course these cowards had fled to the hills on my approach. My Suahilis outran me, and it was with some difficulty that I could call them back, after burning the huts whose inhabitants had done this.

The hills were by this time lined with hundreds of natives who, however, would not come down to attack us. I crawled back to camp after carefully examining the ground, and found the second man, who gave me a circumstantial account of the way in which the other man had been killed.

Thinking the matter over that night, I decided to leave next day. I could not avoid leaving my men alone for a week if I were to attempt any valuable work up the valley, and if left alone they would certainly have attempted reprisals, and I should also have lost men who would have gone out by themselves; for the Suahili cannot be

taught prudence, unless under daily surveillance.
I went down the mountain next morning, and
called on Tengetenge, who had of course fled.
On the way I came across the missing third man,
who had been wounded very severely in the back,
and took him on with me. He was called Mabruki
Manyuema, and had all the stubborn endurance
and pluck which porters of this race often show,
but along with this the corresponding evil qualities.
He was always anxious to steal and bully the
natives. It is no fanciful theory but a definite
fact, which I have often noticed when dealing with
raw tribes, that those which are the most difficult,
restless and unscrupulous raiders, become, when
well brought under control, the very finest races.
It is only necessary to mention the Zulus and the
Sikhs, as compared with the Fingoes and Hindus,
to see the truth of this generalisation.

Mabruki Manyuema, I am glad to say, reached
Ujiji with me, and went to the coast.

I will again draw attention to the curious coincidence that this attack took place very nearly on the
exact site of Emin's camp, just as the other in
Ankole was where I crossed Langheld's route.

Perhaps I may here call attention to the curious
difference between the English and German
Governments. These two large armed German
expeditions passed through our sphere of influence
without saying a word to the English authorities;
they attacked natives and made, as I have good

reason to know, the very name of "white man" odious wherever they went. I, on the other hand, went through German territory and gave full information to the nearest station of my movements, taking a pass from Uganda and doing everything in my power to pay for everything. And the result was that the German Government stole my guns. I hear from my agents, "the German authorities positively refuse to give them up, and say that you failed to attend to the Government regulations when it was in your power to do so." And this, after their officer would not even deign to reply to my letter or return an enclosure received from the German Foreign Office before starting (for which I had to thank Professor Engler)! In fact, the courteous manner in which the English Government treats others, and the extreme want of courtesy with which Englishmen are treated by the German and French Governments, is almost beyond belief.

On my arrival at Tengetenge's, no human being, of course, was on view; but at last a man, who had been living near us, and knew the mildness of my disposition, turned up, and I sent the diplomatic Taratibu to interview him. He sent word that he wanted me to come with five men, and unarmed! I told him by Taratibu not to be silly, and to come at once. So he appeared, shaking with fear and guarded by two hundred equally alarmed warriors. He is a short, fat and bloated man, who seemed to me untrustworthy, and not at all a good ruler.

A short time before this Karakwanzi's army had come with only two guns; whereupon Tengetenge and all his people fled without firing a single shot.

At this interview Tengetenge again, speaking just as the chief of every village I met had done, begged and implored to be put under the white man direct and not under any native chief, whether Kasagama or any one else.

Those who have read the preceding account will understand how the government of any native chief is not by any means a velvet-handed one. It is neither strong nor just nor impartial: it is always a government founded on oppression and cruelty, and never, so far as I know, an old established one.

It is very easy to talk of the "Gospel of Mr. Maxim," and the "Rights of the Aborigines," but by the time the British people have learnt that justice brought to their minds by the exhibition of overwhelming strength, means peace, prosperity and security of life and property to those who, being under their own chiefs, do not know what these phrases mean, by that time they will induce the Government not to shrink from its obligations and to show a proper disrespect for the so-called "rights" of people like Mwanga and Kasagama.

The destruction of Kabbarega's power (involving perhaps the death of 500 brute-beasts in human shape), means life, health and prosperity to perhaps 100,000 of the tribes round Ruwenzori, of whom far more than 500 were yearly destroyed by his ruffians. Justice is certainly, with natives, a form of mercy. To this I have only to add that amongst Englishmen there is perhaps one in a hundred who is disposed to err on the side of severity.

A very curious question, which can only be solved in the future, is that of how German methods of dealing with natives will eventually turn out. Probably if anything approaching my experiences had happened to a German expedition, Tengetenge and possibly the headmen of all the villages within ten kilometres would have been hanging on the nearest trees, before the sun set.

There are two or three important chiefs who live higher up in the mountains to the east and south of the Butagu. "Hange" appears to rule a large country, apparently the headwaters of the Meronji river. He also sent to tell me that he wished to be under the white man directly.

CHAPTER X.

GEOLOGY.

THE difficulty of African geology can only be understood by those who have unsuccessfully attempted to understand it, amongst whom I include myself. There is not a single clue to the structure of the continent as a whole so far as my experience has gone; and I am afraid that the whole of my work has been more in the nature of contradicting other people's theories and adding to the number of inconvenient and irreconcilable facts, than of constructing any plausible suggestions.

Thus in Egypt one finds in a section from Alexandria to the Second Cataract, first limestone hillocks, then nummulitic limestones, and then the Nubian sandstones. In West Africa I found an Archæan series near the coast, and subsequently a rock at about 3,000 to 4,000 feet, which somewhat reminded me of the Nubian sandstones.

In South Africa, after passing the complicated

coast formations, one enters on the Karoo sandstones, and then in the Transvaal on a curious mixture of Archæan rocks and porphyritic diorites.

In East Africa, on this last expedition, one enters, soon after leaving Mombasa, an Archæan series of gneisses, which in the Masai highlands are covered by masses of lava flows, and reappear in the Victoria region, extending to the base of Ruwenzori and, as shown in the map, ending on its eastern side.

These are overlaid by a probably unconformable series of clayslates, sandstones and quartzites, which seem to extend very far to the south, probably reaching South Tanganyika, and which form what I call the Central Watershed. There is, besides this, Ruwenzori, which is not a pure volcanic mass like Elgon, Kenia or Kilimandjaro, but probably a "block" mountain, consisting mainly of schists and a central core of gneiss or granite, and which also possesses round the base another quite different series of comparatively recent volcanic rocks.

Neither the Karoo sandstones, the Nubian sandstones, nor the sedimentary rocks of the Central Watershed are, at any rate to an ordinary observer, in the least similar to one another, but appear to be quite distinct and separate formations.

It is excessively difficult, therefore, to understand in what condition the continent of Africa was in any preceding geological age, and without

GEOLOGY.

data of this kind it is entirely impossible to solve the interesting questions which underlie the present distribution both of plants and animals.

I do not intend to speak of the first section of my journey across the ordinary caravan route from Mombasa to Uganda, as Dr. Gregory has treated this at great length in his paper (Proceedings Geological Society, 1894). On my return to England I handed to him all my collections, and in what follows I am very greatly indebted to his kind assistance. I hope that a paper, chiefly written by him, will shortly appear in the Quarterly Journal of the Geological Society; in this my collection is most carefully and thoroughly described.

The geology of my journey admits of being easily divided into the following districts:—1. The Victoria region. 2. Ruwenzori. 3. The Central Watershed of Ankole, Karagwe, and East Tanganyika.

Of these, the Victoria region does not require a very long description. It may be taken as extending from the Nandi range and Elgon probably across the whole of Uganda westwards to Ruwenzori; on the north it probably extends to the Albert Nyanza; on the south-east, considerably beyond the Victoria Nyanza, though I have not been able to obtain a definite idea as to how far it extends south-east of it. The mouth of the Kagera nearly limits its extent along the south-west shore, and a line drawn from this point to a place called Kiarutanga, near the east shore of the Albert Edward, represents roughly its south-western border.

I have attempted on the map to show its extent in more detail. It only reaches the east side of Ruwenzori about Butanuka, and from there northwards; but it is even in this part interrupted by a volcanic chain at Vijongo. South of Buta-nuka it is separated by the ancient level of Lake Ruisamba from the mountain and, further down, at the Kaihura straits, by a considerable district which is covered by recent volcanic tufa and olivine basalt.

This enormous area, which I estimate at 360,000 square miles, represents the erosion of the Nile, and the sedimentary rocks which may have formerly covered it are probably now portions of Egypt and the Soudan.

It is a country fundamentally of gneissose rocks, which not infrequently form very curious detached hills, as, *e.g.*, between Mumia's and the Samia hills, where their appearance is fantastic to a degree. Usually speaking it is an endless succession of low rolling hills, separated by inconveniently abundant swamp-rivers. These hills are, as a rule, covered by laterite which, so far as I understand, is a baked crust of rock due to sunlight, the carbonic acid of rainwater, and iron salts combining with the under-lying rock to form a shell which greatly resists denudation.

GEOLOGY.

The average level of the hills of the Victoria region seemed to me to be from 4,100 to 4,300 feet above the sea. But on mounting the rivers which enter the Victoria Nyanza, the average level both of the river valley and, in a less marked degree, of its neighbouring hills, rises considerably, and the latter may nearly reach 5,000 feet.

Over the whole of this region there is very rarely anything to be seen but gneiss rock and laterite. There are, however, in places deposits of iron, which occur in sedimentary rocks, probably of a recent age.

I noticed such ironstones at the following places:— Berkeley bay station, near the Sekibobo's town in Uganda (Koki was not seen by myself), and Tiasimbe. At Berkeley bay these iron pockets occur in a patch about 40 yards in diameter at the foot of the Samia hills, and I thought they formed a syncline as shown on the sketch (see Fig. 9, p. 38). They also occur at two if not three places further along the shore of the Nyanza. I estimated roughly the thickness of the beds to be 200 feet, and the strike to be N.N.E. and S.S.W. (see chapter iii. p. 39).

It is possible that these gneisses are not uniformly spread over the whole area mentioned above; Captain Lugard gives mountains from 4,600 to 5,000 feet between the valleys of the Katonga and Ruizi rivers, which appear to separate the Kyojia and Rusanga watersheds.

The geology of Ruwenzori is most curiously different. Captain Stairs, who ascended the mountain to between 10,000 and 11,000 feet, believed that it was an old volcano, of which a further account is given by Mr. Stanley ("In Darkest Africa," 1890, vol. ii. p. 257).

Dr. Stuhlmann in his book "Mit Emin Pascha," p. 298, points out that this theory is not borne out by facts. He gives as his explanation that it is a "faltungs-gebirge," situated between two lines of dislocation.

I found, however, that in my ascent by the Nyamwamba valley, the most central rock which I could reach was not, as one would suppose, according to Dr. Stuhlmann's theory, a diorite, but a rock which Dr. Gregory describes as either a granite or a granitoid gneiss, and he suggests that it is either an intrusive gneiss or a part of the old Archæan or Victoria region series faulted up. In this case Ruwenzori would be simply an orographic block or "scholl." The figure is intended to show how the central block could have been forced up.

The mountain sides until this central core is reached consist of a series of mica schists and epidiorites. The former greatly perplexed me on account of the manner in which the strike seemed perpetually to vary, but I found on comparison afterwards that my observations of the strikes all seemed to fit in with the theory that

GEOLOGY. 167

they were parallel to the tangent of the central elliptic core of Ruwenzori at the particular place.

The epidiorites mentioned above seem to have been originally intrusive bands or dykes, and to have been greatly altered. Gneissoid syenites, representing what was originally a series of intrusive dykes, occur in the Yeria and other valleys,

Fig. 26a.—Diagram of Ruwenzori.

but for full mineralogical details see Dr. Gregory's (l. c.) paper.

There has been, however, quite another era of volcanic activity on Ruwenzori, which is probably long subsequent to the formation of the mountain and may have been comparatively very recent. I was able to find quite a number of little volcanic craters and crater lakes. Some of these are quite perfect little cones, with a deep blue lake in the centre and composed of whitish volcanic tuff or agglomerate often dipping away from the centre. I notice on Captain Lugard's map the word "cones" near one of these at Vijongo, which shows that the credit of discovery is due to him.

I am not at all surprised that he did not notice others, for I passed and frequently saw one hill, named Kyatwa, without the smallest idea that it was a volcano until my return journey when I ascended it and saw on the other side a perfect crater-lake which it probably once enclosed.

These recent volcanoes may be roughly grouped as follows:

1. The Vijongo series.
2. The Butanuka series.
3. Kaihura straits area.
4. The Karimi volcano.

To which it is extremely probable that the following outlying hills, not visited by me, may have to be added—Ruansindi, Ibanda, and Kivari.

Besides these evidences of volcanic activity I found two hot springs on the mountain. One of these was a small tributary of the Winni river, and the other was on the west side of the mountain not far from the Butagu river.

The Vijongo series seem to consist of four or more little cones and one rather large lake of which the cone has disappeared.

GEOLOGY.

The next series are probably the cause of the curious loop (eastwards) taken by the Mpango river. They appear to be separated from Vijongo by the ordinary granitoid gneiss of the Victoria region, on which Kasagama's town is situated, and run in a somewhat curved line from Kyatwa hill towards the east. They form the northern boundary of the low uncultivated plain which seems to be the former bed of Lake Ruisamba.

After leaving Butanuka on my southern journey towards the Salt lake, I first came across a salt river just before the Muhokia, and shortly after crossing the latter, entered the Kaihura straits area. A large crater lake occurs at Chukarongo, the point where the curve of the land eastwards towards the Kaihura passage begins. On the road from this point to Katwe, two deep holes are passed, occupied by poisonous salt lakes, which appear to be undoubtedly volcanoes; and I should imagine there are others in the neighbourhood. Then there is a ridge of olivine basalt, obviously very fresh as compared with the old intrusive beds of Ruwenzori, and after descending this, one passes another clearly volcanic crater lake. Climbing up the lip of this after about a mile's walking over white tuff rock, one reaches the ridge on which the Salt lake fort is placed, and which separates the Salt lake, consisting as I think of three craters, from an arm of the Albert Edward which is probably another, broken into and partially

destroyed by the water of the Nyanza. After
leaving Katwe the white tuff rock ceases at
the Nyamgassa river. At the other side of the
Kaihura straits, I think probably all the lakes
mentioned by Captain Lugard are of the same
formation; and I saw myself similar whitish tuff
rock as far south as Visegwe's village along the
Albert Edward shore.

The Karimi hill, which looks exactly like a
volcano, is towards the end of the ridge that

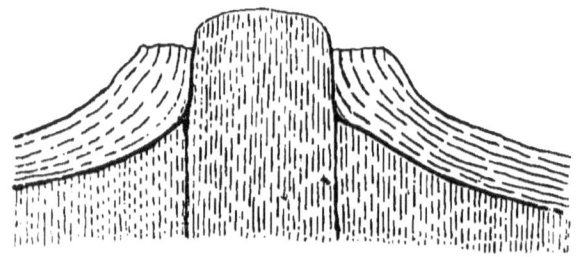

Fig. 26b.—SECTION OF FIGURE 26a.

stretches from this place to the shore of the
Albert Edward Nyanza, and separates the low
flat valley of the Semliki from the similar flat
plain which extends towards the Salt lake as far
as the Nyamgassa river.

It is now possible to give a clear account of how
Ruwenzori may have come into existence. We
may suppose the site to have been once a part of
the original Victoria region plateau. Thus it consisted of underlying gneissose rocks, covered by

mica schists, amongst which were intrusive bands or dykes of lava.

Then an elliptic area (now the central core) was elevated relatively to the surrounding region. The mica schists were carried up with it, and now slope away from the ellipse, and their included bands and dykes have become greatly altered epidiorites (see Fig. 26*b*).

This elevated mountain mass, surrounded by the depressions of the Semliki valley, Albert Edward, the Ruisamba, could not have been formed without the production of lines of weakness or dislocation. The recent volcanic cones probably appeared afterwards along these lines. Thus of the four groups mentioned above, the Vijongo chain is almost north-east; Butanuka is nearly due east; while the Salt lake area (which may have formed the curious narrowing of the entrance of Ruisamba at Kaihura) lies roughly south-east, that at Karimi being approximately south-west. I should be very much interested to know if there are any similar lines of weakness to the north-west of Ruwenzori, but I cannot find evidence of this.

The appearance of the soil, not to speak of the lakes, is very different to anything seen elsewhere. It has a curious resemblance to the blue earth of Kimberley, but I regret to say that I did *not* find any trace of diamonds! In fact, I have never seen any valuable minerals excepting iron in the British East African sphere, and I am disposed to question their existence.

Another curious feature of Ruwenzori which seems to be much doubted by geologists is whether there is any evidence of glaciation. Personally I am inclined to think that three of the valleys have once been occupied by glaciers to a level of about 5,200 feet—that is to say, 7 or 8 miles in one case.

Two of these valleys, the Mubuku and Nyamwamba, have a broad open U-shape in transverse section; another, the Butagu, has the following appearance (Fig. 28).

Now all the other valleys on Ruwenzori which I saw have the typical V-shape of erosion valleys in a tropical rainy climate.

The shape of these three valleys is, it seems to me, very much what one would expect in them if they had once been filled by a glacier.

In the Nyamwamba there is a very curious ridge, apparently consisting of small boulders and stones, which runs obliquely across the valley; the section and plan in Fig. 28 will make its arrangement clearer. I thought this might be of the nature of a moraine, although the flat bed of the valley continues some distance below this point.

Another point which may be taken as in favour of glaciation is the occurrence of numerous large rounded boulders having all the appearance of *roches moutonnées;* some of these are 10 feet high.

Fig. 27.—GORGE IN WIMI VALLEY.

GEOLOGY. 175

It is also only in these three of the valleys visited that one could expect glaciers, because the others which I saw do not lead directly to the highest snow-covered portion of the ridge.

Here I should like to point out again the disadvantage of not knowing what may have been the condition of the Sahara in miocene times, for if the Sahara was occupied by a sea, it does not

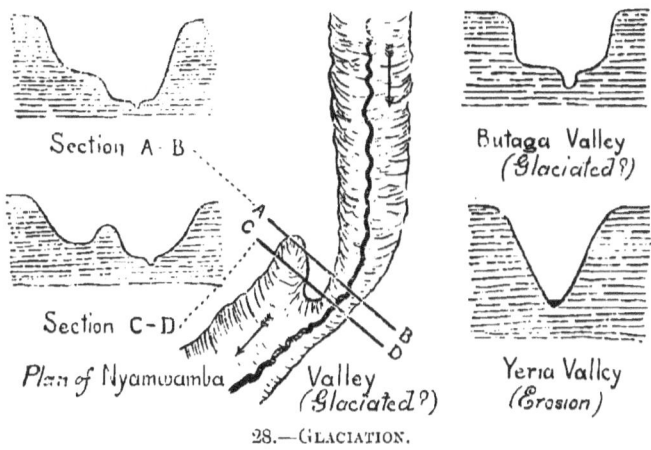

28.—GLACIATION.

seem improbable that the amount of snow might have been so much greater that the present difference between the level of the snow, 15,500 feet, and that of the valleys, 5,200 feet, would not be so overwhelming in amount.

Emin Pasha seems to have found traces of glaciation in this district, as also Casati, but Dr. Stuhlmann has not been able to confirm this. The question is certainly one worth investigating by future travellers.

The Central Watershed rocks are not by any means so interesting as those of Ruwenzori. It gives me a great deal of pleasure to record that Speke, with that extraordinary power of seeing all that was of importance and setting it forth without additions, practically said as much as is required with regard to them. These hills begin close to Kiarutanga, and extend along the southern side of the Ruizi river, by Antari's hill, and round the corner of the mountains behind Kitoboko to the point where the Kagera issues from them, not far from my camp at Butunguru. They then keep on the south side of the alluvial plains of the Kagera until they appear to again approach it not far south of Kitangule. They extend, therefore, over the whole of Karagwe and a large portion of Ankole. On the northern and eastern side they approach the alluvial and volcanic rocks of the Albert Edward, and I entered them before Rubata's on my way south. They are apparently interrupted near Latoma, where the watershed between the Rufni river, which is said to enter the Albert Edward Nyanza, is not more than 300 feet above the Kagera valley level; and from this point they probably proceed southwards till they reach the chain of volcanoes, of which the active volcano, Kissigali, and Mfumbiro are the most prominent members. They then turn south and appear to follow the east shore of Tanganyika; forming the watershed between the latter and

GEOLOGY.

the various branches of the Kagera, *i.e.*, between the Congo and Nile ultimately.

Their appearance is throughout very uniform, and resembles an intricate maze of deep and narrow valleys, often 1,000 feet below the level of the hills.

The lowest rock is usually a black or glistening shale, or ranging from this to a well-cleaved Killas. Above this follows—(2) a series of red or brown sandstones; (3) a coarse schistose sandstone; (4) a white granular quartzite.

These rocks were so much folded and usually at such a steep dip that I was unable to form any idea of their thickness. The coal, which has been said to exist in Karagwe, will, I suspect, turn out to be a black shale, corresponding to the lowest rock.

Dr. Gregory considers it probable that these are part of the series described by Mr. Joseph Thompson about Lake Bangweolo, and by M. Cornet, from the upper basin of the Congo. They are not by any means promising, geologically.

CHAPTER XI.

METEOROLOGY AND CLIMATE.

THE meteorological notes which I obtained are, I find, of but little service. This science is a very exact one, and it was my experience, like that of many others, to find that in the interval between my departure and return, quite new instruments and observations were found to be absolutely essential. I ought to have slung my thermometers to take the temperature, and I ought also to have taken it at hours which I found to be in ordinary circumstances quite out of the question. Thus, it is, of course, far too dangerous to carry thermometers on the march, where they are liable to accidents of all kinds, and the hour, 9 a.m., which seems to be usually considered correct, is just in the middle of an ordinary day's march or excursion. I do not suppose that, except on Sundays, or during illness, I was ever in my camp at that time during the whole expedition.

I also found that it was really too dangerous to leave my thermometers out at night when I was starting the next morning. The plunging about of the boy in the early morning, in a dark tent,

METEOROLOGY AND CLIMATE.

results always in the breakage of anything breakable.

My instruments were lent by the Royal Geographical Society, and consisted of two boiling-point thermometers, a maximum, minimum and wet and dry bulb thermometers, prismatic compass and plane table.

I tried to take daily observations of temperature at 2 p.m., when usually in camp, and at 7 p.m., before packing up for the night. As regards climate, British Central Africa and East Africa may be roughly divided into four main divisions: 1. The Cocoanut or Oil-palm zone, which is below 3,000 feet. 2. The Coffee zone, which lies between 3,000 and 5,000 feet. 3. The Colony zone, between 5,000 and 7,000 feet. 4. The Cloud-belt, above 7,000 feet.

In our East African sphere the first division breaks down, however, for it includes two very different climates. The first is that part of the coast immediately bordering the sea, which is below 1,000 feet in altitude. Most of the large rivers carry the physical conditions characteristic of it for a long distance inland, so that its outline is very irregular. In a natural state it is a dense tropical jungle, with the Rubber vine and many creepers.

The second is the remaining portion of the eastern coast, below 3,000 feet in altitude. This is covered naturally by Euphorbia trees, Acacias, and other thorny scrub. It is an excessively dry, waterless region, while the former subdivision is very wet and humid.

The boundaries of these two sub-districts are extremely difficult to draw on a map, because the second reaches the sea towards Somaliland, and even much farther south; Mombasa Island is very similar to the Euphorbia region, and Kilindini harbour is quite a typical example of the coast jungle.

It is a matter of enormous practical importance, however, to point out this difference, as the first sub-district is extremely fertile, while the second is, so far as one can see, of *no commercial use whatever*.

The second division is the Coffee zone, of from 3,000 to 5,000 feet, which begins before Kibwezi and ends before Matschakos. This is in nature a scrub region, but does not contain a large proportion of those thorny shrubs which are characteristic of the second sub-district of the Cocoanut zone already alluded to. The scrub is quite of an ordinary character, showing traces neither of a very humid atmosphere nor of a very arid one.

The third division, or Colony zone, contains the Masai highlands, by which term I mean part of Ukambane, the whole of Kikuyu, and the Masai country above the level of 5,000 feet or more clearly from Nzowi to the western side of the Nandi range, along the ordinary caravan route.

METEOROLOGY AND CLIMATE.

The Victoria region, by which I understand the drainage area of the Victoria Nyanza, so far as that is comprised between 3,900 feet (the level of the Nyanza) and 5,000 feet, falls of course within the Coffee zone.

The Central Watershed, which includes the Ankole, Karagwe and Urundi hills, and probably may be held to extend along the eastern side of the mountains bordering Tanganyika to the east as far as the Malagarazi river, may be taken as a portion of the Colony zone.

This is simply the watershed of Tanganyika and the Nile, in the wider sense of the term, and is a hilly region, probably nearly everywhere well above 4,000 feet, and in most places over 5,000 feet in altitude.

The climates of British Central Africa may be roughly divided into four: 1. Tanganyika shore, from 2,700 feet to 5,000 feet, which is in the Coffee zone. 2. The Congo-Zambesi watershed, which is in the Colony zone. 3. The Oil-palm region, consisting of Lake Nyassa, the Shiré and Zambesi river valleys from sea level to 3,000 feet. 4. The Shiré highlands from 3,000 feet upwards, are, of course, the typical Coffee zone. In drawing out this paper I have adopted the level given by Sir John Kirk, at the Geographical Congress, of 5,000 feet for the Colony zone, instead of that which I have worked out myself, viz., 4,000 feet. Of course, taking these three regions marked by the oil-palm, coffee, and prospects of colonisation as universal, means a slight inaccuracy. Thus the coffee zone probably descends to 2,000 feet in the Shiré, and ascends to 6,000 feet in the Masai highlands. But this is more than counterbalanced by the clearer idea of the subject.

It is a very difficult matter to draw a good natural dividing-line between the coffee and colony divisions, but it is necessary on account of the difference in health, rainfall, and consequently of the vegetable products of the country. In fact, to estimate rightly the value of British Central Africa, it is above all things important to bear in mind this difference which, so far as I know, is not usually clearly shown.

The leading features of these divisions I shall now try to point out in detail, but before doing so, it may be as well to draw up a tabular statement of the leading characteristics of these climates.

The observations on which the accounts of the first four stations are based, may be found in the excellent " Report on Meteorological Observations in British East Africa," by Mr. E. G. Ravenstein. Those at Bandaue were taken by Rev. Dr. Lawes, and published in the *Nyassa News*. Those at Zomba were taken by Mr. Hyde Wyatt, and published in the *British Central African Gazette*.

The columns of fever and climate are on my own authority.

MEAN TEMPERATURE.

	Year.	Hottest month.	Coldest month.	Rains begin.	Lesser Rains begin.	Rains end.	Greater Rains end.	Rains days.	Rainfall inches.	Climate.	Fever.
Zanzibar	79.8	82.6	76.8	Oct.	Until		May	113	61.34	Very bad	Severe
Coast, Mombasa	78.1	81.9	74.5	Nov.	Dec.	Mar.	June	106	50.7	Trying	Considerable
Masai highlands, Kikuyu	61	66	57	Nov.	Dec.	Mar.	June	118	59	Very good	None
Victoria region (Natete)	71.4	74.1	69.3	Nov.	Dec. Jan.	Feb.	May	114	47.6	Trying	Slight
Ruwenzori	No observations.			Rains	all	the	year.			Do.	Do.
Central Watershed	Do.		Probably	similar	to	Kikuyu.				Excellent	Do.
Tanganyika	Do.				Nov.	No observations.			29.78	Very bad	Severe
Congo-Zambesi Watershed	Do.				Dec.	No observations.				Very good	None
Nyassa, Bandaue	Do.			Nov.			April			Bad	Severe
Shiré highlands, Zomba	Do.			Dec.			Mar.		41.06	Fair	Slight

From the preceding it is at once obvious that there is a very curious difference between Nyassaland and Eastern Africa. The rains in East Africa last from November to June, with a long dry interval of one or two months. On the other hand, the rains in British Central Africa appear to continue without any dry interval at all, and end in April.

I was very much impressed with the fact that in Zanzibar the commencement of the rains coincides with the change of the monsoon, both in March and in November. From July to the end of September seems to be the dry season in all these districts; which, it will be observed, is the season of the south-west monsoon. Of course, on the east coast it is obvious that this wind cannot bring any rain, as it must blow across the land.

In Nyassaland, according to Captain Robertson, the south-west monsoon begins in April, and of course, blowing over the highlands of the Transvaal, cannot bring with it any rain. Hence the rains stop in that month. I am convinced that if it were possible to obtain thoroughly satisfactory observations of the direction of the wind, the beginning and end of the rainy season would be found to follow upon the wind changes exactly.

The following rough table is interesting in this respect.

	Jan.	February.	March.	April.	May.	June.	July.	Aug.	Sept.	Oct.	November.	December.
West Coast Region	W.	W. & S.W.	S.W.	S.W.	W.	W.	W.	W.	W.	W.	W.	W. & S.W.
Angola	W.	W.	S.W.	S.W.	W.	W.	W.	S.W.	S.W.	S.W.	S.W.	S.W.
Cape Town	S.	S.	S.	S.W.	W.	W.	W.	S.W.	S.W.	S.W.	S.W.	S.W.
Nyassaland	N.E.	N.E.	N.E.	S.W.	S.W.	S.W.	S.W.	S.W.	S.W.	N.E.	N.E.	N.E.
Mombasa	N.E.	N.E.	N.E. & S.W.	S.W.	S.W.	S.W.	S.W.	S.W.	S.W. & S.E.	S.E.	S.E.	N.E.
Zanzibar	N.E.	N.E.	N.E. & S.W.	S.W.	S.W.	S.W.	S.W.	S.W.	S.W.	S.W.	S.W. & N.E.	N.E.

The authorities for the preceding are chiefly the maps given in the *Challenger* reports. For Nyassaland, however, I have copied Captain Robertson's report: *vide British Central African Gazette*, vol. i. p. 14. For Mombasa I have used results given me by Captain Coathupe, formerly in command of the *Indus* in Kilindini harbour; and for Zanzibar I have copied from the *Zanzibar Gazette*, Nov. 14, 1894.

The climate of Mombasa itself and the whole of the dry Thorn-tree Acacia desert, as far as Kibwezi, is probably not at all a bad one. This is part of the curious waterless zone of East Africa, which occupies a very large proportion of the German territory and ends northwards in the unmitigated deserts of Somaliland. This is the second sub-division of the Cocoanut zone noticed above. It is, of course, the drought that renders it comparatively healthy. Mombasa island, though it should have a climate almost as bad as Zanzibar, consists of coral rock and has no appearance, so far as the vegetation goes, of the dense tangled and moist jungle which seems, according to Captain Lugard, to mark the Sabakhi valley. On the other hand, the heat is extremely trying. During my journey I had at Buchuma a temperature of 102 degrees in the shade of a double-roofed tent, and at Ngomeni of 104! The average maximum temperature, as far as Mto Andei, being as much as 93 degrees. Such temperatures never occurred during the rest of my journey till I reached Lake Nyassa. Of course, the worst feature of this desert zone is the scarcity and extremely objectionable nature of the water. Dysentery ought to be most carefully guarded against, and water should always be boiled before use. The extraordinary feat of endurance mentioned by the late Mr. Joseph Thomson, who walked fifty miles in a day, shows that, at any rate, some Europeans can support great muscular strain in this region; but it cannot be supposed that the country is one suited for Europeans to colonise and work with their own hands.

The best part of the Colony zone in tropical Africa is undoubtedly the magnificent country which extends from Matschakos to the Nandi range, close to the Victoria Nyanza, which may be called for convenience the Masai highlands. I have myself walked fifty miles in thirty hours in this region, and Dr. Gregory performed feats of this kind which completely throw mine into the shade, and would be even in England worth mentioning. In reality, one is quite in as good a condition physically as in Great Britain.

This is chiefly due to the cold nights, when a fire is frequently pleasant. Sometimes the daily range is very great (*e.g.*, 80 degrees in the afternoon and 46 at night), but considering the manner in which one has to travel, Europeans may safely be said to have every prospect of being able to colonise and bring up children. The work which they would find necessary would most certainly be far less severe than that of travellers under present conditions.

The Coffee zone begins again on the western flanks of the Nandi hills. I think that in this Victoria region the climate is very much more trying than is generally supposed. Making all due allowances for the discomforts and privations of Europeans at present in this part, there are some irreducible facts which go, I think, to prove that it is not a country where Europeans should remain for more than three or, at the most, five years at a time. Nor would it be possible to do continuous manual work, though it is not likely that this would ever be required of a European. It is probably better than most parts of India, but the presence of swamps, and the absence of horses, makes a very great difference to the health and comfort of those who would be obliged to remain permanently in Uganda. Cases of hæmaturic fever also occur. At present a very severe scourge is the "jigger." Every morning at Kampala, a long row of miserable beings, with toes in all stages of ulceration, used to wait for treatment, and though, with reasonable care and attention, it can quite easily be avoided, there is no doubt that this, amongst other things, shows poverty of the blood and a bad state of health.

On Ruwenzori itself the climate is a very pecu-

METEOROLOGY AND CLIMATE.

liar one, and no doubt is very different in different situations.

Fever of the ordinary Uganda type certainly prevails up to a height of 5,000 feet all round the base of the mountain. I do not think that there is any true malarial fever above this altitude. I myself did actually suffer severely from fever when living at about 6,000 feet, but this had been contracted on the plains.

On the other hand, in the Colony zone, at a height of 5,000 to 7,000 feet, there is a curious kind of rheumatism, or "dengue" fever, which affected many of my men. It seemed to begin with headache, followed by pains in the knees and legs, which were accompanied by great lassitude and fatigue. This appears to become acute at night, and in the early morning and during the day seems to disappear almost entirely.

I found that the ordinary treatment for malarial fever was far the best remedy for this "dengue," or rheumatism.

The chief objection to Ruwenzori as a sanatorium lies in the rain and cloud. In a hot climate it is moisture that is dangerous, and on Ruwenzori it is always moist almost everywhere.

The rainfall must be very heavy, for though I had no means of actually measuring it, rain fell on about 40 days out of the 126 which I spent upon the mountain. There is, however, a great difference in different valleys. The Wimi and Butagu valleys are very wet indeed, while the Mubuku, Yeria, and Nyamwamba, as well as the low hills, *e.g.*, about Butanuka and the Salt lake, are in comparison dry. It is not, however, so much the actual rain as the persistent mist and cloud that makes the climate unpleasant.

The cloud mentioned above (ground fog?) seems in the morning, about 10 a.m., to condense and collect at from 6,000 to 7,000 feet, according to whether the particular spot is a narrow sheltered valley or exposed ridge. It completely fills such valleys as the Wimi, but blows over exposed bluffs like the Yeria. It then begins slowly to crawl up the mountain, reaching the level of the bamboos about midday; and at about 5.30 p.m. it begins to dissolve away (as a rule), allowing one to see during perhaps a quarter to half an hour the beautiful snow-clad peaks, the highest summits of the range. Even on the best days it is not a clear view that one obtains, but very tantalising glimpses; now one snow-peak, now another, appearing, and then being again enshrouded in a pall of mist.

This, in part, explains why Ruwenzori was not seen until Mr. Stanley approached it from the north. The history of the discovery of Ruwenzori is a most curious one. Emin Pasha, so far as his letters enable one to judge, never saw the snow, but was well aware of what he called the mountains of Usongora. Mr. Stanley, when speaking

Fig. 29.—FOREST OF WIMI VALLEY.

of the discovery of Ruwenzori, makes the following extraordinary remark ("In Darkest Africa," vol. ii. p. 290): "It is quite a mysterious fact that from the localities reached by Sir S. Baker, it ought to have been as visible as St. Paul's dome from Westminster Bridge."

It is almost impossible to believe that Mr. Stanley could have permitted himself to speak thus of Sir S. Baker in view of his own experience.

In "Through the Dark Continent," vol. i. p. 438 (1878), he says: "The opposite coast was the high ridge of Usongora, which I should judge to be about 15 miles distant." At the place of which he is here speaking, Mr. Stanley must have been within 25 miles of Ruwenzori; yet it is quite obvious that in Stanley's own map, the site where the mountain ought to be is covered with a lake.

Mr. Stanley then was himself within 25 miles of the mountain, without suspecting the presence of anything but a ridge; yet he quarrels with Sir S. Baker for not perceiving it at a distance of from 50 to 60 miles! Moreover, it is evident that the Blue mountains, of which Sir S. Baker speaks, were, in fact, Ruwenzori, and the lake in Sir S. Baker's book shows great affinity to that in "Through the Dark Continent."

The name Ruwenzori has no existence whatever in the country. I have retained it on account of its euphony, in which the real name Runsororo is conspicuously lacking. Most of the natives simply speak of it as "Kiriba," a word which I take to mean a high peak, and which seems to me of Wahima origin. This name is also given to any high peak far away to the south in Urundi.

It is unpleasant to criticise Mr. Stanley's works, but when I find loose and unaccredited statements

Fig. 30. THE BARK CLOTH FIG.

of his quoted as classics against me, and have to fight hard with my own mapmaker to insist on what does not exist being not included in my own map because Mr. Stanley states that it ought to be there, then it is necessary to make a stand.

Mount Gordon Bennett, Mackinnon Peak, and Mount Lawson are not mountains, but quite insignificant hills, if they have any existence at all.

METEOROLOGY AND CLIMATE.

The curious lifting of the cloud at the rate of about 1,000 feet an hour is, as I have mentioned before, the leading clue to the arrangement of the Floral Zones. The cloud in the morning covers pretty nearly that portion of the mountain which is occupied by the forest and bamboos. Its lower and upper boundary corresponding to the beginning of the forest and the upper limit of the bamboo region. From this it follows at once that the heather region receives the sunlight in the morning, and only at that time, and hence the flora is of a comparatively temperate type. The true forest receives the full heat of the afternoon sun, and this, together with abundant moisture, explains the main features of its plants. The bamboos, on the other hand, receive scarcely any sunlight worth mentioning.

A very curious phenomenon is a violent wind, sometimes almost of hurricane force, which sweeps down the valleys, particularly those leading directly to the snow peaks, at about 6 to 7 p.m. It is a phenomenon very closely related to the land breeze, and the figure copied from Dr. Mill's excellent work, " Realm of Nature " (Fig. 31), very exactly represents it. Dr. Mill says : "When a range of mountains rises near the sea, very strong winds are produced, the mountain slope acting like a flue, aiding the ascent of hot air by day and the descent of cold air by night."

I believe the data on which these figures depend

were first discovered during the *Challenger* Expedition by the detection of strands of dry air descending. I have myself noticed, just at the time when my porters were trying to prevent my tent from being hurried down the valley, clouds in a high stratum of the atmosphere drifting gently towards the top of the mountain.

Both this evening wind and the ascent of the cloud are, I think, pretty easily explained. The lower slopes of the mountain are rapidly heated by the sun, more rapidly perhaps than the plain, and the hot air rises, carrying with it, and perhaps partially dissolving, the cloud At about 6 p.m. the whole side of the mountain is clear of cold air, and the stratum in contact with the snow rushes down to the heated lower ground. I noticed also—and the fact seems to bear out this theory—that when rain is falling or has fallen during the afternoon on the lower slopes, this wind does not blow down the valley with the same force.

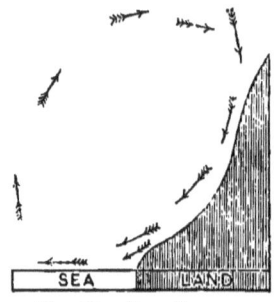

Fig. 31.—Sea Breeze.

I do not know enough of meteorology to be able to explain several other points which I noticed. For instance, rain is most unusual in the lower levels till the afternoon, and the greatest quantity seems always to fall during the night. Again,

I have watched from my camp on Kivata a thunderstorm apparently doing its best to reach the mountain, but passing northwards and coasting it 8 or 9 miles away. The plains were deluged with rain, but scarcely a drop fell in my camp. On another occasion a horizontal bank of clouds tried during the whole of an afternoon to reach my camp, and only succeeded at about 7 p.m. In both these cases there must have been some vertical motion in the atmosphere which prevented their approach.

The climate of the Central African Watershed, by which I mean the highlands from 4,500 or 5,000 feet upwards, which form the backbone of the continent dividing those streams which eventually fall into the Kagera river from those which enter Tanganyika and the Albert Edward, is probably a very fair one for Europeans. It is true that there are numerous swamp-rivers, and my own experience was anything but favourable; still, the altitude is very considerable in most places, and, what is of more importance, much the largest part of the country consists of dry grassy hills and plateaux, having all the appearance of a rather low rainfall. My own condition was probably due to constant fevers and two or three slight touches of sunstroke. It is, therefore, with some hesitation that I place this district within the Colony zone.

Unfortunately, as usually happens, this climatic

advantage is very largely counterbalanced by the extremely poverty-stricken appearance of the country on the whole. Karagwe and Ankole (*i.e.*, the higher plateaux) do not afford much prospect for Europeans. Urundi, of course, is a very fertile country, and probably all along the chain of high hills which culminate in Mfumbiro, and which I crossed near Mwesi's, there is a dense population and plenty of cattle, as well as a fairly heavy rainfall; but just in these places the climate will very probably turn out unsatisfactory. Still, these hills, like the Masai highlands and the Nyika and Stevenson Road plateaux, might possibly form colonies for Europeans: a very unusual condition of things in Africa. It is, of course, satisfactory to reflect that this is in German territory. If, as there are some grounds for hoping, the future trade of this district will pass down through British Central Africa, there will be, at any rate, the passage money of emigrants going there.

For Tanganyika I am sorry that I have very little to say of an encouraging nature. Captain Hore ("Tanganyika," p. 146) gives a very good account of the climate. My own experience is so diametrically opposite to the impression that one would draw from his work, that I feel obliged (though I do not like to contradict one who had such ample opportunities of judging) to quarrel with every one of his statements.

The lassitude and weakness which overcame me

immediately after crossing the Kiriba mountains into the valley of Tanganyika, persisted until I entered the Stevenson Road plateau, and was varied by attacks of the very worst fevers which I ever endured. The Roman Catholic missionaries have had most sad and terrible experience of the deadly nature of the climate. Fever of the very worst kind (hæmaturic) is prevalent, and the water of the lake is, I am convinced, most dangerous. It is only at Kituta, where a good stream of fresh water exists, that even moderate health is preserved; and the London Missionary Society have, I understand, very rightly decided that their stations should be removed to hills and plateaux some distance from the lake. Fortunately the steamer which obliged them to remain near the lake will now be used for ordinary purposes, where it will be of inestimable value, and my kind friends at Niamkoria will soon shift their position to some less trying spot.

As for the water, I cannot understand Captain Hore's remarks. The taste is like nothing in the world except itself, and that Dr. Frankland should report it as "much the same as Thames water, but with very much less organic impurity," is to me inconceivable. No one can fail to perceive the white incrustation which the lake water has left on the rocks bordering the shore. If I had known that no analysis had been published, I should certainly have brought some home with me; and I must most emphatically warn every traveller never to drink it unless after boiling, and, where possible, to avoid it altogether.

The climate may be most safely put half way between that of the West Coast of Africa and that of the Zambesi valley. I do not propose to give a long account of the remaining districts, for which excellent materials for a thorough report will probably be soon available. I must, however, carefully point out that there are three very distinct climates of very different kinds in British Central Africa. The high plateaux of the Stevenson Road and, according to Mr. Johnston, parts of Angoniland and Nyika—that is, the Colony zone—are perhaps as good in every way for Europeans as the Masai highlands. It is only in these districts which are probably of rather small area that Europeans can hope to maintain full working efficiency for indefinite periods and make permanent homes. It gives, however, a peculiar value to British Central Africa that there are such places, however limited in area they may be. It means a supply of European food, vegetables, and comforts of all kinds, as well as a refuge for a few months to those who are settled in the less healthy places.

The Coffee zone, above 3,000 feet, which one may roughly call the Shiré highlands, is very difficult to understand. Many Europeans seem never to have fever at all, and there are a few who seem to preserve their health in spite of very great and continuous strain; but on the whole I do not think any one should remain for a longer period than five years without a holiday, and I am afraid permanent homes are out of the question. It is a country of the very greatest value to Great Britain, for young men can go there even now and by coffee planting, and probably other things in the future, obtain enough to form a comfortable livelihood for themselves, on which they may retire.

The advantage of a colony in this respect is incalculable, and, of course, though it does not appear directly in any statistics, is sufficient to make probably three times our expenditure on British Central Africa justifiable.

As for the oil-palm region, which contains the alluvial valleys of Lake Nyassa and the Upper and Lower Shiré, there is, I am afraid, no doubt that the climate is bad. It is probably not worse than, *e.g.*, Mombasa, but it is very easy to see that it produces great lassitude and loss of energy in Europeans. There is also fever, which occasionally is of a very bad type; and I think no one should remain on these lower grounds for a longer period than three years at a time. Still it is necessary to make a very large deduction for the discomfort and privations which most have to undergo at present, and what I have heard of Calcutta in the early, almost prehistoric, factory days seems infinitely worse than the present state of things, *e.g.*, at Chiromo.

It must not be forgotten in connection with the general question of healthiness of climate that heat has practically very little to do with the presence or absence of dangerous fever. Egypt, where the temperature is sometimes very high indeed, is one of the healthiest climates in the world. The West Coast of Africa is probably more unhealthy than any other spot, yet the temperature is not, as a rule, abnormally high.

It is *moist* heat which is really dangerous, and a camp should always, if at all practicable, be planted on a high and exposed situation—in fact, on the driest and barest spot one can find within reasonable distance of water. A curious instance of this advantage occurs at Freetown, Sierra Leone. By far the healthiest place in the town is the barrack, which is on a bare, grassy hill, kept clear of trees, and much below the so-called sanatorium of Lester Peak.

Of the fact I do not think any observer can be at all doubtful, but the cause is more difficult to explain. One undoubted reason is that at night on bare exposed ground there is far more radiation of heat, and consequently a refreshing coolness in which one can recover from the exhaustion of the system which follows a high temperature during the day.

A very interesting statement is given by Dr. Mill (" Realm of Nature," p. 112) : " Were it not for the dust motes and condensed water catching and retaining most of this heat, the radiation of a single clear night would chill down the land far more than the solar energy received during the day could heat it."

The life history of malaria germs is not by any means completely known. A very excellent account by Dr. P. Manson will be found in the *British Medical Journal*, April 15, 1893. There is also a good summary in *Natural Science*, vol. v., No. 31, September, 1894, by Dr. Gregory. From these the life history of the germs within the body can be easily understood. I do not think, however, that our knowledge of the manner in which they are introduced into the blood is at all satisfactory. Dr. Manson has a most attractive theory that the mosquito receives malarial germs—a most gratifying idea to every one who has suffered from mosquitoes, as I have done!

As far as I can understand, for the question is certainly one which is not by any means fully explained, the mosquito, like man, suffers from fever, and is able to extract the malarial germs with human blood; this is, of course, obviously possible. The disease may then be passed from mosquito to mosquito, and thus kept alive. It may become encysted on the death of the mosquito, and may be in this condition swallowed or breathed by travellers.

Personally, I supposed that the marriage flight of mosquitoes occurs just before sunset, and that the female after this commences to feed; then I supposed that she laid her eggs and died. Dragon-flies and a kind of sand-wasp are the only creatures that prey upon them, to my knowledge.

Still, the association of malaria with the mosquito suggests the remark that there are numerous places in Africa where (to my own knowledge) fever is very bad and mosquitoes almost or altogether absent (Tanganyika). There are also many places in which mosquitoes abound and yet fever is not present at all or very rare (Salt lake).

The answer, of course, may be that, when one enters Tropical Africa, the mosquito belt must inevitably be passed through, and it is very possible that the germs are in reality present for months before unfavourable conditions of health bring matters to a crisis.

Fever is most usually produced by a chill, usually the result of sitting or sleeping in damp clothes, but it may be produced, as I know from experience, by sunstroke or over-exertion. It is a general theory amongst planters everywhere that clearing a jungle results in fever; and I have heard, *e.g.*, in the Shiré highlands, so many instances of this that I am disposed to believe in it. It does not seem to be generally known that malarial fever occurs amongst animals, but I think this is the case amongst cattle, dogs, and even poultry and turkeys!*

* I have heard so on good authority in Tamatave.

METEOROLOGY AND CLIMATE. 205

All this shows that the manner in which fever germs are introduced into the system is a most important matter for inquiry.

A moist heat probably interferes with perspiration and respiration, and so brings about a lowering of the system, which renders it unable to resist fever. Whether this is due to the wind bringing with it fever-stricken mosquitoes or malarial germs which obtain admission to the blood by some other means, the effect is the same, and the presence of marshes near a station is most dangerous.

It may seem strange that a non-medical traveller should lay stress on these matters, but they are not by any means realised in practice.

Fort Johnston, on Lake Nyassa, is almost surrounded by a marsh, and is therefore, as one would expect, probably the most unhealthy station in British Central Africa. Generally speaking, in a climate where fevers occur, no trees, no marshy ground, but a perfectly bare clearing on, if possible, an exposed dry knoll is by far the best station for Europeans.

I am astounded that so obvious a fact should be so frequently neglected in practice.

In my journey I noticed the following stations built in a radically bad situation: Kibwezi, Lubwa's, Kituta, Fort Abercorn, Karonga's; at this last, however, as well as at Chiromo and Matope, there is no really good position close at hand.

The effect of trees, even a banana patch, is to afford protection against wind, which is the main agent of health, and to preserve in the neighbourhood a permanent humid atmosphere, leading to chills, and generally weakening the system.

Mr. Rome, at Chiromo, Shiré highlands, remarked to me that whenever the wind blew across the marshes towards Chiromo everybody in the place became ill with fever. I have also noticed the same thing in West Africa and Madagascar.

CHAPTER XII.

BOTANY.

AMONGST the very great difficulties in the way of studying botanical distributions, one of the most serious is that he who puts forward either theories or explanations does so only at the peril of his reputation as a scientific botanist. The wind of evolution has not yet stirred the dry bones of systematic botany, and many are unable to realise the main leading fact of evolution, namely, that all genera and species of plants must have had a definite origin in space. A species must have either become differentiated in the particular spot in which we find it, or it has wandered to that spot from its original home.

I do not think any field-botanist will quarrel with the assumption that every particular species is restricted to a definite climate, though the conditions which a certain set of species (very limited in number) require may be fulfilled throughout very wide areas.

The flowering season of any particular plant

depends upon the commencement and duration of the rains and on temperature.

After our English flowers have received a definite amount of sunlight (called by Körner *the thermal constant* *) and moisture (which is rarely lacking in England) they bloom; and perhaps as much as thirty days may separate the period of flowering in an abnormally cold and an abnormally hot year.

Now imagine some kind of plant which is travelling from the home of its parents; it is easy to see that if it enters a physically different climate it will not bloom at the same period as its parents. The moisture and amount of heat will be different.

Most flowers remain in bloom for a comparatively short time. So, assuming that the wanderer does not blossom till the 1st of May, and remains in flower one month, it is obvious that if its parent begins flowering on the 1st of April, even if insects or wind can pass freely from one to the other, no cross fertilisation can take place. The two are separated as widely as if the broad Atlantic rolled between them.

If there are different physical conditions, these will affect *the main body* of a species entering the country. The extreme conservatives and over-rash radicals, who either refuse to alter their habits or alter them too thoroughly, will be exceptional and will leave no descendants.

* See " Natural History of Plants," Körner and Oliver.

All these newly isolated colonists will be affected by the physical characteristics of their new home, and, of course, all will either adapt themselves in some way to them or die out. It does not follow that these adaptations will be the same in every case. There may be two or three or more main directions in which they are made to vary.

Thus, to recur to the original instance, plants which have been accustomed to flower, say, in the beginning of the rainy season may, if they arrive in the Victoria region, begin to flower either in November or in February. Under certain circumstances the differences in, for example, temperature between November and February may produce in both these sets of the same species visible differences which may be sufficient to make them in an ordinary botanist's eyes species, distinct both from their parent and from one another. Under no circumstances can they cross if they are specialised to flower in these different months.*

From this one sees clearly that the first essential

---

* In the preceding remarks I am obliged to assume what has never been questioned by any one except Professor Weissmann. Those who have studied Darwin's "Plants and Animals under Domestication," or who have watched the curious wrigglings and formation of new heads which Weissmannism adopted under the strain of adverse facts, will not require any further apology. Mr. Herbert Spencer has very satisfactorily buried its remains in two articles in the *Contemporary Review*. Professor Henslow has, since the above was written, proved most of the theory which is embodied in the above "Origin of Plants."

in marking out floral regions is a knowledge of the facts connected with the beginning and duration of the hot and rainy seasons. These will be found at greater length in the preceding chapter. Our knowledge of these simple facts in Central Africa is chaotic as compared with our knowledge of the plants of different regions.

I am not going to subdivide Africa into a large number of divisions. There is a German paper by Dr. Buchwald, in which the continent is divided into 38 districts, each of which is subdivided, so that there are in all 109 subdivisions marked by abbreviations. "B" may stand for Berber, Bongo, Baringo, Benue, Barombi, or Bachila, &c.

The simplest way of grasping the facts, as I hold them, is to start by imagining a subsidence of 3,500 feet all over the continent. If this took place the Niger and Congo valley would be almost entirely submerged. A ridge of high land, beginning in Abyssinia and Lower Egypt, would pass due south by Ruwenzori and east of Tanganyika, and somewhere in the neighbourhood of the Stevenson Road plateau would turn west along the watershed of the Congo and Zambesi to the sea in Angola. The whole country to the west of this would be submerged, except for little islands such as the Cameroons and Kong mountains. This submerged district is our first botanical region.

The ridge—which is of course what I have called the Central Watershed—or a branch of it, probably extended originally right across the Victoria Nyanza to Kenia and Kilimandjaro, and it may have extended southwards across the Zambesi valley to the highlands of Mashonaland and the Transvaal. The Central Watershed, therefore, will form our second Floral region, though it can be divided into marked sub-districts.

On the eastern side of this ridge the valleys of the Sabakhi, Rovuma, and Zambesi have cleared away a great portion of the soil, so that a submergence of this amount—3,500 feet—would cover a very large and irregular area, eating up to within 200 miles of Tanganyika along the course of the Zambesi and Rovuma. This will make our third great division.

Now for the ocean which we have imagined as submerging the first and third regions, let us substitute a warm and humid climate all over Africa below the level of 3,500 feet. The facts, then, are closely represented; and we have in Tropical Africa two humid climates—west and east—and a central watershed which is comparatively dry. These may now be considered in detail.

The *Westerly* Wet Climate, or Niger and Congo Flora, now extends across the Nile to the foot of the Abyssinian mountains. It includes many of the valleys of Ruwenzori, the Semliki valley, and Tanganyika. It is limited on the north by the border of the Sahara. Throughout the whole of its area (though there are probably many elevated dry spots, or climatic islands, enclosed in it), it is marked by the same characters, being usually a dense tropical forest with abundant moisture and general steaminess, exceedingly unhealthy, and deserving even to be called the worst fever district in the world.

The rains here are brought from the Atlantic ocean by westerly and south-westerly winds, which prevail during the whole year. It has thus a most marked characteristic flora. The same plants range from Ruwenzori and Tanganyika to Sierra Leone and the Gambia. There is no earthly reason why they should not, for the same climatic conditions prevail everywhere. Thus Ruwenzori belongs in part to the Western Flora, and even up to about 7,000 feet altitude there are upon its flanks deep, steamy, forest-clad valleys, such as the Wimi, where I found numerous characteristic forms belonging to the West.

Of these plants many are creepers with broad, rather thin, membranous leaves, with very long stalks. There are numerous ferns, but very few annuals or small shrubs of any kind. All those plants which are specially adapted to heat and moisture together occur frequently.

As to the origin of this very distinct flora, which is one of enormous size, it is extremely difficult to orm any opinion. It is not European, for I find no similarity to European or Mediterranean genera

Fig. 32.—WATERFALL ON THE WIMI RIVER.

whatever. It is, however, quite certain that it must have come from somewhere, unless it originated in the region; and therefore one is obliged to suppose that it arrived either from South America or some part of Asia, or from the Cape of Good Hope. Of these the most probable is certainly Asia, and there is a resemblance between the genera of Malaya and those of Congese Africa.*

I entered and left this region in two places during my route, and in all my experience I have never seen so well-marked a line of distinction. When I came into the Wimi valley, I could in some places have supposed myself near Sierra Leone; and again, on descending the mountains bordering Tanganyika on their western side, to about 3,500 feet, I immediately noted that I was in a Western Flora. On leaving the lake at Kituta, I found myself at once out of it after ascending not more than 1,000 feet above the level of the lake (*i.e.*, 3,700 feet).

Now let us consider the *Easterly* Wet Climate. All along the east coast, beginning at Kilindini, lies a series of river valleys such as the Sabakhi, Rovuma, Zambesi, and Shiré, which latter includes Lake Nyassa. These have all of them a very moist, unhealthy, and feverish climate. Their plants are quite different to those of the westerly wet side. Perhaps this can be most easily shown by the statistical method.

* I believe Professor Oliver holds this view.

In the "Journal of the Linnean Society," vol. xxx. p. 67, I have attempted to determine by the statistical method the most natural African floral regions.

Taking the figures there given, I find that 498 species of the order Rubiaceæ found in Tropical Africa occur as follows :—

The Westerly Wet District contains 280 species, or 56 per cent.

The Easterly Wet Division contains 58 species, or 11.6 per cent.

Abyssinia and Angola, which may be regarded as parts of the Central Ridge, contain 39 species, or 5.8 per cent.

The exceptions, that is plants common to East and West Tropical Africa, are 18 in number, or 3.6 per cent., and amongst this small proportion are such weeds of cultivation as Oldenlandia, &c.

The most interesting region of African botany is the third, the Central Watershed, or ridge of highlands that extends from Abyssinia by Ruwenzori down to the Livingstone mountains and Stevenson Road, and may even be traced, I think, to the Cape Colony.

It consists usually of a series of grassy ridges, though in some places it is covered by scattered trees, not dense enough to constitute forest and not isolated enough to form the park-like country which one occasionally sees in the lower levels. The river valleys are often, or usually, covered with forest, but it is not the dense steamy jungle of the east and west wet low-level country, but what one may call river woods, without bringing the German term "Galeriewald" into requisition.

The most curious feature of this central ridge is the manner in which the flora changes as one proceeds from north to south. Excluding for the moment the true sub-alpine plants, belonging to the region above 7,000 feet altitude, there is a gradual transition observable from Abyssinia to the Transvaal. The flowers of the Shiré highlands, and particularly Mount Mlanje, are very like those of the Transvaal. Those of the Masai highlands show a less marked but still a perfectly clear resemblance, while those of Ruwenzori and Abyssinia have only a very general and perhaps scarcely perceptible similarity. The explanation is simple enough, on the hypothesis that the ancestors of the present plants travelled down the ridge from Abyssinia before the present basins of the Nile (*i.e.*, Victoria Nyanza), Congo, and Zambesi had been eaten out to their present level, while by the subsequent excavation of these and other valleys different portions of the ridge have since been isolated from one another by the interposition of climatic barriers.

Thus the Malagarazi river has burrowed out a large valley, which is colonised by Tanganyika, or rather Congo plants. North of this valley, on the east side of Tanganyika, are the hills of the Kiriba chain, Ankole and Karagwe, while to the south are the high plateaux south-east of Tanganyika, which are probably inhabited by the same plants as the Stevenson Road and Angola. These two areas show a most marked similarity to one another, but at the same time there is just the difference one would expect. To prevent confusion it is best to state clearly the apparent main stations along this north to south migration :—

1. Abyssinia.
2. Ruwenzori.
3. Central Watershed.
4. Stevenson Road.
5. Angola.
6. Shiré highlands.
7. Victoria Region.
8. Kenia.
9. Masai highlands.
10. Kilimandjaro.
11. Usambara (in part).
12. Somaliland and Taru Desert.

If we imagine instead of plants an immigration of human beings, it is much easier to understand in what sense these districts ought to be taken. Supposing some Abyssinian race, which is obliged to remain at a height of at least 3,500 feet for the sake of health, to have colonised Central Africa; then every one of these 12 sub-colonies would in course of time become different from one another.

If we suppose that they colonised the country *before* the Victoria Nyanza was excavated down to its present level, it is easy to see that those parts of the tribe which inhabited its site might conceivably remain on its shores; but when things became as they are at present they would have to live in quite a different way to their relations on the much higher country of the Masai highlands to the east and Karagwe hills to the west, and would become like the Waganda—a people quite different from any Abyssinian race and also different from the people of Ankole and Karagwe.

Now this is what has happened to the plants of the Victoria region. The country occupied by it lies between 3,900 feet and 4,500 feet altitude. It is a fairly dry climate, but not a desert one. The rainy season is from October to April. It follows from this that the plants there could not have come from the Congo area, for their climate is a very wet one, and their rainy season is from April to October.

Therefore we find in the Victoria region, along with plants which belong to the Masai highlands and the hills of the Central Watershed west of the Victoria, a large number of kinds which are not found elsewhere, but which are modified forms of high altitude plants adapted to the special physical conditions.

Something of the same kind has occurred in the twelfth area, Somaliland, and the dry thorn-tree desert which passes between the coast and the more rainy Masai and Ukambani highlands. The droughty conditions have produced a very large number of new forms which were originally settlers from these moister uplands, or perhaps from the Easterly Wet valleys.

The Central Watershed, the Masai highlands,

Usambara,* and the Stevenson Road colonies are very closely allied. They are chiefly steppe or grassy countries, though often covered by scattered trees; they all lie on an average at an altitude of between 3,500 and 6,600 feet; the climate is not as dry as the Victoria region, but it is a warm one, and the rainfall also occurs between October and April. Those parts of Abyssinia, Ruwenzori, Kenia, and Kilimandjaro (to which one may add Mfumbiro and Elgon) which lie between those altitudes (3,500 and 7,000 feet) possess many of the forms which are found in the Central Watershed, and perhaps also in districts 4, 9 and 11; but the inhabitants of the very wet and cold Cloud regions of Ruwenzori, Kenia, Kilimandjaro, and the Kiriba above 7,000 feet are for the most part utterly different to anything found on the lower levels, and are obviously a separate migration which has followed the same course as that of the Central Watershed plants at a time when there was probably a continuous ridge above 6,600 feet from Abyssinia to Mount Mlanje and Mashonaland. This explains why some of them also extended to the Cameroons and Fernando Po, where, so far as I know, the plants found below 7,000 feet have not penetrated. Thus the district may be summarised as follows:—

* I use this name to designate all parts of German East Africa, except the Central Waterhed, which are over 3,000 feet in altitude.

BOTANY. 221

A. Westerly Wet region, Niger-Congo; very hot with April to October rains and below 3,500 feet.

B. Easterly Wet region, Zambesi and other valleys; very hot, with October to April rains, below 3,500 feet.

C. Central ridge which is above 3,500 feet and fairly dry, with October to April rains.

Of this last the following sub-districts are all above 4,500 feet and are each occupied both by a low-level flora, 4,500 to 6,600 feet, which is in a fairly dry and warm climate, and a high-level flora above 6,600 feet which has extremely wet and rather cold conditions of life.

1. Abyssinia. 2. Ruwenzori. 3. Central Watershed. 6. Shiré highlands. 8. Kenia. 9. Masai highlands. 10. Kilimandjaro.

When better known probably both (4) Stevenson Road (including south-east Tanganyika), and (5) Angola will be found also to contain a high-level of the wet and cold-loving Alpine forms. (11) Usambara is in the same condition. Of the two remaining districts, the (7) Victoria region lies between 3,900 and 4,500 feet and has rather a different rainfall, while (12) Somaliland and Taru is a desert with extreme drought.

The question remaining is therefore to know how all this came about. Here we are met on the threshold by a barrier at present insurmountable. There is no definite knowledge of the condition of Africa in miocene times.

If we take the period when natural orders and the leading genera of plants were pretty well differentiated, and if at that time we assume a sea in place of the Sahara stretching across the whole desert country which now extends from Beluchistan to the Atlantic, between Morocco and Senegal, an explanation can be given. There would, of course, be islands in this sea, but the most important point is that the range of mountains about the Red Sea, with those of Abyssinia, would form a climatic bridge to the ancestors of the Mediterranean flora; hence there would be no difficulty in understanding the distribution and affinities of the Alpine flora of Africa—(high level, wet and cold-loving plants) which probably came across at that time. At this period the ancestors of the low-level steppe flora may have covered the whole of the continent south of 15 degrees N. latitude.

Along the southern shore of the Sahara sea would be a continuity from the coast of the Indian Ocean to Timbuctoo; at this time neither the Niger, Congo, or Nile would have excavated their basins, but all Africa south of 15 degrees N. latitude might have been fairly high ground.

Now, under these circumstances, *first*, the Coast Jungle Flora of India and Malaya, *as it existed at that date*, would colonise the southern shore of the Sahara sea.

Now, if we imagine the rivers beginning their

excavations: The Niger and Congo valleys would be occupied by the ancestral Coast Jungle Flora of India which would rapidly multiply its species as the valleys broadened and deepened, and finally occupy, as they do now, the whole Niger-Congo area, with pioneers in the valleys of Ruwenzori and the Malagarasi. The Nile would deepen the Victoria region and the steppe forms would colonise it.

The Zambesi, Rovuma, and other rivers on the east, are very insignificant as compared with the Nile and Congo, and I think it is safer to assume that they were colonised at a much later date when the Coast Jungle Flora was nearer its present condition. At any rate, it is simpler to suppose that these valleys are inhabited by plants whose ancestors came originally round the eastern coast, *viâ* Zanzibar, and which now reach even as far south as the coast of Natal.

This may seem a gigantic and baseless speculation, but I think it is possible. If true, it would at any rate account for certain facts which are to my mind absolutely proved, but cannot be explained on any other hypothesis; namely, first, the strange fundamental difference between the Niger-Congo Soudan area, and the Zambesi and Zanzibar district, and, secondly, the distribution of the steppe flora and the Alpine flora. It may at any rate be considered a working hypothesis; though ultimately it can only be tested by increasing knowledge of the geological facts.

The following table is an attempt to give the height of the forest, bamboos, and snow, on the more important African mountains :—

	Beginning of Forest.	Beginning of Bamboos (or Teneriffe pines).	End of do.	Snow level.	Highest point.
Teneriffe (Berthelot) 28° N. Lat.	Sea level (?)	6,000 feet	7,500 feet	10,000 (?) feet	12,182 feet
Ruwenzori (Scott Elliot) 0° Lat.	7,400 feet	8,700 ,,	10,000 ,,	15,500 ,,	16,700 ,,
Kenia (Gregory) 0° 6′ S. Lat.	7,300 ,,	8,000 ,,	9,800 ,,	15,300 ,,	18,400 ,,
Kilimandjaro (Meyer) 3° S. Lat.	6,232 ,,	(?)	8,856 ,,		19,500 ,,
Mlanje 16° S. Lat.	3,500 ,,	3,700* ,,	(?)		10,000 ,,

* *Widdringtonia Whytei.*

It will, of course, be noticed that the preceding floral divisions are almost exactly those given for climate. The Westerly Wet Flora occupies very nearly the Oil-palm region of the west coast, and the Easterly Wet Flora the Oil or Cocoanut zone on the east coast.

The Central Ridge and its branch to the Masai highlands contain the remaining climatic regions, viz., Coffee zone, Colony zone, and Cloud belt, but of course in every sub-division these are differently represented.

The division of Africa is, in fact, the same, as of course it should be, whether one divides it according to the meteorology, botany, or economical facts. Materials are, however, non-existent to give satis-

BOTANY. 225

factory definitions of the sub-districts. Even in the botany, which has been more studied than the other two sciences, I only know of three collections worth mentioning on the Central Ridge and Ruwenzori.

There is a curious similarity between South America and Africa which may, perhaps, be explained by meteorologists.

Fig. 33.—IN THE VICTORIA REGION.

Starting from the east coast, north of Mombasa, and crossing the continent one finds the following floral characters:—(1) A very wet jungle; (2) a dry thorn region, in parts desert; (3) a fertile mountainous country of woods and steppes; (4) a much drier country (Victoria region); (5) a mountainous region with woods and steppes and cloud belts; (6) a very wide wet jungle area (Congo) reaching to the Atlantic.

Starting from the *west* coast of South America one has (1) A littoral strip; (2) a dry, or in parts desert country (Peru or Chili); (3) a fertile mountainous region with cloud belts and woods; (4) a dry desert valley; (5) another mountain chain with woods and steppes; (6) a very wide wet jungle (Amazon, &c.) reaching to the Atlantic.

It is only in the jungle character of No. 1 being less marked in South America, and in the cloud belt being in No. 3 instead of in No. 5 that these sections differ.

The similarity is, to my mind, too close for mere coincidence, and the meteorological phenomena should be the reason.

CHAPTER XIII.

MPORORO AND EAST SHORE, ALBERT EDWARD.

ON the 4th of August, 1894, I left the Salt lake on a journey of which I knew nothing, and which had never been traversed by a European. Just at the last moment I found that two of my best men were unable to come. They had developed horrible sores on the feet, and I was obliged to leave them in charge of the headman at the Salt lake station. I had forty men and one woman. This woman had married one of my askari at Kampala and was allowed to come on condition that she looked after the cattle *en route*.

I think, now, that it was rather a foolhardy thing to start with so few, as a journey of this kind has usually been undertaken only by caravans of not less than a hundred men. Still, I certainly could not have managed to go by the same route with a larger number on account of the difficulty of supplies; and as I did bring all except one to Ujiji in safety and health I have no right to complain of my fortune.

The forty and myself were packed into three huge dug-outs at the Salt lake, and, after paddling 1½ hours, we arrived safely at Kaihura's (Kwa Kaihura means " of, or belonging to, Kaihura ").

The position of this place is wrongly put on most maps, Kaihura having moved very much to the north.

I found it to be a most miserable little collection of huts, and his people to be a puny, half-starved race, apparently living chiefly on fish. Kaihura was very much alarmed on account of what had happened to some deserters from Mr. Grant's caravan. These men had attempted, on their way back to Uganda, to make slaves of two guides who had been supplied to them by a neighbouring chief (in the ordinary Suahili manner) and in consequence had lost their lives. Poor old Kaihura was also in great fear of Antari, whose people came and raided him when they had nothing better to do.

In fact, the general balance of power in this corner of Africa is in a state of great instability. A corner of Waruanda people is pushing up from Ruanda along the eastern border of the Albert Edward Nyanza. This seems to be a race in a state of expansion, and is at present pushing on all the tribes which surround it. As is usual in such cases, their pioneer colonies are in course of separation from the parent race, and friction is beginning to occur between Makowalli, the head of this north-eastern prolongation, and the original people. The country Mpororo, which occupies a large space on the map, is now a very insignificant district. Makowalli's people separate it from the lake, and Antari's people also make raids upon it from Ankole, so that its chief, Seribombo, is between two extremely uncomfortable stools.

The countries of Visegwe and Rubata are both small districts between Kaihura on the north and Makowalli on the south. They seem to be raided by the Ankole people from the east, and probably also by Makowalli and Kaihura, as well as by each other.

African politics are a complicated matter, but I fancy these two districts, as well as Kaihura, may be regarded as pioneer colonies of Ankole broken loose and turned independent.

I have tried to win the gratitude of readers of books of travel by avoiding the daily journal method of writing, but here I must employ it, to give some idea of this almost unknown region.

After leaving Kaihura's, we passed at first over a series of low rolling hills, which are, I think, part of the Victoria region plateau. Then, close to Visegwe's village, there was a sudden descent to the shore of the Albert Edward Nyanza, and we saw, sweeping away to the south-west, an enormous plain, for the most part covered by dense Acacias, and almost entirely uninhabited. This is the old level of the Albert Edward, and considerably below that of the Victoria region plateau. This plain is broken by lakes and lagoons, and is still a haunt of the ever-retiring elephant. I am inclined to think a considerable part of it is of recent volcanic origin, and quite similar to that of the country round about the Salt lake. I myself noticed no craters, but Captain Lugard, whose route crossed mine, mentions several lakes (Nyamsigira, Kibona, Ruamiga) which lie to the east and north-east of my route. I was much impressed by the volcanic appearance of Ibanda mountain when descending from the Ankole hills, but as my route was direct to Chansingaira, on the shore of the Albert Edward, I did not see any of these lakes or any definite evidence of volcanic action. The tuff-like appearance of the soil, however, near Visegwe's, which is quite similar to that of the Salt lake, as well as Captain Lugard's account, which I did not then know of—it is my rule to attempt to be perfectly impartial by *not* reading what others have said *before* seeing for myself—lead me to believe now that both Ibanda and Ruansindi are volcanic cones, and that the area of recent volcanic activity on the east side of the Albert Edward is a very considerable one (*vide* chap. x. and map).

Just before Visegwe's, we coasted the Albert Edward shore for a short distance. It is fringed by giant bulrushes, and there are quantities of herons, white ibis, ducks, and geese, as well as a white and black kingfisher with an enormous head. In these rushes the natives set up hippopotamus traps, of which a sketch is given. We saw a few fishermen in small canoes very ingeniously made of rough planks lashed together by banana fibre.

Most of this part had been recently burnt, and had a very desolate appearance. Such cultivation as I saw seemed to consist of wimbi, "hungry rice," and sweet potatoes. There seemed to be very little game anywhere.

Just before Rubata's village, this old lake bottom is left, and after a short interval of low rolling hills and swamp-rivers, which are probably a southerly strip of the Victoria plateau fringing the Albert Edward Nyanza, the Central Watershed (or Ankole-Karagwe hills) is again entered.

Fig. 31. —Hippopotamus Trap.

It was in this part that I found what seemed to me the characteristic schists of Ruwenzori; but they are certainly not spread over a large area, as, immediately after this, one enters the characteristic white marble-like quartzites of the Karagwe series.

From this point until the top of the Stevenson Road plateau is reached, the same formation of sandstone and quartzites, with occasional shales, continues, so far as I can see, without variation. There was only one place where I thought that a different rock occurred, and that was in the valley of the Kagera at Latoma.

The people at Rubata's were very much like those of Ankole generally. They are very poor and miserable, and most rapacious and determined beggars. Some of those I saw had been mutilated; just as used to be the case in Uganda, where I have seen at Buddu a man without nose or ears—a punishment inflicted by the chief for gross misbehaviour. The man had been thrown out as dead, and subsequently recovered; during the prevalence of an epidemic of "jiggers," he had found rather a nice-looking young woman who had suffered severely from them and had been similarly thrown out to die. He had carefully washed and attended to her sores, so that she recovered and married him, presumably out of gratitude. He seemed rather proud of his horrible appearance, and was a great favourite with the French missionaries. Here at Rubata's there were several similarly mutilated. One had the nose cut off as well as an eye put out. Besides other bad habits, these people smoke almost all day long, and, as in Buddu, divide the day as follows:—When the women smoke their first pipe; when the women smoke their third pipe; after or before that important period; and so on down to the fifth pipe.

They are clothed usually in skins, though they are very anxious for cloth when they have a chance of obtaining it. They also wear heavy wire anklets, and frequently amulets of various kinds round the neck.

They are rather above the medium height, though slender, and many have the rather high and prominent foreheads characteristic of the Wahima. They are undoubtedly more intelligent than most native races; some of their paths are neatly engineered through the hills, and stepping-stones and even bridges across the small streams are not infrequent.

They appear to be quite ignorant of European ways, and a petty chief once followed me with an armed band to extort "hongo," which, of course, I refused. The most powerful of all the chiefs is Makowalli, whom I did not see. He was very angry with me because I only sent him seven pieces of cloth, whereas Mr. Stokes had sent him thirty-three cloths. I sent to tell him that he had sent *me* nothing, and that I was not Mr. Stokes.

These people are so cranky and rapacious, that travelling is not safe with a small caravan. The country seems in many places well adapted to cattle. I saw one very large herd in Mpororo, and the above-mentioned Makowalli is said to possess two hundred cows, but I am afraid cattle ranching would not be safe until the chiefs have been brought under control.

The chief cultivation seems to be millet, "hungry rice," or wimbi, sweet potatoes, and beans.

The strata of the Karagwe series seem to be folded in such a way that the fertility of the soil is quite different in different places. Sometimes one passes an outcrop of rich brown loam, and then perhaps over a considerable extent of very sandy soil. This makes it even more difficult than usual to estimate the value of the country, but on the whole it is probably very fairly good, and certainly far better than Karagwe.

Just before reaching Seribombo's place, a messenger came from a chief called Kasiliwamba to see me and to show me a very curious letter of which I here give a copy.

Deutsche Ost Afrika,
Ekatoka den 29 August, 1893.

Der Sultan Kasiliwamba vom Katoka (Mpororo) steht unter deutschen schutz.

(Signed) LANGHELD
Kompagnie Führer.

Gesehen, 28/7/94

This was also sealed with the seal of the Deutsche Antisklaverei Komite. The peculiar coolness of this letter very much impressed me, for Katoka is a long way within the English sphere of influence, as " Kompagnie Führer Langheld " must have very well known. Of course, as no English official has ever been near the district (excepting Captain Lugard, who did not come nearly so far south), and as two or three German officials have passed, the natives cannot be blamed for putting themselves under their protection.

In fact, the Germans are along the whole border quite prepared to pounce on our territory when they get the opportunity. If we were to throw up Uganda and the neighbouring territories, it would be under German control, probably, in two months. Other countries generally realise far more than we do the advantage, in the future, of our East African possessions.

Just before reaching Seribombo's I was seized with a sharp attack of fever, and was obliged to remain a day or two on the route.

Seribombo himself, and the people of Mpororo generally, are very much more friendly and agreeable than Makowalli's ruffians, and I was extremely sorry to learn that shortly after I had passed a raid had been made upon him by Antari's warparties. It is, of course, our duty to put down this sort of thing in territory everywhere within our sphere, and it is to be hoped that it will not be long before a European official is established in this district.

A good situation would be about two days' journey from the Kagera river, on the high mountain spur which ends the Ruampala mountains to the west. Probably this point would only be three days' journey from the Albert Edward Nyanza, and one could obtain as much labour as would be required by utilising the salt from the Salt lake in payment.

The road leaves the mountains at Seribombo's, and enters the Rufue valley. This river is said by the natives to enter the Albert Edward Nyanza, a point of very great importance, since a short day's march over two or three rolling hills, none of which are more than three hundred feet above the Kagera plain, leads to a stream, the Kakitombo, which falls into the Kagera just below Latoma. It follows, therefore, that there should be a very easy road to the Albert Edward Nyanza from this point, probably not more than 60 to 70 miles long.

This river, Kakitombo, is about 15 yards wide and 2 feet deep, and has a small belt of forest on its banks. The Kagera itself is about 40 yards wide, very deep, and has a moderately swift current (two miles per hour). The belt of papyrus is about 80 yards wide on either side, and the water is, as usual, full of hippopotami. We crossed in six canoes, each of which was capable of carrying a man and two loads at a time. These were formed of two small dug-outs lashed together. The banks of the river are very steep, nearly 40 feet above the water. The river is curiously similar throughout the whole of its course, from Bugufu to Kitangule and Musonje.

Emin Pasha's description of the Nile below the Albert Nyanza applies almost exactly: "The mighty stream winds in curious curves between papyrus masses often 12 feet high; its current is made apparent by the Pistias which float along its surface."

The water is usually yellowish-brown and it is always deep, and never, where I saw it, interrupted by islands. The breadth is also almost always the same. The valley is usually a flat alluvium, sometimes of enormous width, as about Kitangule.

Often when wandering along the banks I have wondered if there was in this part another Egypt lying dormant for want of population, intelligence, and good government.

I do not see why there should not be a great future for these vast plains. There is sometimes 30 to 50 feet of rich alluvial soil, which is too dry from April to October for any great amount of native cultivation. The Wakaragwe have no idea of "shadouf" or "sakkieh," and have absolutely no inducement to work. If they became rich, the Arabs or the Wankoli would plunder them, so they simply live on in their fathers' banana plantations.

Higher up the flat alluvial part of the valley narrows to about a mile in width. This is usually covered with scattered thorn-trees of various kinds, chiefly Acacia and Erythrina. Underneath there is dense matted grass often two or three feet high, and at the season when I passed yellow and scorched by the sun. This is intersected in every direction by the broad paths of hippopotami. This animal is extraordinarily agile in Africa. I have seen a regular road down the river banks, so steep that I could not understand how so clumsy a creature could manage to ascend.

Very often there is a narrow fringing wood just at the edge of the bank, what is called in Germany a "Galerie" wood.

A stroll through one of these was always interesting. One could obtain a glance through the bushes and perhaps see an enormous crocodile floating lazily on the surface. Some kind of waterfowl would be running about the papyrus roots. If there is a withered tree along the banks, a darter will be sitting on a branch glancing sideways, backwards and downwards at the water. This bird, from mechanical reasons, has to keep its bill tilted high in the air, which gives it a most supercilious appearance.

Perhaps an enormous python will glide out of the brushwood and coil itself noiselessly into the sluggish stream.

Hippopotami heads are to be seen everywhere, and every now and then one will give an enormous yawn, exposing a most capacious gullet. I used, from a sense of duty, to sit down at the bank and fire at them, but this was quite an innocuous amusement on my part. The amount of nostril and head exposed was far too small for me to do them any harm.

I remained a day at the crossing Latoma (a little above Kavingo) as I found the people very friendly, and I wished to lay in supplies for my march through Karagwe. They brought me quantities of beans and peas to sell, and I found them entertaining and pleasant.

There are some hot springs at a place called Mtagata, a few miles below Latoma, and salt springs occur also at a point about 20 miles north-west of it. According to Dr. Stuhlmann there are also hot springs, not very far to the west. There is therefore, very probably, an area of recent volcanic activity, slightly to the west of Latoma, which may be in connection with the active volcano Kissigali of the Mfumbiro chain. At Latoma itself, however, one is, I think, on part of the Karagwe series, or Central Watershed mountains. Here I was very unfortunate in obtaining a guide who was full of incorrect information, and during the rest of the way to Karagwe's capital was perpetually leading me off the track which I wished to follow.

CHAPTER XIV.

KARAGWE.

THE country of Karagwe was in a marked decline when I passed through it.

If one reads Speke and Grant's account of the district, it is easy to see that it was then in a very prosperous and thriving condition.

The present state is so much the reverse that it serves as a good object lesson of the rise and fall of an African native kingdom. A true and thoroughly unprejudiced account of the changes in a small community like this would be of use even in European politics.

It is really a case of individuality. Rumanika, the former ruler, was a kind of African Gustavus Adolphus. A man of extremely strong character, energetic, exceedingly shrewd, and hampered by no scruples whatever, he pushed forward the limits of his country beyond the point at which its real resources in men and products were able to maintain them. All these characteristics, as well as Rumanika's humour and imagination, appear quite clearly in his interviews with Mr. Stanley, who came away with the impression that Rumanika was truthful, benevolent, mild, and altogether a fine character.

When the master-hand was removed, and a youth, Kajeti, brought up in a dissolute and licentious court, came to the throne at an early age, then things at once fell to pieces. A colony of Arabs established themselves at Kitangule and dominated all the neighbourhood of his northeastern border, though now these will probably be soon driven out by the Germans, who have the whole eastern border under their control.

On the south the two districts, Buhimba and Kakaruka, being driven to extremities by the exactions of Kajeti's weak and unprincipled favourites, have thrown off all allegiance.

Along the whole western border, that is along the Kagera river, the country is completely uninhabited. I passed numerous banana plantations, which are neglected and becoming overgrown with weeds, and destroyed. The two fringing semi-independent states on the west bank of the Kagera, Kishakka, and Sangwe, have by their continual raids produced this effect. The people received no protection, and were obliged to go.

In the immediate neighbourhood of Werowangi, Kajeti's capital, I saw the manner in which the labouring classes were oppressed by the exactions of the Court. My guide from Latoma, after receiving his present, bolted homewards so as not to be robbed of it. The country people brought me plenty to sell until Kajeti's people appeared on the scene, when they departed; and if by chance one remained near the camps, he was a poor man according to his own account.

Kajeti himself, when he at length summoned up courage to visit me, proved an arrant coward. He would not enter my tent, although it was raining. I offered him some sugar and salt, but he would not taste it. He and his large following of dissipated boys and youths were all half drunk with pembe, and when he had at last discovered that I did not intend to hurt him, he began to beg and demand guns in such an insolent way that I had to tell him to go and leave me alone.

Oppressions and robbery of the poorer people, as well as licentious and drinking habits in the king's *entourage*, are an inevitable consequence of a warlike and raiding state. They have in Karagwe, as usual, produced utter destruction of the community after a very few years.

The journey from Latoma to Werowangi was rather tiresome. After Kisozzi, we had to leave the Kagera on account of the enormous lake or lagoon of Karaingy. This is a vast sheet of water which must have once extended fully 20 miles further inland amongst the hills, and is now apparently drying up. It has numerous floating islands and patches of papyrus in it, and is probably very shallow.

KARAGWE. 243

Some Sangwe people in a canoe were too afraid to land, and I saw no canoes or inhabitants except these anywhere near.

The hills, amongst which broad, flat valleys penetrate in curious winds and curves, are extremely stony. The grass had recently been burnt, and

Fig. 35.—EUPHORBIAS OF THE ALBERT EDWARD PLAINS.

the country had a very dry and desolate appearance. This was the only spot on the journey in which I had to feed my indomitable cow with manioc and sweet potatoes.

Both hills and the dry alluvial valleys are covered with scattered bushes of Acacia. This part is well to the east of the Central Watershed, and the kinds of Acacia are quite different to those about the Salt lake. The characteristic Euphorbia of the Albert Edward does not occur. There is in most of the valleys no water whatever. Where it does occur, it is either in the form of a stagnant lake which has been left by the retreating waters of some tributary of the Kagera or towards the head of the valley, where it is found in a few shaded, stagnant pools or occasionally as a minute running stream.

These latter do not, I think, occur unless in the last mile of the valley, where its level is above 4,500 feet.

Thus a fairly good idea of the country may be formed by imagining these winding, thorn-dotted, flat valleys, usually some 10 miles long and one or two miles wide, and which occasionally spread out into wide alluvial plains, with here and there an unpleasant marshy pool, bordered by hills and ridges which may be about 1,200 feet above their level (*i.e.*, 5,000 to 5,500 feet high).

The country remains quite similar throughout Karagwe, and in Kakaruka and Buhimba.

The really fertile parts are the narrow ravines at the heads of the minor valleys, for instance at Mgaira and Butenga, where a little stream of water drops down three or four miles through a narrow valley covered and shaded by banana plantations and thin forest.

There is plenty of iron in the country everywhere, and particularly at Butenga, where I saw some very pure specimens of ore. It is hard to see what could be done with it. If the valleys were filled with swamp-rivers, as in Uganda and Urundi, and as no doubt they were originally, then it would be just as fertile; but these swamp-rivers have become dry alluvium, and the only chance of utilising them would be either by building broad tanks or by making wells wherever possible.

I crossed the watershed of the Kagera and Uriji lake at Butenga. It is at least 6,000 feet high, and the descent is as usual extremely steep.

The shortest distance from Tanganyika to the Victoria lies a little south of Uriji, and is only about 180 miles according to recent maps!

This line, however, after keeping pretty close to the Kagera river, crosses the headwaters of a branch of the Malagarasi, and then over some mountainous country to Amranda, at the head of Emin Pasha gulf. It would probably be extremely expensive and difficult to build a railway along it.

If there had been an outlet from Uriji to the Victoria Nyanza, which does not seem to be the case, then the nearest approximation to this direct line would be by the route that I followed from the Uriji basin.

After leaving Kakaruka, which is within the latter drainage area, I ascended a long, flat valley of the usual type to Mgaira. Then a very steep climb of 400 feet led on to a broad, gently sloping hill, from which there is probably a long gentle descent to the flat valley which leads to the Kagera.

It is probably some 220 miles from Tanganyika to the Victoria by this route, but this is not a matter of much importance. I know nothing of the country between Uriji and the Victoria; but they appear not to be in connection with one another, besides which there could be no competition with the Kagera route.

Game in Karagwe is usually conspicuous by its absence. The most important animal is the rhinoceros. The day I left Karaingy lake and followed its shore, passing over numerous little ridges and alluvial bays extending from it, until I camped on the shore of the next lake at Kangennyi, was remarkable on account of the number of these animals. On starting early in the morning we saw two of these creatures looming large in the mist. I at once sallied forth to shoot, and had advanced within 100 yards when my enthusiastic little dog spoilt everything by rushing in and barking. It will scarcely be credited that these huge beasts, after running wildly to and fro for a minute or two, fled precipitately, with little Bobby barking courageously after them for a quarter of a mile.

After proceeding a short distance we came across another, which did not wait for us. I was walking behind my guide and crossing a flat valley studded with ant-hills, when I was surprised by his suddenly springing back nearly upon me and pointing at an ant-hill. I went forward, looked over it, and was surprised by the sight of a rhinoceros lying asleep on the other side, so near that I could have touched it. Unfortunately I had not a rifle with me, and before one could be produced the animal awoke and went off.

We saw two more near the end of the march and went after them. I was just kneeling down to get a good aim, when one of my men, who wore a white shirt, rushed forward, and the animal saw him and charged us both. We both fired and the discharge turned him. After we had fusiladed him, and he had been charging us with an activity which I should never have suspected, during perhaps 20 minutes, he had had sufficient exercise and went off to some quieter place.

This day's experience showed me conclusively that as a rule these animals do not charge out of sheer wickedness. In this country, however, the natives appear sometimes to collect in large bands and spear them, and this may account for their timidity. I am sure that they cannot see clearly for more than 50 yards or so.

I also saw them on four or five other days in Karagwe and Buhimba. The reason of their abundance is probably connected with a kind of thorn bush, of which there is a great variety all over the district.

I supposed them all to be the common "black" two-horned rhinoceros, although they were nearly white in colour. The long horns of the white species are often found for sale at Zanzibar: I should have supposed that these specimens had probably been brought by the Arabs from the Zambesi river or Portuguese Africa. I hear, however, that this form (*Rhinoceros Homewoodi ?*) has been reported from the German Territory to the south-east of the Victoria Nyanza—practically, it appears, the same country as Karagwe—and it is possible that I was mistaken.

Other game is very rare. I once saw a troop of zebras, and on two or three occasions we came across hartebeest. Guinea-fowl were curiously common near the plantations at Kibwera and Kakaruka. I saw one flock, which must have contained at least a hundred, and Bobby for once made himself useful by rushing in and barking. They took refuge in the trees, and were so occupied in gloating over his futile wrath, that I had no difficulty in getting as many as I wished.

The little lake which Speke called Windermere is one of the pleasantest spots that I have seen anywhere. It lies amongst some very steep hills, and its surface is dotted with two or three beautiful little islands. Kajeti's capital lies on the banks of a wooded ravine to the south-east corner, and there are several small valleys and

Fig. 36.—Canoes on the Kagera River.

banana plantations at various points round it. The hills, however, are grassy and rather bare and arid looking.

A narrow gorge leads out of the lake into a very wide flat valley, which is bounded in the distance by a line of blue hills, really the limit or watershed of the Kagera. This valley is broken by irregular lakes and marshy lagoons; as to the number and position of which I could not obtain a definite idea. It seemed, however, certain that the Kagera river has a distinct course of its own, and that these lakes lead into it without being on the main course of the river.

After leaving Kajeti's capital, we passed over the hills by Kibwera to within a short distance of Uriji, which was quite clearly visible, and is a lake of much the same appearance as Windermere, though much bigger; then, turning up an interminable flat thorn-covered valley, in which were numerous wild pig, we at last reached Kakaruka.

This is a small colony under a chief who is nominally, but not really, under Kajeti. It is a very curious place, consisting of the headwaters of three or four valleys, and is covered by forest patches and many plantations. Here my health broke down through another slight touch of the sun, and for three days I had to be carried in a hammock. For those who should ever be subjected to such an experience, it may be useful to mention that the best plan I could discover was to douche the head in a large quantity of cold water whenever possible. This removes the throbbing heat in the temples and at the back of the head, and I *think* often keeps off fever attacks.

I fancy the reason why I did survive the journey was a habit of taking a cold bath whenever I arrived in camp, and avoiding the sun from the moment I reached camp till at least five in the afternoon. I found a curious progressive weakening as the journey went on. At first I used to go out and botanise after reaching camp till sunset, then it was too much strain to go more than a few yards from the tent, and about this period I found myself unable to stir from the tent after reaching my camp; while even such light labour as writing out labels for my botanical specimens required an amount of effort and determination which I could not explain.

I am bound to say, however, that the cold bath is condemned almost always by those who have wide experience of Tropical Africa, and this is probably another instance of the manner in which climate affects different people in quite dissimilar ways.

Buhimba, which I reached soon after leaving Kakaruka, is the outpost (I think) and limit of the southward extension of the Wahima or Wahuma people. So far as I understand it, they must have travelled south from Abyssinia, and after conquering Unyoro, reached Uganda and the Victoria Nyanza. They do not seem to have been able to advance against the Wa Nandi and Masai, to the east of the Victoria, and so travelled along the west, conquering Ankole, Toru and Karagwe. Here they came in contact with the Warundi on the west, and probably the Wanyamwesi and Wahha on the east, and their further advance southwards was prevented. At any rate, here in Buhimba one finds the whole population of the tall, slim, athletic type which characterises the race. They have also the prominent foreheads and good features seen in the best examples of the people.

I liked the appearance of the people greatly, and they seem to have plenty of exercise, both in hunting the rhinoceros and resisting the attacks of Kajeti and all the tribes which surround them. I was not, however, in a condition to make many observations.

We then turned more directly west, and at last had a good view of the Kagera, just 2 miles below the point where the Akenjaru branch, which is here called the Kagera, unites with the Ru-Vuvu.

I found the Ru-Vuvu here a broad stream at least 40 yards across, and with a narrow fringe of papyrus and alluvial banks 4 to 5 feet in height. The current was about $1\frac{1}{2}$ miles an hour, and the bed was very deep. The usual cabbage-like Pistias were floating down it, and the snort of the hippopotamus, called by the natives "ufufu," was to be heard at frequent intervals.

CHAPTER XV.

BUGUFU AND URUNDI.

CROSSING the Ru-Vuvu, which is certainly the most important branch of the Kagera, I entered the country Bugufu, which I was apparently the first European to visit.

Fig. 37.—KARAGWE HILLS.

About two or three miles north of the crossing, the other, or Kagera proper, branch unites with the Ru-Vuvu to form the main river. Stanley's Observation hill was not noticeable in any way, but it should be on the right-hand bank, almost opposite the meeting of the waters. I only once found the name Akenjaru to be understood by the natives, and I spent much time and trouble in trying to discover where on earth the enormous freshwater sea, discovered and christened the Alexandra Nyanza by Mr. Stanley, could possibly be. This, of course, it is now clear, has no existence whatever; apparently the name is applied to a papyrus fringe on the course of the Kagera proper.

The Alexandra Nyanza may therefore be put down to another stroke of imagination on the part of Rumanika.

The country Bugufu is a very hilly little district. It is bounded on its eastern side by the Ru-Vuvu. In pronouncing this word, there is a distinct pause between Ru, which seems to be a prefix denoting water, pretty common in the Bantu group of languages,[*] and Vuvu, which may be an attempt to represent the sound of flowing water; hence it should be spelt as is here done. On the north the boundary is probably the Kagera branch proper; the left-hand bank of which is part of a country called Kishakka, apparently a small independent piece of Ruanda. On the west Bugufu appears to be bounded by a swamp-river, in Visanganwi's country, of which I failed to obtain the name, but which joins the Ru-Vuvu

[*] *E.g.*, Ruo, Ruizi, Rufue, &c.

BUGUFU AND URUNDI.

some 10 miles below, and separates it from Urundi.

It would thus seem to be an independent pioneer colony of Urundi.

Uhha appears to lie on the eastern side of the Ru-Vuvu entirely.

The hills, which I call Kiriba, send a prolongation westwards, which divides the Kagera-proper branch from the waters which eventually fall into the Ru-Vuvu. Bugufu consists of a number of little valleys and ridges, which terminate this prolongation. The soil is a rich red loam and very fertile. Cultivation is chiefly carried on in the bottoms of the valleys, which appear to be quite free from the white alluvium so common on the Kagera. The average level of these valley bottoms must be some 4,500 or 4,600 feet, and I estimate the hill summits of the prolongation, referred to above, as being at least 7,000 feet altitude. In consequence of this there seems to be no lack of permanent water, and all these little valleys are occupied by running streams. The country is also healthy, and probably will be at some future time of very great importance.

The people are simply delightful and I think the very nicest race I have met anywhere.

Here I enjoyed an experience which I shall always remember with profound satisfaction. I was supposed to be the "Man in the Moon."

The original ruler of Urundi was a "Mwesi"

(*i.e.*, moon) who seems to have brought an enormous district under his control. In fact, the original Urundi probably stretched from Ujiji to about 2 degrees S. latitude, and was bounded on the east by Tanganyika and the Kilimanyambi country, and on the west by the Ru-Vuvu, and, perhaps, to the south by Uhha.

The part directly under Mwesi's control is now very much reduced. Bugufu is quite free, and several chiefs between it and the capital are almost independent, and will no doubt form separate little kingdoms shortly.

This is due to the death of the original Mwesi, who is supposed to have been translated to the Moon. The people thought that I was this individual returned from that elevated position, and they told me that now I had returned the locusts and the jigger would flee away and their land would be at rest. This idea I did my best to suppress, but the porters I am afraid encouraged it for financial reasons. In consequence, my march was a triumphal progress; everybody came from miles to form my bodyguard, and the whole population gave themselves up to dancing and singing.

From the moment I started, they thronged round me in hundreds; a view of the scenery was quite impossible on account of the crowds that ran along beside the caravan. The women used to stop every 500 yards or so and collect in a small circle, clapping their hands and dancing, while one or two in the centre went through the usual body and wrist motions of the West African dance. The performance would end in a long, drawn-out, melodious squeal. Then they would bundle up their babies and run on for another 500 yards or so, to go through the whole of it again. The men would collect on any bare piece of ground in a semi-circle and stamp and posture dance, keeping time with feet, bodies, and neck; every now and then they would jump into the air coming down with a unanimous thud which made the earth tremble and the dust fly. They had also many horns which gave forth a frightful sound. The noise was quite indescribable.

When I stopped, one after another would come and kneel down before me clapping their hands; every one would bring a small piece of grass or a bit of banana leaf or barkcloth fig, which they would lay at my feet. I presume this was intended to symbolise that the country was completely at my service.

They are a healthy, athletic set of people, and I fancy well able to hold their own though they are attacked by the people of Kishakka and the Warundi. They are not Wahima, being much shorter and with more hair on the face. In character they are also very different. The Wahima are sulky, selfish, and keen at a bargain; but these people are very emotional and passionately fond of song and dance; in fact, rather of an Irish temperament.

They are fairly industrious, and I often noticed that the land was carefully irrigated.

Their spears are extremely long and have a small lance head at the top. The arrows have a very long curved barb, often with a blob of poison attached. They seem to be superstitious and are fond of charms. A very common thing is a curious, almost complete, ring of wood worn round the wrist. This is about an inch and a half in diameter, and usually of ebony, often with curious patterns inlaid. It is difficult to imagine how the wrist is introduced, but a man after great persuasion showed that with great exertion the ring could be opened sufficiently to slip off.

They are also fond of wearing amulets, goats' horns, or a small piece of ivory on a string round the neck. Very often one finds curious little brass cylinders hung on these necklaces. These appear to contain a charm. They are also fond of all kinds of beads. Many shave the head, leaving only a longitudinal strip or sometimes a horizontal semi-circle of little clustering curls. They wear barkcloth only, which is usually dyed black, probably in the swamps. The country is almost certainly a good one for cattle, and I should fancy well suited for coffee and other plantations.

After a very pleasant time amongst these delightful people, I passed over a long, rather barren, hill

BUGUFU AND URUNDI.

to the swamp-river referred to above. I had a great deal of difficulty in inducing the Wagufu not to accompany me into Urundi as they obviously thought it would be a good opportunity of paying off old scores; but after some trouble we managed to cross alone and saw the 2,000 or so Wagufu warriors gazing regretfully after us to see if we should be attacked.

We found the people of Urundi in this part did not recognise the present Mwesi. They were at first fairly pleasant, and we had more dancing. In this part, however, and also in Kilimanyambi's country they used to dance on our first arrival with long peeled wands instead of spears, probably to show their pacific intentions. Urundi in this part is not at all well known by Europeans.

It is therefore, perhaps, best to give a short account of its geography.

Mfumbiro is really the end of a great range of mountains, of which the importance appears to have entirely escaped the attention of geographers. I call this range by the native name, Kiriba, as it would be recognised under that name by any native near its position. Mfumbiro is about 10,000 feet high, and the Kiriba, even where I crossed it, was about 8,000 feet. It extends in, I think, a south-easterly or almost southerly direction along the east of Tanganyika till it is interrupted by the Malagarasi valley. After that river is passed the chain, which there takes on a plateau character, again appears, and rising to a height of from 8,000 to 10,000 feet is continued to the extreme south of Tanganyika. After the interruption of Lake Nyassa, the same central ridge of high land is continued by the Livingstone mountains, and does not finally end till the isolated summit of Mlanje.

Few seem to realise that there is this extraordinary Central Ridge which is almost everywhere from 8,000 to 10,000 feet high, and which may be said to be about a thousand miles in length.

Urundi consists of the eastern slopes of this range, which are enclosed by the Ru-Vuvu and Akenjaru branches of the Kagera.

Ruanda, or more properly Kishakka, occupies the left bank of Akenjaru, and so far as I have been able to discover, Uhha occupies the right bank of the Ru-Vuvu.

From this main Kiriba there are two minor transverse ridges. One of these is that already noticed as dividing the Akenjaru from a swamp-river which occurs in Visanganwi's country; Bugufu is situated on a part of it.

The other separates Visanganwi's and other branches of the Ru-Vuvu from an important stream, Nyankulu. This minor ridge is the one on which Mwesi's capital is situated, and is called "Misossi ya Mwesi." The actual site of his town is apparently on the southern side of a bold conspicuous hill, which is about 15 to 20 miles (at a guess) from the main Kiriba chain.

BUGUFU AND URUNDI.

It will be seen, therefore, that the part of Urundi which I traversed lies between the Bugufu and Mwesi's prolongations or promontories of hills. This country is a most curiously difficult one to cross.

Visanganwi's swamp-river and its numerous branches have cut the whole district into narrow valleys, perhaps as a rule, 1,000 feet deep, separated by ridges which are usually not a mile wide. These valleys are mainly occupied by swamp-rivers perhaps 500 yards across. There is, however, one running stream into which most of them fall. I crossed it about 16 miles north-east of Mwesi's capital at the only ford which I could hear of. This was in the dry season, and yet the river was about 4 feet 6 inches deep and fully 50 yards wide. The altitude of this spot was 5,050 feet. The general level of the ridges seems to be almost 6,000 feet.

It will thus be seen that the country is full of water; in some places I found a curious transitional condition in the valleys. The stream, which was an ordinary brook higher up the valley, had become very broad and shallow, and was covered with a sort of crust of rushes and sedges which bent and yielded under the foot in crossing; lower down the valley it could be seen to have changed into a regular swamp-river of papyrus.

Sometimes these ridges are of laterite covered

by dry and bare grass, but usually there are banana groves fringing the crest of the ridge. The women have to descend 1,000 feet to fetch water and return three or four times a day. In many places, and especially towards the Kiriba chain, the ridges are covered with an endless series of banana groves and plantations of millet.

On rising to a height of over 6,000 feet, one finds that the plantations are chiefly of beans (Maharagwi) and it is here that one sees herds of the big-horned cattle which these people seem to have brought from Abyssinia. The country has all the appearance (*i.e.*, between 6,000 and 7,300 feet altitude) of being well adapted to cattle and sheep.

The forest on the Urundi or eastern side of the Kiriba chain has been nearly all cut down and is only found almost on the summit. On the western or Tanganyika side, however, it is very dense, and covers most of the flanks (see chap. xvi.).

My journey through this country was the most dangerous and difficult attempt that I have ever undertaken.

At first the people were not unfriendly, though suspicious, and entirely refusing to tell me the road or sell me food. They did not know the name of Tanganyika until I had gone four days' journey by compass towards it. Then they described it as "Kule Tanganyika." During the first few days, however, while passing through the countries of

Busikosa and Visanganwi, both of whom are semi-independent, I had no very great difficulty except such as was due to my ill-health, which forced me to be largely carried every day.

The first night I encamped in the country directly under Mwesi things became worse.

I was sitting exhausted in my camp when I heard a shot. I immediately came out but could see nothing. Then there was a second, and I at once hurried off with five men to the valley where it appeared to have been fired. I found a respectable old porter, Mirambo, with three bad spear wounds, lying on the ground half conscious. I found he had been stealing maize, and had been attacked from behind by three of the people. Never in all my life have I had to exercise such self-restraint. I wanted to punish them, but what could I do with 40 men? There were at least 2,000 people, each armed with two spears and bow and arrows, who followed me daily. I was in the centre of the country, and though I could have punished them, I must have lost more men, or at any rate had more wounded. I was obliged to restrain myself. Now let me again point out a curious coincidence.

My men were attacked in only three places during the whole of my journey of some 2,500 miles. The first was in Ankole, just at the spot where Captain Langheld killed 35 people in his fight with Antari.

The second was at Tengetenge's, almost on the site of Emin and Stuhlmann's camp.

The third was in Urundi, just where I entered the particular district crossed by Dr. Baumann. The conclusion is obvious.

After this things became worse day by day. I had to walk in spite of great weakness, as poor Mirambo was being carried; no food could be got from the natives; no one would show us the road; and I expected hourly to be attacked.

The character of the country has had a curious effect on the people. It is so fertile that the population is extraordinarily dense. This is, perhaps, also due to the fact that no Arabs have ever obtained entrance to Mwesi's and hence no slave raiding has occurred.

Moreover, the manner in which it is cut up by valleys and swamps has very much isolated the different villages. Each is perched on its own ridge and, through the struggle for existence, is perpetually fighting with all its neighbours. The boys and young men of each village form a standing army perpetually on the watch and ready for anything.

My caravan of 40 (one of whom was carried in a litter) looked absurdly forlorn amongst the huge crowds of armed ruffians following us in serried masses and running alongside the caravan. They greeted me with cries of "Where's my cloth?" I was very weak, and while keeping a careful watch on the natives and on my own men, I had to count my steps and take bearings with a loaded Winchester on my shoulder. One day I estimated our following as 3,000 fully armed men.

On that night things came to a crisis. Mirambo died; all our goats were stolen, and we had no more food after the day's posho was given out. I therefore told the quietest old man I could see that I was going to Mwesi, and that I would fight him if he did not give me food and show me the way. I started with this intention, and found Mwesi's headmen and an enormous army awaiting me.

I explained to these people my intentions, and they promised on the Sultan's part to give me food and goats, and three took us under charge and conducted us to a camp. They brought us food; and as it was Sunday, and my men were exhausted, I rested there one day, and then under their guidance went on to the Kariba chain. There armed crowds still followed us, though they only scowled when Mwesi's people took their bananas to give us food. In fact, they followed us almost to the very summit, and I did not get rid of them till I clearly showed that they would be fired on if they dared to follow us any longer.

These people are active and vigorous, but appear to suffer greatly from smallpox and syphilis. The jigger is also very common. They usually wear a piece of barkcloth round the shoulder and strips from the waist; their arms and legs are covered with coils of wire, and many wear a small piece of ivory from a necklace. When two meet they salute one another by interlacing their fingers and murmuring a long formal salutation. If a woman salutes a man, he embraces her under the

Fig. 38.—BANANAS IN MUBUKU VALLEY.

armpits, and both murmur a salutation with the greatest propriety.

Politeness is always most marked in lawless and dangerous countries.

As to their character, they are certainly liars of the most perfect description. I had no opportunity of learning to know them well.

Mwesi appears to be a boy of some twelve

years old, though I heard rumours that he was really an image or idol; he appears to be completely in the hands of the usual dissipated ruffians who form an African court. He has a very slender control over these turbulent villagers, who detest his chief men. These courtiers do just as they like, and probably greatly oppress the smaller places. The banana, on which the people live, is the one used for native beer, and my men did not at all appreciate it.

It is, perhaps, needless to remark that Mwesi's promised goats did not arrive, but I was only too thankful to get out of the country.

The valley or pass up which I ascended is a rather narrow and steep gorge, probably seven or eight miles long. It is covered with bush, with many clearings for beans and the edible arum. Up to 6,600 feet the plants are quite similar to those of Ankole and Karagwe.

CHAPTER XVI.

THE TANGANYIKA BASIN.

ON the summit of the Kariba chain I posted sentinels, and we rested for half an hour in the forest before descending. The altitude by boiling-point thermometer was 7,896 feet, but I judged that the actually lowest point of the ridge at this point (a little south of us) was only 7,700 feet.

This was the source of a tiny burn, and it was strange to think that some of its water might find its way through the Victoria Nyanza and past Khartoum and Cairo to the Mediterranean!

Many peaks of the chain, both north and south, were much higher, and some may have reached 8,500 feet. On a few of the higher ones I noticed bamboos, which were certainly growing at a somewhat lower level than they do at Ruwenzori, where I do not think they occur below 8,700 feet; this is to be expected, as the latitude is fully 3 degrees south. I was not surprised, therefore, to find characteristic high-level plants, such as a tree Senecio, *Viola Abyssinica*, the tree heather (*Ericinella Johnstonei*), and the gigantic Lobelia, all growing several hundred feet lower than they occur farther north.

From the position where we began the descent, Tanganyika should have been visible, but was shrouded in mist; I could, however, distinctly see

Fig. 39.—HILLSIDES.

the main course of the ridge on which I stood. This was curving round in a north-westerly direction, until it nearly reached the ridge on the opposite side of the valley, which latter forms the boundary of Tanganyika on the west, and is continued almost due north for, at any rate, 40 miles.

This puts me (now that I have seen Dr.

Baumann's works *) in an unpleasant position. The country, according to these observers, is quite different from what I supposed. The Mfumbiro chain is said to run east and west, whereas from my observations it should be almost in the line of the Kiriba chain where I saw it—that is to say, it should lie N.N.W. and S.S.E.

Certainly from the top of the Kariba chain the Tanganyika valley does not appear to extend for more than 30 or 40 miles north of the lake, and it appeared to me to end at about that distance in a pass not more than 15 miles wide. This valley is perfectly flat and covered with thorn-trees, and the Rusige river, which seems to be a very insignificant stream, winds down it from this pass until it enters the lake.

This flat valley is bounded on the eastern side by the Kiriba chain, on which I was standing, and on the western by a prolongation of the mountains of the western shore of Tanganyika.

The importance of the question lies in the character of the country between Tanganyika and the Albert Edward, but I do not think this question can be solved until an expedition has passed through this country to the Albert Edward Nyanza.

From our position one could see clearly that

* Most unfortunately Baron Von Gotzen's work and map have not yet been published, and the rumours I hear of it are most perplexing.

within the crescent formed by the north-westerly trend of the Kiriba chain lay an intricate mass of little hills and valleys, which ended suddenly in the flat thorn-tree, valley of the Rusige. The steepness and intricacy of these little hills we had oppportunities of experiencing somewhat severely during the next two days. Starting again on our way down the mountains we plunged into a dense forest, and in the course of probably less than two miles descended 2,250 feet. We found ourselves then in a banana grove, at the level of the smaller hills alluded to. At first every one fled, but after cajoling and coaxing a brave but very insufficiently clothed old man to be our messenger, the young chief Maboko appeared, and hearing that we would not allow Mwesi's men to accompany us, he became quite enthusiastic and we had dances and singing.

Enormous pots of banana beer were brought to us, and small jars of palm oil. My men had a big drink, and were all as happy as possible.

The people here belong to a chief called Kilimanyambi, who is almost or quite independent of Mwesi. It is a very rich district, and densely peopled. It consists of an enormous number of little steep hills with quantities of banana groves, and in the lower valleys many oil-palms. Above these smaller hills rises the steep Kiriba ridge, which is on this western side covered with dense forest. It is full of running streams, and the people were friendly and pleasant everywhere. Every little chief came out to conduct us through his territory. Arabs seldom visit this country.

I have never seen so marked a line between different floras as occurs on these mountains. Below a certain level the plants are wholly western, and obviously the whole basin of Tanganyika is simply a subdivision of the enormous Congo-Niger, or Westerly Wet Flora.

We spent two days going up and down these little hills, and then emerged on the old level of Tanganyika.

This is a very sandy plain, often with banks of shells; there are many Euphorbias and trailing creepers; Manioc seems the favourite food, and cattle and goats are also very common. At last, on the 28th of September, after marching through an enormous market-place, and about three interminable miles of bananas, we encamped on the shore of Tanganyika.

Then I collapsed utterly. It had taken us 55 days from the Albert Edward, and the last month had been a most anxious and trying experience, while my health had been gradually getting worse and worse.

Here I had to say farewell to my indomitable cow. This gallant animal, the present of Captain Gibb, at Kampala, travelled with us everywhere, even up and down the break-neck paths of

Ruwenzori and through innumerable swamps. I only once had a difficulty with her. This was at a very deep narrow gully by the Kagera. We threw some tree logs across, but she absolutely refused to have anything to do with them. Then I had the branches covered with a tarpaulin, but it was still unsafe in her eyes. Her offspring was then dragged bodily over, and having been blindfolded, she was at last, amidst general rejoicing, hauled across. She used to take her place in the caravan, as she thoroughly understood the signals of the drum, and used to follow me about the camp for bananas.

All this district—that is to say Usige and these outlying hills north-west of Tanganyika—is extraordinarily rich and very densely peopled.

The day that we arrived, an Arab, who was settled a little to the south, sent a messenger to me, and I told him that I wanted a dhow to go down the lake. Next morning the boat appeared, which was a most extraordinary piece of good fortune. It is true that it sailed on one side, and my caravan was packed like sardines, in most uncomfortable and ungainly attitudes, but it was most providential that it arrived just at that moment.

We started at dusk, for at this season a southerly wind usually springs up about 11 a.m. and lasts till sunset. It was a delicious change to lie on the deck in the cool of the evening after the day's unutterable heat, and to listen to the chorus of the Ujiji rowers in the moonlight. Their songs are very beautiful, with an alto solo and both bass and tenor parts. There is often a melancholy, pathetic tinge in them.

The voyage was not, however, at all a pleasant one.

The second day the rowers, all slaves of the Arab, were anxious to land at a point belonging to a chief who was hostile to the Arabs and run away. After we had gone some distance they mutinied. They would not obey orders, and twice let the yard of the sail down with a run, in an attempt to crack my skull. I therefore adopted strong measures, and succeeded in quieting them. Then the waves became larger, and a storm began to rise, until the overladen boat was in considerable danger. We ran her ashore, and in spite of the heavy sea, I thought it necessary to land with three askari. I did not know where we were, and the last news I had had from home was a very alarming letter from Mr. Swan, saying that the Arabs were going to cut the throats of every European on Tanganyika. I got soaked to the skin in landing, and spent a very miserable night in a wet shirt beside a small fire, watching the lantern of the dhow tossing on the waves.

Next morning the sea had gone down, and we arrived at the place where Salim, a rich Arab, had established himself. Instead of cutting my throat, as I had expected, he was most friendly and hospitable. He gave me a house, goats, chickens, cakes, and honey, and was most kind to us all. It was at this place, formerly called Rumonge, that several Roman Catholic missionaries were murdered by the Arabs.

We stayed a few days and then went on to Ujiji, where I was the guest of Sefu bin Raschid, the most hospitable and friendly Mussulman that I have ever known. He loaded me with gifts and presents, and was most kind in every way. He did not even swindle me, as he could very well have done. Here I despatched most of my men to the coast. They were very glad to go. I was told that there was no difficulty whatever in their going alone, and Captain Hore and others had also sent their men back from this place. I therefore gave them all "chits," or letters, and posho, and with much regret said good-bye to the thirty stalwarts, who had behaved in a most gallant way throughout our dangerous journey. Nine sick and personal attendants I took on with me to Kituta. The others, excepting four or five, who were detained by the German authorities, appear to have arrived safely.

For the cloth I paid Sefu partly with the English sovereigns which had accompanied me and partly by a draft on Kituta, to which place I had sent funds before starting.

After a very severe attack of fever I was carried on board the dhow, and we started for Abercorn, or

Kituta, in one of Sefu's dhows, which was a really good boat.

During this journey I was very weak, and scarcely able to move. One effect of the Tanganyika fever is to produce loss of memory and sometimes other curious things. For two days I had a series of horrible mental visions over which my will seemed to have no power, and which succeeded one another continually.

On passing Cape Kabogo, which is a very prominent double headland (called by the Arabs husband and wife), the boatmen recited a long address to it, and flung into the water a little flour, a few beads, and a doty of cloth. At and from Kungwe promontory the hills come down to the water's edge and are covered with scrub. Amongst these hills are many curious little rockbound harbours, usually with shallow water and a strip of sand. At last we again met Europeans at the mission station of Karemi, where there is probably the best house in all Central Tropical Africa; it is two stories high and built of kiln-dried bricks, and roofed with tiles. The mission is on the edge of a rich alluvial plain of enormous extent, but is not, I am afraid, at all a healthy place. After receiving great kindness from the French missionaries, the first Europeans I had seen since leaving Buddu, we started with a strong wind southwards.

We kept on till dusk, making an enormous day's sail, and eventually reached a small island. A sailor, who said he had been there before, induced me to try and pass between a little islet and the shore, and in trying to do this we ran on a ledge of rocks. A strong wind and tide was blowing us on to this ledge, and I never thought we should get off. All our poles broke, and the whole crew were turned into the water to keep her from being broken to pieces on the rocks. At last the waves went down sufficiently to enable us to force the dhow back and get her round the islet.

Soon after this we reached another French station at Kala; I was almost dead by this time, but the extreme kindness of the missionaries, and a bottle of wine which they gave me from a very scanty store, enabled me to pursue the journey and at last to reach Kituta. Here, to my inexpressible delight, I found myself amongst my fellow-countrymen, who gave me the best they had, played music to me, and told me stories. Mr. Law could not possibly have been kinder to me.

The history of Tanganyika seems to have been rather needlessly confused. Commander Cameron discovered the outlet by the Lukuga river into the Congo; Mr. Stanley eventually confirmed this discovery.

As for the theory of a former barrier between Kahangwa and Kungwe, and that the northern half of Tanganyika was of a later formation than the southern, no evidence worth mentioning is brought forward by Mr. Stanley, and certainly from my own observations, I cannot conceive for what possible reason any such theory should have been published. There is no geological difference between the northern and southern half, and no reason to suppose that the lake is not what it appears to be, namely, a rift valley like that of the Mau. It is, in fact, simply a pool on the Upper Congo region.

The changes of level may be most simply explained by the supposition that the outlet by the Lukuga is in some places extremely narrow and liable to be blocked.

Data for ascertaining the changes of level—due probably to the opening or closing of this outlet—may be obtained from three sources.

There is first the obvious difference between Captain Hore's careful map and the present outline of the shore. There is also the height of the occasional alluvial plains, *e.g.*, that about Karemi; and there is, finally, the level of the white incrustation due to the deposit of saline matters from the water on the rocks near the lake.

From observing these points I was able to be sure of one fact, that the level of the lake was at one time 21 feet higher than its present condition. It appeared to me very unlikely that this high level could have been maintained for a long period.

For the last three years the level has been

nearly stationary, though probably it has been on the whole sinking.

The simple inference is that some local accumulation, perhaps remaining in action for four or five years, temporarily blocked the Lukuga, which is now cutting down its cataracts and gradually lowering the lake.

The state of my health quite precluded any really scientific study of this question, but the former highest level of Tanganyika could be easily recognised from a study of the ravines in the hills immediately surrounding it; and from those which I saw I should be much surprised to learn that it ever rose more than this amount—21 feet above the present condition.

Sometimes the lake is very beautiful; little rocky islands and small cliffs rise boldly out of the water, for the hills in such places usually reach the water's edge and are covered everywhere by trees not very close together, and usually some six inches to a foot in diameter. In the narrower valleys which wind amongst them, one still finds dense forest and a little fine timber, but the supply of the latter seems to me limited and bound to diminish rapidly.

Every here and there, as at Rumonge, Ujiji, and Karemi, one finds a large flat plain usually of alluvium, though sometimes of a very sandy character. Probably these will have considerable value in the future, for the Arabs and French missionaries give a very favourable account of coffee, figs, tobacco, rice, wheat, &c. At Ujiji pomegranates, oranges, lemons, guava, mango, cashewnut &c., are common. These plants, and the presence of oil-palms, show clearly that it is a part of the Congo-Niger area. It is therefore a very rich country, but, like that of the Congo, exceedingly unhealthy.

The plants appear to be (up to 3,500 feet, or towards the north up to 4,500 feet) simply those of the Congo. According to Professor Engler, they have advanced considerably east of the lake along the Malagarasi valley.

Above this height (3,500 feet) the plants towards the south are simply those of the Tanganyika-Nyassa watershed.

Probably the most interesting district left now in Tropical Africa is the high plateau region and mountains from the Livingstone range to the north as far as the Malagarasi. This is said to be in places 10,000 feet high, and I suspect will produce the high Alpine forms.

It seems almost necessary to point out here the decline and fall of the Arab in Africa.

In the days of the early travellers the whole country was overrun by Arab slave-traders, who appear to have started from the East Coast and Zanzibar.

The hospitality of the Arab, his courteous manners and clean, flowing robes, appear to have very favourably impressed most people, and to have hidden from them a few obvious facts which are of great importance.

One of these is that Arab or Mussulman life

Fig. 40.—Suahili Women.

means slavery, and involves the ruin, morally, mentally, and physically of every native race with which it has been brought into close connection. Like all Mohammedan peoples, a native race controlled by Arabs is wholly incapable of mental development. No Western ideas or methods can be introduced until the Arabs are expelled. The treachery, dishonesty, and cold-blooded cruelty of the Arabs are innate. Their profligacy, leading in its train all kinds of disease, means destruction physically and morally of the subject peoples. Another fact lost sight of is that competition by Europeans with slaveholding Arabs is impossible. The expenses of life for the white man are infinitely greater, and he is obliged to pay his porters and treat them with, at any rate, some regard for their life and health. The Arab has no compunction or obligations whatever. Unfortunately Europeans in some cases actually assisted to establish the Arab power on a firmer basis. Tippu Tib, although he coolly deserted Mr. Stanley in 1878, was placed, apparently through the latter's advice, in such a position that he nearly wrecked Mr. Stanley's last expedition.

Fortunately both the Belgian and the German authorities now understand that if you enter a strong man's house you must first bind him; and during the last few years, the turning point of African history has been reached and the Arabs are now nearly turned out.

Rumaliza, "the man who destroys utterly," the strongest of them all, after tearing down a German flag, crossed Tanganyika, fought, and was thoroughly beaten by, the Belgians. Returning to Ujiji he was not allowed to remain there by his own compatriots, and attempted to reach the Wahehe, then at war with the Germans, but was not allowed to pass through the territory of quite an insignificant little people on the road. He then turned south towards British Central Africa and apparently entered Portuguese territory, and has now reached Zanzibar.

In fact, in the whole of German and Belgian territory the Arabs are almost completely absent. There are some still at Kitangule, Rumonge, Ujiji, and perhaps one or two other places in the whole German sphere; in the extreme south-east and north-east of Belgian territory there are also a few, but their teeth are drawn and they are unhappy.

Formerly they used to obtain by credit (at 33 per cent. interest) a supply of guns and powder, cloth, and ruffians from Zanzibar. Their caravan then proceeded inland and finally reached some native chief, who received a present; he gave them in return a few slaves costing nothing and, of course, asked for help against some enemy of his.

Such raids are secretly planned several months before they come off. When the force actually starts it travels at the rate of 30 or more miles a day. On the first news of arrival every one flies to the bush, for such raids are only undertaken with quite overwhelming superiority in numbers. Those who do resist are speared;

so are the very old people and young children, while all who can be caught are carried off as slaves.

Ivory was also obtained either by barter or by shooting; and in former times, the slaves would then carry the Arab trader's ivory to the coast, where he would sell both the slaves and the ivory, making a profit of about 300 per cent. Or he would make himself Sultan of some territory and have a very good time. Now the ammunition dealing is illegal, and so is the slave-raiding. They are in a bad way and, as Sefu told me at Ujiji, they are eating their cloth, and when it is done, they will return to the coast.

In British East Africa Arabs are fortunately absent except perhaps at Kabbarega's court, and of course along the coast. In British Central Africa they are, unfortunately, still powerful and able to do great harm. All our enemies there, the former Jumbe, Mponda, Makanjila, and Kawinga, were backed up by coast men. If Mr. Commissioner Johnston had followed the policy of Captain Lugard instead of subsidising one of the most powerful Arabised chiefs, they would probably be also absent from his district. From Mr. Johnston's report, however, I find that he realises that the "Arab must go."

It is very unfortunate that we of all people should be upholding the Sultan of Zanzibar instead of crushing his domination out. Moreover, it is very difficult to see how one could in any way utilise the Arab. Even if employed under careful supervision he will use slaves and replace them by raiding, for he cannot live without them.

CHAPTER XVII.

BRITISH CENTRAL AFRICA.

AFTER a few days' rest at Kituta, I said good-bye to my kind host and started for the mouth of the Zambesi. Here I at once realised the perfection of porter arrangements as evolved by the African Lakes Corporation. No more wearisome marching was required; instead one was swung rapidly along in a roomy hammock or machila by a crew of eight men, who replaced one another frequently. The journey across the Stevenson Road to Nyassa was, however, anything but pleasant.

I had noticed a sort of haze over my eyes for two or three days, but when I started this developed into iritis so severe that I had to spend a fortnight almost in complete darkness. I used to remove my bandage for a second or two, in spite of the intolerable pain that followed, to look at the country, but naturally I could not see very much.

The Stevenson Road is now badly overgrown

BRITISH CENTRAL AFRICA. 289

with trees; in fact, most of the plateau is covered by isolated trees, not quite thick enough to form a regular forest. Fine large timber only exists (*e.g.*, at Kituta) in the valleys near the lakes or narrow ravines. I took a fortnight in crossing over this plateau, which is usually from 4,000 to 5,400 feet high (Appendix). It is, of course, the Congo and Zambesi watershed, and is extremely healthy. Cattle thrive everywhere, and wheat can be grown in any quantity. Mr. Carson, at Fuambo, amongst other kindnesses, gave me some excellent strawberries and cream; and I think it may be considered quite certain that this watershed plateau, which seems to extend southwards and a little west through the Awemba and Angoni country, is a district which will be of great importance. Europeans would be able to live at any point in it above 5,000 feet, and by growing wheat and raising and training cattle, should be able even now to make a comfortable livelihood. The demand for these articles will almost certainly increase rapidly during the next few years.

When one descends from the plateau to the wide alluvial plains of Lake Nyassa the difference in climate is very marked. In fact the whole of these alluvials, which begin at Nyassa and accompany the Shiré and Zambesi to the sea, are distinctly unhealthy and dangerous. Their level appears to be 1,700 feet at this point. We may say that the unhealthy part of the country is roughly all that portion which is below 3,000 feet in altitude (see chap. xi.). As usual, however, this low-lying part is probably very fertile and capable of growing cocoanut-palms, cotton, sugar, and other valuable things.

At Karonga I took the steamer *Hermann von Wissman* to Fort Johnston, with a pleasant visit to Likoma *en route*, and then descended the Shiré with painful slowness in a boat to Matope. From here I was again carried in a hammock to Mandala.

During my stay at Mandala I was in a continual state of bewilderment at the progress and level of civilisation already reached in so young a colony.

I then decided to try and see something of Mlanje, but on arrival had a severe fever, which left me too weak to do any work in the rainy season, which was then just beginning. The Scotch missionaries at Mlanje were very kind indeed to me during this illness. I then went on to Mr. Moir's station at Lauderdale, where I spent a happy Christmas, and, finding myself incapable of serious work, started for Chiromo.

This short hammock journey was marked by two curious experiences.

I had the narrowest escape from drowning which I have ever experienced in crossing the Likumbuliyu. After a little difficulty this torrent, which was very deep and extremely rapid, was successfully crossed by Mabruki Sirkali, to whom we had tied a rope. We fixed this rope across a branch, and, in order to give the others courage, I crossed first. I caught hold of it and went hand over hand, but I lost my footing in the first ten yards, and never expected to reach the other side. Eventually we got all the loads hauled over and every person crossed, but it was with great difficulty.

I crossed the Tutschila river in a punt, the like of which does not exist anywhere else; it is simply two cases nailed together with a tarpaulin stretched below.

At Chiromo I eventually got a steamer, and arrived safely at Chinde, from which I went to Zanzibar, said good-bye to the nine men still remaining with me, settled up my affairs, and came home.

The total expenses of my expedition come to £1,300, of which £700 were supplied by the Royal Society. I hope that the results were worth this expenditure, but when I think of Suliman Msudi and Mirambo, as well as the numerous sick who were left at stations on the way, I feel doubtful whether any number of new species of plants can make up for the losses. At any rate I am clear on this point, I did the best that was in my power, though hampered at every turn by want of funds. The only part of my expenditure which I regret I might have avoided by not appointing any agent till my arrival at Mombasa. I am proud also of having given every man his regular day's food the whole time he was with me, and posho when he was sent home, and also of never leaving a sick man behind unless at a Government or missionary station.

It is not necessary to say more of my personal experiences in British Central Africa; but of the place itself something further must be said.

This little colony has been made by the personal exertions of about nine or ten men, all of whom were Scotch. These are Livingstone, J. and F. W. Moir, J. Buchanan, Rev. D. C. Scott and Dr. Scott, Dr. Laws and J. Monteith Fotheringham.

These men, with scarcely any capital and by their own dogged perseverance and pluck, have won for Greater Britain a new colony which may be in time as valuable as New South Wales.

The history of Mr. Buchanan, which is that of coffee planting in British Central Africa, is most interesting.

He went to Blantyre as gardener to the Established Church of Scotland Mission, without money or experience in any tropical cultivation. There were at the mission garden three coffee plants sent from the Edinburgh Botanic Gardens. Two of these died, but from the third sprang almost the whole of the enormous number now growing in the country. This celebrated shrub unfortunately died and was made into walking-sticks. Buchanan, in introducing the cultivation, had the usual experience of pioneers; he was at first unsuccessful, but now he owns probably half a million of acres, and has mastered the production, not merely of coffee, but of tobacco, sugar, and other things.

The progress of the country may be judged by the following table:—

Year.	Exports.			Imports.			Total.		
	£	s.	d.	£	s.	d.	£	s.	d.
1893	10,201	10	0	9,147	15	0	19,349	5	0
1894	22,236	10	0	13,737	10	0	35,974	0	0
Inc. in 1894	12,035	0	0	4,589	15	0	16,624	15	0

As to the future one may only guess, but to my mind there is every reason to expect a continually increasing success. There are probably now at least four hundred Europeans finding a livelihood, and probably many making a fortune, in a country which a very few years ago was harried by slave-dealers and entirely destitute of white men. At present coffee is the main article of export. The prospects appeared to me good. The yield seems to be as heavy, if not better, than that in Ceylon. The low price of land and labour as compared with that country more than counterbalances the slightly higher freight. There are places in British Central Africa where the rainfall is perhaps scarcely sufficient, and, of course, many plantations were formed by people without experience, in windy or otherwise unsuitable places, and must be expected to fail. Still, allowing for all these drawbacks, there is not, I think, anywhere in the world a better prospect for a young fellow not afraid of work and with £500 or £1,000 capital than to go coffee planting in the Shiré highlands.

In order to see what the future may be expected to bring forth, it is, perhaps, best to give a short account of the physical features of the country.

The Stevenson Road plateau or the Congo-Zambesi watershed has been already mentioned. It rises to about 5,600 feet at Mambwe Mission, and thence appears to continue across a country of which very little is known.

The part which is now being opened up by ourselves is really the Shiré and Lake Nyassa valley. It is bounded on the west by a high plateau ridge, which starts in the highlands of Nyika at some 7,000 feet high, and is continued southwards through Angoniland and the Kirk range.

On the other side of this ridge are the different tributaries of the Luangwa branch of the Zambesi.

On the east of Nyassa is a similar watershed, which separates it from the various branches of the Rovuma river, flowing due east through German and Portuguese East Africa to the sea near Cape Delgado. This begins with the Livingstone mountains, which are of a plateau character and some 10,000 feet high. They sink greatly in height, however, as one proceeds southwards by Mtonia, and eventually become at Zomba, Chiradzulu, and Sotchi, a series of scattered, isolated summits, the farthest south being Mlanje, which is from 9,000 to 10,000 feet high.

Below Mlanje there is only the flat valley of the Zambesi, with occasional hills, such as Moramballa, rising to 4,000 feet.

It is obvious, therefore, that if coffee succeeds well in the Shiré highlands, on the slopes of Mlanje and the other mountains, it ought to succeed equally well on the slopes of all these mountains east and west of Nyassa at the same altitude—that is to say, on the zone between 3,000 and 5,000 feet. This gives a strip about 400 miles long on either side of Lake Nyassa and the Shiré; and that is quite sufficient, though, of course, the soil may not be equally fertile everywhere.

The country below 2,500 feet is for the most part the flat alluvial valley of the Shiré and old lake level of Nyassa. This is usually a grassy plain, broken by clumps of woodland and occasional marshes. It is not densely inhabited, but there is a considerable population, chiefly Manganja and Yao.

The Coffee zone seems naturally to be covered with scrub, not forest, but it is full of ravines and river valleys, often with a very moist climate. So far as I can gather there is more rain and permanent water in those parts which have not been planted than one finds in the Shiré highlands, and this is most promising.

Lastly, there are the higher plateaux and mountain summits such as the Stevenson Road and Mlanje. The former, as I have tried to show, are most promising so far as the climate is concerned. The high plateaux of Mlanje (6,000 feet) would be probably a disagreeably cold and moist place to live in, but I cannot speak of it from personal knowledge.

Coffee land at the time of my visit was worth from 3s. 6d. to 5s. an acre freehold, but I have heard of £35 being given for a single acre at Blantyre, and the price has probably greatly risen since I was there.

Still there are so many places in the Coffee zone, that the amount of land suitable for coffee is probably, for all practical purposes, unlimited, provided native difficulties are avoided.

I cannot help thinking, however, that too much reliance is placed on one article; the experience of Ceylon planters should force every one to cultivate one or two other things in case of the appearance of the coffee disease.

In the valley country below 3,000 feet, or on the hills above 5,000 feet, there is no difficulty in suggesting articles to replace coffee.

The enormously rich alluvials below 3,000 feet are probably capable of growing oil-palms, cocoanut-palms, cotton, sugar, rice, cocoa, and tobacco to any extent.

About 5,000 feet on the drier places wheat and cattle and all European vegetables seem to thrive, and probably oranges, figs, &c., would also grow. I found on Sotchi, and it is probably also the case on Mlanje and the Nyika country, an extremely moist and humid ravine, just such a place as one would suppose suited to tea, pepper, vanilla, and the Landolphia rubber.

On the exact zone of coffee, however, the climate is too dry for tea, at least in most places; too valuable for wheat or cotton, and not exactly suited for sugar or cocoa.

Tobacco can certainly be recommended, for when one smokes a really good cigar produced by the first pioneer in tobacco-growing, whose knowledge of that art is derived from books and rule of thumb, then one forms a very high idea of its future.

English potatoes and tomatoes certainly do well, but they are very far from a good market. It is possible merino sheep might be a success (*vide British Central African Gazette*, vol. i. p. 3).

Besides these may be suggested as well worth trying beniseed or sesame, Cinchona, Indigo, jute, and hemp.

Such plants as nutmeg and rubber trees (*Manihot* and *Ficus*) take so long to mature that they can scarcely be recommended nowadays.

In none of these eight articles are there sufficient data on which one can report with certainty. Erythroxylon Coca, yielding the valuable drug *Cocaine*, and the Papaw, which also yields a valuable medicine, certainly grow in this zone as well as they could possibly grow anywhere.

There is an enormous demand to be expected for indiarubber, and in moist, humid, and forest-clad valleys experiments on the rubber vine (*Landolphia spp.*) should be tried; no one has, so far as I know, attempted the regular planting of Landolphias. It should not be difficult, as the bush should *not* be cleared except of undergrowth and other creepers.

The native population consists of many different races, which are of slightly varying characteristics, though not very different in disposition.

This country is one of a very few places where Europeans of a good stamp (not the coast variety) have been able to deal with natives who were not previously corrupted by generations of slavery and Mohammedan domination.

The results are wonderful. Thus when, say 600 loads have to be forwarded from Karongas on Nyassa to Kituta, the men flock into Karonga from the neighbourhood, and their names are written down; each receives a yard of cloth for posho (food), shoulders his load, and starts under charge of a native headman. When he arrives at Fife, which is half-way, he receives his six yards of cloth, and goes home with or without a return load. A fresh set of men at Fife take the loads on to Kituta; the 240 miles being covered in about fourteen days! If a native finds his load too heavy he lays it down on the road, *folds up his posho-cloth, and leaves it on the load*, and then goes home with a clear conscience!

Some of the races, *e.g.*, the Yao, seem capable of any development. In that magnificent church at Blantyre, which was designed by Mr. Scott, and erected by native labour under his superintendence, one sees that these native boys, fresh from barbarism, have learnt and practise carpentry, wood-carving, brickmaking, tilemaking, and building, with really good results.

Mr. Johnston's paper, the *British Central African Gazette*, is as well turned out as most of our London evening papers, and it is printed and revised entirely by native boys from Nyassa.

It seems to me most unfortunate, therefore, that the development of these promising races should be in any way hindered by the introduction of natives of India, which has been inaugurated by Mr. Johnston.

The cost of Indian labour in Natal seems to be from 25 to 29 shillings per month, including passage out and home, but even supposing that Indian labour costs only half as much again per head, and is worth in work three or four times the amount produced by natives *at present*, it is a very great pity that the whole future of the natives of British Central Africa should be spoilt by introducing this system.

There is an enormous supply of labour in the Angoni, Awemba and Atonga peoples, which is just coming into training. The relatively small amount available near Blantyre is due to the fact that this was a happy hunting-ground of the slave trader. Moreover, most of those who still live near Blantyre grow maize and produce for sale. An enormous increase is to be looked for in the native population under our settled government. The population in the Ruo district, *e.g.*, increased from 8,000 in 1892 to 13,000 in 1893!

It is possible locusts may interfere with the food supply, for last year there was a severe famine in British Central Africa. They seem to have come from the country between Mwero and Tanganyika, and thence to have travelled over the Stevenson Road and down the Shiré. The older natives remember a similar plague as having occurred apparently about 1860, and this leads one to hope that it only happens occasionally. It has been suggested that it was due to the fighting on the Congo in 1893, but this can scarcely be the case. More probably it was due to exceptionally favourable, bright, sunny weather in December, 1892, and January, 1893. Dr. Gunther informs me that heat and sunlight are necessary for the eggs to develop. In January, 1894, this was the case in Uganda, and there were numbers of locusts. The female lays all her eggs close together, and the young ones at first are unable to fly, and only gradually spread out in a circle from their birthplace till they unite with those from another female, and form a flight.

The moral character of these natives seems high. Mr. W. P. Johnston mentions that a woman and boy became slaves of their own free will in order to redeem their chief.

The manner in which native caravans were sent off with only a native in charge, or occasionally a single man sent with a load for 240 miles, filled me with astonishment.

It did eventually occur to one body of 43 Angoni that there was no reason whatever why they should not walk off into the bush with their loads; this would probably have made every man of them as rich as their own chief. They carried out this brilliant idea, probably introduced to them by some half-caste, but the loads have, I believe, been all recovered through their chief expostulating with them.

I am afraid difficulties with the natives are not by any means finished.

All along the eastern or Portuguese border are a number of chiefs, more or less under Arab influence and fond of slave-dealing, who not unnaturally detest the white man. These are Makanjila, Zarafi, Mponda, Kawinga, Matapwiri, and others. Unfortunately, they are only now beginning to realise that they have no chance against us. Captain Edwards, with 31 Sikhs, 9 Makua and 70 untrained men belonging to Jumbe, attacked and completely routed 1,200 of Makanjila's warriors. The very recent defeat of Kawinga last February cannot have been forgotten. Mr. Fletcher, with 16 men, kept 500 employed for two hours; when he had only five rounds left he charged, and with 30 Atonga, who came up at the time, put them to flight!

This ought to be a lesson to all these chiefs, and I fancy Kawinga is now pretty well crushed.

On the west side there are still Arabs near Karongas, and these are bound to give trouble in the future. It is most unfortunate that Mr. Johnston made terms with these people after Captain Lugard had been wounded; it is a common impression amongst those who took part in the struggle, that very little would have been required to turn them out of the country.

There is still a very powerful and warlike race, the Awemba, to the west of Nyika. These appear to have only been visited by Livingstone, Giraud, and Mr. Thomas. They appear to be much oppressed by Ketimkuru, who objects to Europeans, as he probably understands that his absolute power cannot be permitted if we get the predominance.

Further south is the enormous country of the

Angoni, a Zulu race who are said to have crossed the Zambesi in 1825, and who appear to be a very warlike people.

Most people in British Central Africa seem to think that these races will never attack the white man, but I think all experience leads one to the belief that sooner or later a conflict must occur.

It seems a pity that we should still trust so much to Sikh soldiers. Both Makua and Atonga seem to have behaved with extraordinary pluck in these recent wars, and the Germans habitually engage Atonga from our territory as soldiers. Moreover, the Angoni, if really Zulus, are probably excellent fighting men.

At the same time, British Central Africa is so new that it is of course much less trouble to bring soldiers and workmen from India; yet surely it is a pity that when our missionaries and traders have brought on these races so far, they should suddenly be dropped, and no further development attempted.

A very few suggestions may perhaps be permitted me.

The chief needs of British Central Africa are, first, a railway from Matope to Chiromo, and another from Karonga to Tanganyika; secondly, a covenanted civil service, in which knowledge of native languages should be encouraged by solid cash. Other less important requisites are a good map on a 4-mile to the inch scale, roads, and experiments, on an economical scale with every valuable tropical plant, accompanied by very stringent rules as to the import of seeds from anywhere.

CHAPTER XVIII.

TRANSPORT.

AFRICAN transport is apparently just now on the verge of a great and important change.

The old Arab method, adopted by Europeans, of conveying goods on men's shoulders is doomed to vanish.

Of all beasts of burden man is the most unsatisfactory. He requires wages besides his food, and he can carry only half the load of a donkey.

Moreover, the Suahili porter is destined to disappear altogether. The supply of porters in old days was entirely kept up by slave-raiding. Porters, as a rule, have no families, and even if they have children, these are very different in stamina and health to the sturdy Wanyamwesi and Wanyuema savage who was caught young, fifteen to twenty years ago.

Hence at the very outset of the question one is met by an impossibility. The supply of Suahili porters is diminishing daily, while the goods requiring carriage are daily increasing.

In East Africa we are in a peculiarly bad position; for the Germans will not allow Wanyamwesi to settle in British East Africa, and not one of the native races has been proved to yield even fair carriers. Moreover, it is obvious that in the Masai highlands, where a 25 days' march has to be made without provisions, if a man's load is 65 pounds, and his own food for the 25 days comes to 37 pounds, he can only convey the difference, viz., 30 pounds.

The carriage of goods on men's shoulders must be soon, therefore, a matter of the past.

We must, consequently, examine the question from the very beginning. It is first quite certain that no form of carriage can possibly compete with water transport. It costs, roughly, 5s. 6d. a ton to bring goods from America to London by sea, and about 5s. 6d. a ton to send them by land 15 miles to—*e.g.*, Bushey.

If this is the case in the dry, it is far more so in the green.

I find that the Universities Mission steamer on Lake Nyassa can convey goods at probably less than ½d. per ton mile.

The reason of this difference is the fundamental fact that no maintenance of a permanent way is required, and that, unless for canals, no capital is required to make a road in the first place.

Moreover, animals get worn out or die, and have to be replaced. To keep a locomotive in repair is probably not much less expensive than to keep a boat's engines in order, while the cost of making and maintaining barges is far less than that of trucks and carriages.

There is, therefore, no doubt that water transport must, wherever possible, replace any other kind of conveyance.

This is a matter of the greatest importance in Africa; for, by a curious provision of nature, there is no continent which has so many lakes and navigable rivers.

We have only to take the Victoria Nyanza to see the point of this argument. It has a coastline of perhaps 700 miles, roughly, and a single steamer costing to place on the lake £12,677 (according to the curiously definite figures of the Mombasa railway report) would be able to visit the whole of its shore. Taking the cost of maintenance, fuel, and working expenses as £1,200 a year (a very large estimate), a capital expenditure of £53,000 (£13,000 for steamer, £40,000 to yield 3 per cent. interest) would enable this steamer to convey, say, 30 tons at the rate of 5 to 10 miles an hour for £1,600 a year. This makes it nearly possible to convey a ton at the rate of a halfpenny a mile!

While it would require about £53,000 to build a railway only 18 miles long, the same expenditure would enable a steamer to visit 700 miles of coast, not including islands and creeks, which might conceivably bring up the coast-line to 1,200 miles.

Of course this advantage is probably quite realised by every thoughtful person; but I think few seem to know how entirely overwhelming it is without severe examination of the question.

Hence it will be seen that the first essential of African transport is to utilise every mile of waterway, wherever that may be found.

The following are the main African waterways:—

The Nile, as far as and including the Albert Nyanza. So far I have not been able to satisfy myself as to the exact length of the Somerset Nile, between Ripon Falls and Fauvera, which is navigable, but probably there is a considerable length of waterway.

The Kagera river will, as I have attempted to show, probably enable steamers to penetrate to about 50 miles from Lake Tanganyika. The Zambesi and Shiré with one break of about 120 miles, are actually navigable to within 240 miles of Tanganyika. In fact, from Cairo to the Zambesi, one could probably proceed by water with only 540 miles of land transport.

It is absolutely certain to my mind that in the next century this road will be utilised, and I have in spite of repression from every recognised authority, tried to induce the British Government to obtain this route, which is

TRANSPORT. 309

about 4,000 miles long, for British commerce. I am afraid I have advocated it in vain.

From this main line the Victoria Nyanza can be easily reached.

The Congo river with an enormous expenditure of money and life may eventually serve the vast basin of that river. This does not concern us, for it will be reserved as a useful outlet for French enthusiasm; and it is very fortunate that this is the case, as I understand people throughout that vast area are sent down *to recruit* to Banana Point; which last spot has a bad reputation even on the West Coast of Africa, which has again the worst climate in the world.

Now let us turn to the relative advantages of other forms of transport.

They may be roughly divided into two :—

Roads or railways and pack animals.

There can be no doubt that pack animals are a makeshift and economically to be condemned if compared with wheel traffic along made roads. It is, however, very difficult to get at all an approximate estimate of the cost of carriage by draught animals or railways, as in this case we must include the cost of road-making, which varies according to the country and the price of labour, and also the cost of maintaining and repairing roads, all of which vary.

The amount of traffic on the road when made has also a most important bearing on the question;

for with a made bullock waggon track one can convey as much traffic as is required, whether this is five waggons in the year or 500, and in the case of a railway this factor is possibly even more important.

The initial expenditure of a railway is so enormous that I do not think it can be justified in Africa unless there is some present initial traffic to develop.

In America the surplus population of Europe and the markets in the eastern states have made railway development profitable on the whole, but in Africa until pioneer work has been done, and the prospects of colonisation and plantation are sufficiently definite and settled to induce colonists to go out in considerable numbers, it will be ruinous to build a long railway line.

The British taxpayer cannot justly be asked to hand over £3,000,000 for a railway through a country in which there is not one single planter, nor any minerals, at least so far as we can tell at present.

On the other hand, in British Central Africa, it is justifiable; for there is a large daily increasing population, many plantations, and, as I hope to show later on, about 2,300 miles to be opened up by steamers and railways, which latter do not exceed, collectively, 410 miles in length.

Let us, however, first see exactly the relative advantages of bullock waggons and railways.

TRANSPORT. 311

We will take first a length of 240 miles (Stevenson Road, or Mombasa to Kibwezi). The cost of making a bullock waggon track with bridges and ballast in swampy ground we will put down at £200 a mile—a very low estimate. The road requires, therefore, £48,000, for which we will allow 4 per cent. interest and £500 a year for maintenance—probably below the truth.

Now 3 waggons and 50 oxen will cost at the least £600, on which 5 per cent. depreciation must be allowed. The salaries of one European and ten natives will amount to at least £300 per year, during which they might transport 6 tons of merchandise across the road 12 times. There will, however, be only transport upwards at first, as the export from such a country will be insignificant for the first few years. Hence they will only receive at the utmost about 40 tons to carry, which must therefore yield them :—

Interest on £600 ...	£24
Depreciation ,, ...	30
Salaries	300
	£354

That is to say about £9 per ton for the journey of 240 miles.

The interest on the capital spent in making the road itself and maintenance will amount to :—

4 per cent. on £48,000 ...	£1,920
Maintenance	500
	£2,420

So that if we allow a charge of £5 per ton on merchandise carried, fully 484 tons at a total freight of £14 per ton will be required to make the operation pay.

A railway across this country could probably be built for £3,000 per mile which estimate includes rolling stock. That is a capital of £720,000.

As to working expenses, it is impossible to obtain a definite statement, but assuming that they would be about the same as in Natal, one may take 5s. per train mile as near the truth. It is 4s. 10·96d. according to the Government of Natal Railway Accounts. This includes salaries, maintenance, and repairs of rolling stock and the line.

Thus the cost of transporting, say, 20 tons 240 miles would be £60, or £3 per ton. Allowing the same charge of £5 for the use of the road, 484 tons (the amount taken above as necessary for bullock waggon transport to be productive) would yield £2,420 for payment of interest, but 4 per cent. interest on £720,000 amounts to £28,800.

If we allow, however, £11 per ton charge, which makes the total freight £14 per ton (as for bullock waggons), then this would yield £5,324 for this quantity, namely 484 tons.

It is obvious that 2,620 tons at this freight would be required to make it productive, or, on the other hand, assuming 500 tons as the probable amount to be carried, a charge of £57 12s. per ton, bringing the freight to £60 12s. would be necessary.

The present charge per ton from Chinde to Tanganyika is, I believe, £143 per ton, of which, probably, fully £100 is allotted to the Stevenson Road. The margin, therefore, between £60 and £100 is sufficient for a railway.*

It may therefore be assumed that providing 500 tons can be carried either method would at present

* It is a nice mathematical problem to see exactly where the railway prevails over the bullock waggon. It is obvious that—

1. The total freight by rail must be less than that by waggon.

The total freight consists of charge for interest on capital (c^b and c^r) and charge for working expenses both per ton (w^b and w^r) in each case.

2. The charge for interest on capital per ton multiplied by the number of tons (n) must equal the total interest (i^b and i^r) on the capital in each case.

$$\therefore\ c^b + w^b = c^r + w^r\ (w^b\text{ and }w^r\text{ constants})$$
$$nc^b = i^b\ (\text{a constant})$$
$$nc^r = i^r\ (\text{a constant})$$

In the example above :—

$$c^b + £9 = c^r + £3$$
$$nc^b = £2,420$$
$$nc^r = £28,800$$

From which it follows that the number of tons is 4,396, which would require a charge of £6 11s., or total freight of £9 11s. by rail, and a charge of 11s. per ton with the same freight by waggon. In practice it should be built long before this point as the lower freight rapidly increases the amount of tons carried.

be productive, and this quantity, 500 tons, could probably be obtained very soon on the Stevenson Road.

It will be interesting to compare the Mombasa railway and see how much would be required to render this productive.

We have a capital expense of £2,250,000, that is, taking only 3 per cent. interest, an income of £67,500 to make up to which must be added 5s. per train mile; that is for through traffic £166 for a train to the Victoria Nyanza, or £8 3s. per ton of expenses.* On 500 tons one would require a charge of £135 per ton to make up £67,500, or a total freight, adding £8 3s. for working expenses, of £1 433s., which is not so very much less than what is now paid on goods conveyed to the Nyanza by German territory on men's shoulders, and quite destroys the possibility of plantations or general trade.

On the other hand, if a freight of £23 0s. 6d. per ton (that is £15 for interest and £8 3s. for working expenses) were charged, 4,500 tons would be required to make it possible.

This amount might be reached after perhaps 20 years' traffic, but certainly not before.

Moreover, even with this amount there are very few products valuable enough to pay such a price.

* I take 40 tons as the possible amount to be conveyed to the Victoria Nyanza, and as it will have to return empty divide £166 by 20.

In Uganda there are only coffee, ivory, and tobacco. All kinds of cereals, beans, and peas could not even pay the working expenses of their conveyance, namely £8 3s. per ton. Cattle, if bought in Usoga for £3 and sold at the coast for £10 to £12, would just pay expenses of conveyance.*

The Natal Government lines mentioned above are about 400 miles in length and obtained a revenue of £465,871 with an expenditure of £300,000 in 1894.

The Beira railway charges, I believe, £6 per ton on a line 118 miles in length, and its expenses amount to £2,500 a month, or £30,000 per annum, though whether this includes interest on capital or not, I cannot find out.

It is necessary also to examine the question of pack animals to see exactly how African transport is situated in this respect.

The main advantage of pack animals lies in their requiring absolutely no road-making. They can be driven along ordinary native paths excepting only such places as Uganda in the wider sense and Unyoro where the numerous swamps and rivers made their use undesirable.

---

* The Government having apparently decided on a much lower gauge than that recommended in the Mombasa report, this reasoning does not apply, but it is obvious that there is no alteration in the comparison between the two railway routes which follows.

The following table shows the relative advantages of each at once :—

	Load lbs.	Pace miles per hour.	Average journey per day.	Pound miles carried per day.	Cost at Kikuyu.
Donkeys	100	2	20	2,000	15s.
Mules	160	3	20	3,200	£15 ?
Horses	200	3¾	20 ?	4,000	£10 ?
Bullocks	160	2½	20	3,200	£10 ?
Camels	400	2½	20	8,000	£20 ?
Elephants	1,000	3	20 ?	20,000	£100 ?
Man	65	2¾	15	975	£200 *

The figures for the donkey are extracted from my own experience. The remainder are chiefly drawn from "The Soldier's Pocket Book" by Viscount Wolseley.

It is extremely difficult to give any closer approximation to the cost as found in actual practice.

It is too much to expect any animal to proceed day after day through great change of climate, and always carrying a load, for the space of two or three months.

Hence it is not in the least surprising that all animals which have been tried so far in East Africa appear to have proved a failure. Besides this strain, they have never had proper attendants or saddles or fodder on the road.

It is, therefore, not satisfactorily proved that draught animals could not be used with profit, but there is extremely little to show that they could.

* This at 3½ per cent. is equivalent to a wage of 12/- per month.

Still from the preceding it is obvious that the most economical animal is the donkey.

The others in order of merit being probably camel, horse, mule and bullock, elephant and man.

It is only necessary to compare the possibility of transit by donkeys with that by bullock waggons to see the advantage of the latter form wherever no road-making is necessary.

20 donkeys can carry 2,000 pounds
,,   draw 4,500   ,,

This difference is so great, and the strain on the animals so much less, that in a country where a possible track can be found, there is no doubt that pack animals should never be employed.

They are, in fact, simply a makeshift, and should only be employed in extremely difficult and unpromising places.

For wheeled transport there is no doubt that bullocks are infinitely superior to every other animal.

Thus it is quite obvious from the preceding account that the essential point in African development is to utilise every mile of waterway. Where no waterways exist then either bullock waggons should be employed if this is possible or, in rare cases, a railway should be built; the use of pack animals and men being on every reason economically unsound. If men are used, this means an amount of suffering and waste of labour which one has to see with one's own eyes before one can rightly estimate it; and their use also means the perpetuation of slavery.

Now there are at present three railway schemes. These three are competitive, and probably mutually destructive.

The first is the Mombasa to Uganda railway. The second is the German railway, which has actually been commenced. The third is the African Lakes Route.*

The map and elevations here given show pretty clearly the position and leading physical features of each. It is of course at once and immediately obvious that the Mombasa railway cannot possibly compete with the German line in any civilian transport or trade. It is 181 miles longer, and the physical difficulties are very much more pronounced. Moreover, for military transport some form of conveyance from the shore of the Victoria Nyanza to the Albert Nyanza is absolutely essential if it is to be of real importance.

If it is simply a question of carrying a few officers to the Albert Nyanza, we have in this fortunate country so many anxious to go that it is quite unnecessary to build a railway to convey them. On the other hand, to place a British

---

* The German line is derived from Dr. Baumann's "Durch Masailand zur Nilquelle." The Mombasa railway, "Mombasa Survey Report." The African Lakes Route from my table of altitudes.

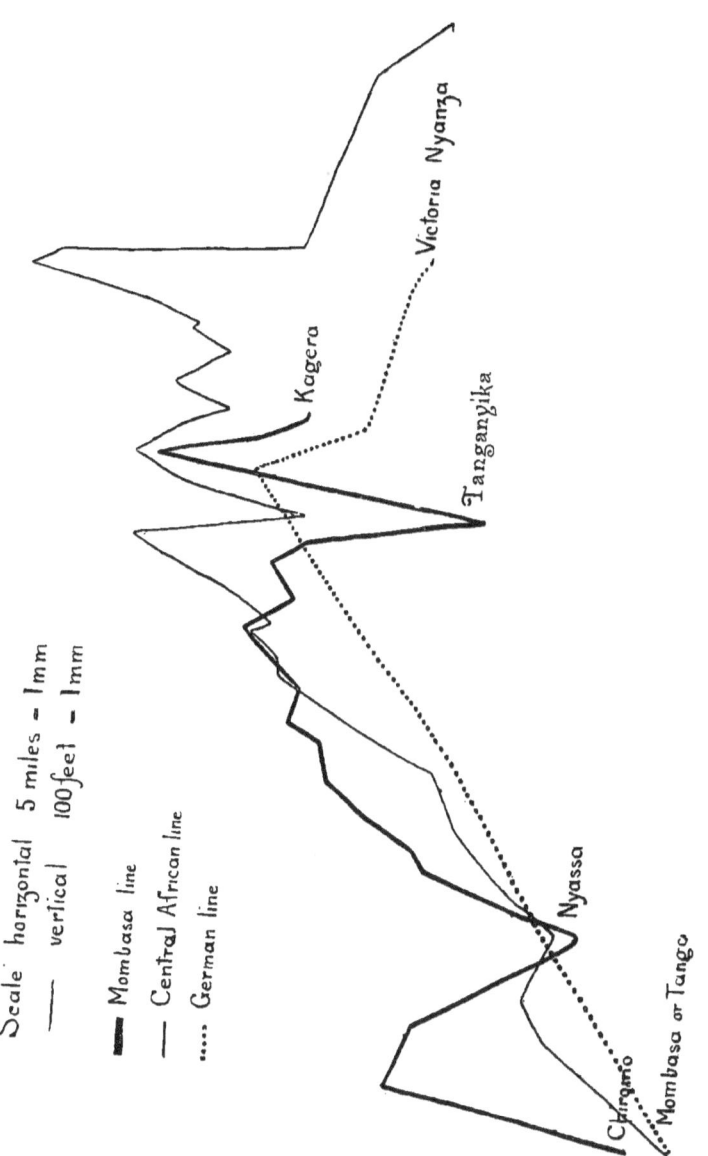

regiment on the Albert Nyanza requires a chain of railways and steamers from the Victoria to the Albert Nyanza.

If we wish to compete with Germany, therefore, in opening up Uganda and the Upper Nile to English trade and commerce, some other way must be discovered, and this is only possible by the African Lakes Route.

This route is not a new idea, and the advantage of it has been noticed so long ago as 1868, by Mr. R. Arthington, of Leeds. Dr. Parkes was also strongly in favour of it; but it appears to have slipped out of public notice in England for some years.

This route is as follows. The important point is simply to utilise the Shiré, Zambesi, Nyassa, and Tanganyika waterways, which altogether amount to something like 1,200 miles of water transport, and build railways across the Shiré rapids (120 miles) and Stevenson Road (240 miles).

This would penetrate to the north end of Tanganyika, and to within 180 miles of the Victoria Nyanza.

It is quite obvious that of the Congo state, German East Africa, and ourselves, to one of whom the trade of Tanganyika must go, we are in by far the best position, as we have only 360 miles land transport.

The advantage of this route so far has not escaped German attention :—

"Noch ein andere Linie ist bestimmt die Tabora-strasse vollig lahm zu legen: die Nyassa-Route. Sobald diese herrliche Wasserstrasse erst erschlossen und die schmale Strecke zwischen Tanganyika und Nyassa irgendwie zuganglich gemacht ist wird der Verkehr bis ins Herz Afrika's dringen können. Länder welcher, wie Urundi und Ruanda heute zu dem Ultima Thule des Tabora-Verkehrs gehoren, werden direkt mit dem Handel in Berührung treten."

("Another line will completely finish the overland road by Mombasa: the Nyassa route. As soon as this beautiful waterway is opened, and the small strip betwixt Tanganyika and Nyassa is made passable, trade will penetrate into the heart of Africa. Countries which, like Urundi and Ruanda, are now the Ultima Thule of the Tabora trade will enter into close commercial union.")

This quotation is from Dr. Baumann in "Durch Masailand zur Nilquelle."

Before starting on my journey I had been very much struck by what I had heard of the Kagera river, and it seemed to me a point of the utmost importance to know whether or not it was navigable; as by it one would, according to the maps, be able to approach close to Tanganyika.

This river rises on the eastern flank of the mountains to the east of Tanganyika, flows about 200 miles north, and then suddenly sweeps round to the east, falling into the Victoria Nyanza.

As the result of my journey I felt convinced that it is navigable from a point 50 miles distant from Tanganyika to the Nyanza.

There appears to be no doubt in any quarter that from the outlet, which appears to be deep, it may be ascended without any difficulty (except such as may occur from the rapid current and numerous hippopotami) as far as Musonje, where I crossed it. From this point I myself followed its course to Kitoboko, where I struck across Ankole to Ruwenzori.

I intentionally left that section between Kitoboko and Latoma, where the river takes the sudden bend in its course referred to, untraversed; as I knew that both Dr. Baumann and Mr. Stanley had crossed it at different places.

If I had been aware that their reports were so extremely unsatisfactory, I should have followed its course right up to Latoma, where, as I intended, I eventually reached it again on my return journey. As is shown in previous chapters, I was only able to follow it a short distance south of Latoma before I was obliged, on account of enormous lagoons, to make a wide detour to the east, only picking it up again at Bugufu, where it was a broad, navigable stream. This point is only 160 miles from Tanganyika.

I think that it must be navigable from this point to Latoma; and all native testimony, as well as that of Mr. Stanley, who appears to have boated over some portion, agrees that this is almost certain.*

Mr. Stanley, however, states that there is a cataract on the river between Latoma and Kitoboko. The real authority for this statement is not, however, Mr. Stanley, but Rumanika, the King of Karagwe (see "Through the Dark Continent," vol. i. p. 459). "You can go up the river as far as Kishakka and down to Morongo (the falls), where the water is thrown against a big rock and leaps over it, and then goes down to the Nianja of Uganda." Mr. Stanley quotes further on (p. 470) a long conversation with the same person, in which Rumanika made himself responsible for at least five downright untruths, and two statements which would force any other traveller to draw a pencil through his notes of the information supplied by an individual possessed of such a fund of humour. Mr. Stanley, however, appears to have allowed it to remain in his mind; and afterwards, on hearing the roar of the river (as I have frequently heard it myself) when passing through a narrow gorge in the hills, jumped to the conclusion that this was Rumanika's Morongo.

It is therefore the deceased Rumanika's statement that I controvert when I say that there is

* Lately I have heard unpleasant rumours that Baron von Gotzen saw a cataract on this portion, which much alters the question.

TRANSPORT. 325

no evidence as yet of a cataract. The following boiling-point observation, taken by myself, show that a cataract is scarcely likely if they are correct, and that they probably are so is shown by the comparison of the levels of the Victoria Nyanza, Tanganyika, and Nyassa, with other sources.*

Kagera river altitudes : —
Victoria Nyanza...	3,900 feet
Kitoboko ...	3,986 ,,
Latoma ...	4,164 ,,
Bugufu	4,394 ,,
Near Mwesi's (a branch) ...	5,050 ,,

Whether by accident or design, I cannot say, but Dr. Baumann has not, so far as I know, mentioned the possibility of the Kagera being navigable. Obviously the point is one which it would not be to the advantage of the German line to lay stress upon. A beautiful view of the river, however, occurs in his book (p. 80) at a point 138 kilometres, or 84 miles, from Tanganyika. This was about 35 miles south of the point where I crossed it.

He makes its height at this place 1,140 metres, that is, 50 metres below the level which he gives (1,190 metres) for the Victoria Nyanza, so that it is certainly a misprint on his map.

At a distance of 65 miles, according to his map,

* See Appendix.

from Usige he found the Akenyaru branch to be 10 metres deep, and had to find canoes to cross.

My own belief is that the Kagera will be found to be navigable by the Ru-Vuvu branch to a point some 47 miles distant from Usige, on Tanganyika, and lying nearly east-north-east from it. I am bound to say, however, that my map is in many ways very different from his.

The route here suggested consists therefore of—
1. Steamers on the Zambesi and lower Shiré.
2. Railway across the Shiré rapids, 120 miles.
3. Steamers on Upper Shiré and Nyassa.
4. Railway across Stevenson Road, 240 miles.
5. Steamers on Tanganyika.
6. Railway to Kagera, 47 miles.
7. Steamers on Kagera and Victoria Nyanza.

Now let us compare this route with the Mombasa railway and the German line.

The only method of seeing the different relative advantages of each is to estimate on the same basis the cost (capital) and the relative values of the country opened up.

Special advantages and disadvantages of either can then be considered separately.

The Mombasa railway was roughly surveyed and mapped (see Government Report, 1893) by Major Macdonald and other Royal Engineers. This is taken as a basis of comparison.

The cost (see pp. 31–35 of this Report) falls as follows :—

TRANSPORT. 327

			Miles.	Cost per mile. £	Total. £
1 Section,	Mombasa–Tzavo	.. ..	123	2,930	360,390
2 ,,	Tzavo–Kikuyu	.. ..	198	3,276	648,548
3 ,,	Kikuyu–Molo	.. ..	125	3,330	416,250
4 ,,	Molo–Nologoselli	.. ..	106	3,925	416,050
5 ,,	Nologoselli–Victoria	..	105	3,677	386,085
			657	£3,409	£2,227,323

The above is for a line 3 feet 6 inches gauge, with stations, rolling stock, &c., included (*vide* Report).

Against this let us consider the three railway lines included in the African Lakes Route.

The first rises to a height of 3,500 feet (from 600) and ends at about 1,200 feet altitude; it crosses no important river, and is probably far less difficult than that of Section 1 of Mombasa railway. (The estimate of the syndicate now making this section is £200,000.)

The second rises to about 5,400 feet, from a height of 1,500 feet, and descends to 2,700 feet, crossing very few rivers of any kind, and none of importance. This must be less expensive than that of Section 2 of Mombasa line, which rises from 1,500 feet to over 6,000 feet, and crosses both Tzavo and Athi rivers.

The third rises from 2,700 to 7,000 feet, and descends to 4,500 feet. The rivers are of no importance. The corresponding Section 4 (Molo to Nologoselli section of Mombasa line) rises from 6,200 feet to nearly 8,000 feet, and passes some extraordinarily dangerous and difficult ravines, then dropping suddenly to a height of 6,000 feet. In order to prevent the cataract of Rumanika being used as an argument, we will also set down the cost of 50 miles of rail along a flat river valley.

If, then, the African Lakes Route is reckoned on the same basis as the Mombasa railway the result is as follows:—

		Miles.	Cost per mile. £	Total. £
1 Section,	Chinde–Chiromo (steamers now exist and pay)..			
2	Chiromo–Matope railway ..	120	2,930	351,600
3	Matope–Karonga (steamers now exist and pay).. ..			
4	Karonga–Tanganyika railway	240	3,276	786,240
5	Tanganyika steamers (2) ..			25,400
6	Tanganyika–Kagera line ..	50	3,925	196,250
7	Kagera steamers (4)			40,000
8	(Cataract, 50 miles railway)	50	2,930	146,500
				£1,545,990
	As compared with the Mombassa line			£2,227,323

The *comparison* is not in the least affected if the cost of the Mombasa railway is reduced by diminishing the gauge.

Thus it appears that the capital required is about two-thirds of that necessary for the Mombasa railway; and even this is not a fair comparison.

Sections 1, 2, 3, and 4 of the Lakes Route are required in any case, so that to develop the Victoria countries and Upper Nile by using the Mombasa

TRANSPORT.   329

line, is much more expensive; the extra cost of the Lakes Route is only about £402,150 as against £2,227,323. Or, if one prefers to put it in another way, the difference between the amount required to develop East Africa by the Mombassa railway and British Central Africa by the two additional lines now required comes to—

	£
Mombasa railway	2,227,323
Shiré railway	351,600
Stevenson Road line	786,240
	£3,265,163
As contrasted with	£1,545,990

This is probably the best manner in which to compare the two, for British Central Africa will inevitably have a railway, quite apart from the prospects of its being utilised for through traffic. Preliminary steps have already been taken with this object.

Now let us consider the prospects of interest on the capital expended.

As to the Mombasa railway, there can be absolutely no data on which one can rely. There is only one article of export—that is, ivory; and probably three trucks in the year would carry all that is at hand to the coast. There is not, I think, a single plantation—that is to say, of coffee or wheat—grown for export. There are, I think, two Europeans at Kibwezi, one at Matchakos, and probably Mr. Watt and his wife in Ukambane, and one at Kikuyu—that is to say, six along the route. The number of Europeans in Uganda itself may be thirty or forty—that is to say, a population of thirty-six to forty-six Europeans to a line of 657 miles in length.

The third course, the German line, is 496 miles long, and probably may be taken as equivalent in difficulty to the Tzavo to Kikuyu section of the Mombasa railway.

	Miles.	Cost per mile.	Total.
Tanga-Nyanza...	496	£3,276	£1,624,896

It is, therefore, slightly, though only slightly, more expensive than the African Lakes Route.

The prospects of the Mombasa line may be summed up as follows:—

The first 10 miles or coast district is fertile, producing cocoanut-palms, possibly cloves, and very likely other valuable plants suitable for plantation. It has considerable forests, and there is a certain amount of rubber. The native population is large, and there are a few Europeans, though the climate cannot be called healthy.

In the next stretch of 240 miles there is nothing of any value so far as one can now tell, and perhaps as little prospect of anything as one could find anywhere in Africa.

The next stretch of 417 miles is one of great

TRANSPORT. 331

value, but it is absolutely untested. No plantations
have been started, and the native population is on

Fig. 42.—ACACIA TYPICAL OF THORN-TREE DESERT.

the whole very small and in a very backward condition.

Let us now take the African Lakes Route :—

The first 200 miles is the alluvial basin of the Zambesi and Shiré. Both coal and alluvial gold have been reported. There are probably at least ninety Europeans now at work. A large sugar factory is working successfully, and, though the climate is not healthy, it is probable that cotton, coffee, cocoa, and tobacco may be grown successfully. The most essential point is that steamer traffic now pays so well that there are at least two, and possibly three, rival companies.

The proposed railway (120 miles) across the Shiré highlands is going to be built simply for local traffic by a syndicate chiefly of Glasgow merchants. It is not necessary to say anything more.

The next section, from Matope to Karongas at the north end of Nyassa, is about 400 miles long.

There are about nine steamers on this section which appear to pay.

There are the two large missionary societies, Universities, and Free Church of Scotland. There is also a German Government station and many British Central African posts. The Europeans may be eighty in number.

The next 240 miles across the Stevenson Road passes through a very new country. It may be declared positively that it is very healthy, and produces cattle, wheat, and strawberries. There may be thirty Europeans in the various mission

TRANSPORT. 333

stations and trading and Government posts. I estimated that I saw five times as many porters during the fourteen days that I spent in crossing as I saw during two and a half months' journey from Mombasa to Uganda. There is still ivory

Fig. 43.—MAUNGU WATERHOLE.

near the route, and it is probably the best way to the Katanga mineral country.

The 400 miles of Tanganyika is at present commercially untried. There are at least six mission stations, and both the German and Belgian Governments will require stations on the lake. Coffee, wheat and rice, and oil-palms grow well however. The climate is bad.

The 50 miles from Tanganyika to the Kagera is densely peopled, and possesses forests as well as a rich cattle country. Probably it is healthy and very fertile.

The 250 miles along the Kagera to the Victoria Nyanza lies through a fairly healthy country, quite untried by Europeans. Most of the valley consists of rich alluvial soil.

So far as one can judge, more than half the German line is similar to the Maungu desert, though it is near Kilimanjaro, and there are, apparently, numerous small hills generally similar to the Teita hills in our territory.

The rest is probably like the Masai highlands, but not quite so valuable.

Thus the—

	Miles.
Mombasa railway opens up ...	657
German railway opens up ...	496
African Lakes Route opens up	1,660

It is obvious, *from this fact only*, that the African Lakes Route can compete with the German line, whereas the Mombasa line cannot possibly do so.

Moreover, the foregoing brief summary of the prospects of the different countries shows that there are most decided prospects of dividends, which are unfortunately necessary in this century, by the African Lakes Route, and by that route alone.

Moreover, it would be in strict accordance with the spirit of British colonisation to develop and foster the present thriving colonisation in South Central Africa, and push upwards and northwards through them.

Moreover, it developes British Central Africa, obtains for us the trade of Tanganyika, and opens up the whole of East Africa. It is only the last that is produced by the Mombasa line.

The policy of enormous initial expenditure, with the hope that something may come of it, is a French, and the pushing forward of railways through a new and unsettled country is an American idea. It succeeds in the United States, where New York and Chicago are at the other end of the line. It is doomed to fail in Africa. That is the lesson which is clearly to be read from the present state of Australia and the disastrous failure of the Imperial British East Africa Company.

There are two distinct advantages in the Mombasa railway. One is the rapidity with which mails or men could be sent into the country; but it must be borne in mind that all military operations in Uganda or towards the north will have to be carried on by native troops led by Europeans, not by British regiments. The Waganda and Soudanese will probably, with training, quite equal the very best Indian regiments. Then, even with a railway to the Nyanza, we should require roads to be made, and the whole transport organised, down to the training of bullocks and their drivers, before we could reach the Upper Nile, on which a sufficient number of steamers must be placed to advance against the Mahdi.

The second advantage is much less important. There are no "breaks of bulk." But breaking of bulk in a country where land can be had for the asking and labour at a penny a day, is quite an unimportant detail, and has scarcely to be taken into consideration.

So far we have only compared the routes to the basin of the Victoria Nyanza, which is the object of all the three roads considered. We must, however, specially in view of recent developments, consider the wider problem of reaching the Upper Nile.

The country between the Albert Edward and Albert Nyanzas and the Victoria is extremely difficult. This arises from the fact that it is intersected in every direction by enormously long, curved, and intricately meandering swamp-rivers. These Mr. Stanley has called "rush-drains"; but they contain scarcely any rushes, and require draining.

A railway or even a bullock waggon track would be a matter of enormous expense in this country, as in whatever direction it is taken, numerous tributaries of these swamp-rivers, which are frequently half a mile broad, must be crossed; and two hills at least for each.

Hence it is obvious that the secret of the future local development of these regions is to turn these obstacles of transport into means of carriage by cutting narrow canals through them.

The Katonga river is utterly and entirely useless for navigation. It is not navigable within half a mile of its mouth where I crossed it, and Captain Lugard also saw it. If Mr. Stanley really means to say it is navigable, it must have changed in every respect since he went there. Captain Lugard, in fact, crossed it without *even wetting his feet*, 25 miles from the mouth.

It may be useful for the local development of Buddu, but certainly is of no use for through traffic.

There are two other methods of reaching the Albert Nyanza. One by the Albert Edward Nyanza, and the other by the Nile from Ripon Falls.

I have not been able to grasp clearly the number of miles of waterway by the latter route, but so far as I can judge there must be 25 miles from Ripon Falls to Isamba, and probably 70 miles from Fauvera to the Albert Nyanza which cannot be utilised.

The other route would leave the Kagera river at the bend mentioned above; at a distance of 60 miles over easy country, it would reach the Albert Edward which thus opens up the rich district about Ruwenzori.

From the north end of Lake Ruisamba to the Albert there is probably 70 miles of land transport.

If we assume these figures to be near the truth and take an equal rate of £3,000 a mile, this would give by—

	Miles.	Cost.
Somerset Nile ...	95	£285,000
Albert Edward ...	130	390,000

Of course there can be little doubt that the latter opens up a much richer country to traffic and settlement, and apparently at not much greater cost.

The time of transit to the Albert Nyanza would probably be twenty-one days by the African Lakes Route and Kagera, twelve days by the Mombasa railway and Kagera, and eight days by the Mombasa railway and Somerset Nile.

It must be, I think, obvious from the preceding, that the African Lakes Route is far superior to the Mombasa railway in cheapness and in the prospect and value of the country opened up.

The disadvantages of slowness of transit only apply if the Mombasa railway is to be extended to the Albert Nyanza, which involves a further unproductive expenditure of £285,000. We could not without this attempt to put a British or Indian regiment on the Albert Nyanza, and certainly such a railway with its extensions would require at least five years to make.

That of breaking bulk is insignificant.

The real and only difficulty is the fact that part of it passes through German territory.

The right to make a line 50 miles long and navigate the Kagera could be easily arranged on somewhat the same lines as the Chinde concession on the Zambesi.

The German Government would in no respect be prevented from crossing this line to pursue a westward extension, in which we would wish them every success.

They would gain by the opening up of the territory *en route* to trade and commerce.

They would also be paid for a concession 50 miles long by 2 miles broad at Tanganyika, and perhaps two stations on ground measuring 5 miles by 5 miles along the Kagera.

They might be allowed such a royalty on goods passing through that it would be well to their interest.

If they refuse to permit this, it can only be out of the simple determination wantonly to annoy and aggravate England when it is against their own interests to do so. Moreover, the right of free transit of goods and men is expressly stipulated for in the original partition of Africa.

German armed expeditions have traversed our territories over and over again without paying duty or obtaining permission. If under these circumstances the British Foreign Office could not obtain, for a fair *quid pro quo*, the concessions mentioned above, then we are incapable of any further extension; we could not build a railway or develop Uganda; and we should say to the spirit which "*stets verneint*" (I mean Mr. Labouchere), "*Ich liebe dich*."

The great argument in favour of the African Lakes Route, however, lies in the fact that it will unite and keep together our colonies in British Central Africa and East Africa.

If the Mombasa railway is built at the present time, then they will be isolated from one another for ever.

If it had not been for the curious hostility of Germany towards ourselves (which seems to date from the Emin Pasha expedition), we should have had the whole of Africa east of 30 degrees longitude in the hands of ourselves or our friends, which were Germany, Italy, and Egypt (for the unhealthy Portuguese coast and the sands of Obock may well be left to their possessors).

Even now, if some sort of arrangement with Germany is arrived at and this scheme is carried through, we should be able to hand over to our descendants this vast territory. It is possible to-day to buy in Glasgow a ticket for the north end of Tanganyika, and if this scheme were persistently carried through, then it will be possible in 1930 to take a through ticket *via* Ruwenzori from Cairo to Cape Town.

CHAPTER XIX.

THE SUAHILI.

THE name Suahili appears to have been first given to the followers of Imam Amu Zaid, at Shangaya, near Lamu. The term is now applied indiscriminately to those half Mohammedan coast-natives who are for the most part slaves of the hybrid Arabs of Zanzibar and East Africa. Like all African travellers, I had full opportunity of understanding these curious people.

They are pure savages domesticated by the Arabs for the purpose of carrying loads, and, in their one particular line, they surpass all other natives except the Wanyamwesi.

Their faults in number and enormity can only be understood by those who have had the misfortune to experience them practically; but it is impossible not to like them, and even to grow really fond of them, after one begins to understand what children they really are. They have been brought up with the hippo-hide whip, and unfortunately cannot be managed even now without its use; the Arabs have managed to destroy almost all the moral nature they ever possessed, and any

Fig. 41.—The Originals—Wahteita.

attempt to Christianise them is almost impossible.

A Catholic priest after spending two hours in describing the probable future state of an old Suahili, was met by the following overwhelming reply: "Mimi Mzee nataka ku karibia moto" (I am an old man, I like to be near the fire)!

In fact, they are totally incapable of looking forward even a day ahead. A man will sell his tent to buy a goat, although he knows this means sleeping in the cold for months, as well as great personal danger from hyenas and leopards. The manner in which some travellers attempt to replace corporal punishment by fines is for this reason perfectly useless as well as cruel.

When an unfortunate porter gets 10 rupees a month for carrying a heavy load some 10 miles a day, it is too bad to diminish that scanty sum; and the man cannot realise that you will do it, even if you have the necessary cruelty in your disposition. Along with this absence of foresight one finds curious, even pathetic, instances of long-headedness. Several of my men carried parrots for months to sell when they reached the coast. One poor fellow was carrying about 10 lbs. weight of hippopotamus teeth, in addition to his load, for several months, with the intention of selling it at the coast for 3 rupees.

Another man of mine, who had fallen into the hands of some Hindu moneylender in Mombasa, was having all his wages stopped under the head of "family remittance" to pay off his debts.

This was only known to me, and I found out he had obtained relatively enormous advances of food and cloth from most of his fellow-porters, promising to pay at Mombasa when he received his wages, although he knew that all these would have been given to his creditors.

The manner in which the now happily defunct I.B.E.A. Co. played into the hands of these Hindu usurers, and obtained payment from those indebted to itself by this system of "family remittance," was disgraceful. As a rule, this family remittance, supposed to support the porter's wife, goes to his master if, as in most cases, he is a slave; but I fervently hope the whole system of paying and engaging porters has been thoroughly reorganised.

The same kind of contradictory qualities appear over and over again when one studies the Suahili character. One of the pleasantest traits in their disposition is the tendency to look on the cheerful side of things. For instance, they were mightily pleased because, on the march, if overtaken by severe rain, I used to make them undo the baggage tarpaulin and remain under it; and while they stood there, shivering all over with cold, they would laugh and howl with delight at the witticisms of the wag of the party. Even when pitching camp, with all their scanty wardrobe soaked through, they would take it as an enormous joke, and never grew depressed and melancholy. Moreover, when they receive a punishment, which they usually take in a very plucky and stoical manner, they may be heard laughing and joking half an hour after it is over. Yet, if treated with injustice, they may sulk for months, and, in fact, never get over the feeling of being ill-used.

They are not constitutionally brave, and are very liable to sudden panics. Even such a great favourite with natives as Mr. George Wilson has been deserted by his whole caravan. But about half my men always volunteered if I wanted to do anything dangerous, and I should never be afraid of desertion if I could get the drum beaten a little and could manage to work up their enthusiasm.

I have never found in them any kind of affection for their masters or their fellows. In fact, their treatment of their own comrades shows their very worst side. They will leave them to die on the road. No Suahili can be trusted to deal out food or cloth for the others. He will always steal, even from the sick. It is extremely difficult to get any sick porter attended to. If you trust his chum to give him medicine, he will very probably sell the medicine to the other porters and go to sleep.

I do not think they ever really care much for their white masters. I have noticed much more appearance of real affection between Suahilis and Arabs than between Suahilis and Europeans; but one is very much in the position of a schoolmaster with a rod to wield, and I do not think many boys have a real affection for a physical-force schoolmaster, at any rate while they are boys.

On one occasion I had great difficulty with a thoroughly lazy porter. The headman and askaris complained that he would not keep up with the rest of the caravan. So I first set apart one askari to look after him, but I found that this was too dangerous, as the two came in long after everybody else had arrived.

I then put him at the head of the caravan, and kept him well up to his work all day. Afterwards I made a long speech to him, saying that I was not going to risk the life of an askari on his account, and that I would beat him more and more every day till he did his duty. He went away rather impressed, and a few minutes afterwards brought me back a few heads of flowers as a peace-offering.

It is, I think, very rare for them to show any real affection for their "bwana." Yet there are some things they thoroughly admire, such as physical courage or extent. A big man has a great influence simply through his size. They have a good deal of the slavish devotion of a dog to a severe master, as can be readily understood from their experience of Arab slave-owners. Yet I have seen and heard of really brave actions amongst them. A native boy has been known to pick an arrow out of his master's neck under a heavy fire!

Along with the extraordinary patient endurance they display in carrying a heavy load for miles under a burning sun goes a disposition to die out of sheer want of pluck when seriously ill. In fact, if a man makes up his mind that he will die on a certain date, the corpse will be there when the time comes.

They are inconceivably stupid. The very night that Mirambo died of his wound, received through stealing food, another man crept out of camp to do the same thing.

I am convinced that a great deal of this stupidity, as well as the unfortunate falling off in intelligence on maturity, of which every missionary has experience, is due to the practice of carrying loads, especially when young. This also produces occasional fits of what seems like madness, pure and simple.

My best man, Mabruki Sirkali, complained one night of severe pains in his head, and then went off his head completely. He called for some salt and water, and drank it eagerly, and then began talking nonsense. Unless every one agreed with him he became frenzied. All night long he remained groaning and moaning, but after two or three days, during which he was very silent and unhappy, he became all right again. This was a very anxious time for me, as he was the strongest man I had. He was always a curious character, often very silent for days; but when he began to talk, he would go on for hours, and, in fact, till he was thoroughly hoarse.

One night, when I was just sinking into sleep after a severe attack of fever, he was on guard, and came to my tent to call me. His face was grey and he was shaking with fear. He said "simba" (lion). I heard the noise, and got my rifle, and we watched for about half an hour. I felt sure that the beast was going to spring over the fence, and was making up my mind to blaze away at it when in the air, when I discovered the noise was produced by a man suffering from indigestion.

Yet this man was always first to swim across a swollen river, and would have done anything for me.

Their chief passion is for dancing, singing, and a big drum. They really possess a musical taste, in spite of the nasal tones and curious monotony of their music.

One of my men possessed a fiddle of a very primeval type, composed of one string, a gourd, and a stick. This instrument yielded eight notes, which he had combined to form a real tune (of course a simple one). After hearing this tune for about an hour and a half every night for 6 weeks, I grew tired of it. Fortunately he sacrificed his aesthetic development to the craving of his appetite, and sold it for a fowl.

I have noticed also in Suahilis, and never in any other natives, a real delight and appreciation of scenery. They really have a distinct, though embryonic, artistic sense, and if we compare the native songs of, say, Tanganyika with the very early music of England, I know, but dare not say, which is the most pleasant to listen to. These songs were of Wanyamwezi or Wajiji origin, but my men were not by any means wanting in talent of the same kind. It was in comedy that they specially distinguished themselves. A skit of the Bugufu song and dance carried on by some of my porters was the funniest thing of the kind I ever saw.

They have scarcely any idea of honesty, and none of truth. They are hopelessly corrupted, both physically and morally, by Arab teaching and example. Yet, in spite of all these failings, one likes them; one trusts with perfect reliance in their pluck and endurance, and certainly it is to them that the real credit of European travelling is due; the strength of the "Bwana" lies really in sitting still (I mean figuratively, not literally), for no natives are so docile and easily managed as these clumsy, strong, and good-natured children.

Their life is, as a rule, very hard and short. Born of some slave girl, taken in the interior, and brought up in the unspeakable corruption of a Mohammedan household, they are, as children, used as hewers of wood and drawers of water. When the master thinks it advisable that a porter should go on a caravan journey, he is sent to one of the

Company's headmen, who, for the sum of two rupees, will take him to the Transport Office and swear that he knows him well, and that he has been several journeys under his control. (I am speaking of things as they were when I left Mombasa, in 1893.) His name is written down, and he receives three months' pay in advance, with which he goes on the spree, and remains probably drunk till it is finished. His master receives three rupees a month out of his wages during the whole time that he is away. If he does not die of illness and starvation on the road, he will turn up after, say, three years, to obtain his wages, which may not amount to more than 200 rupees (about £10) for this hard and wearisome work.

The master will be waiting in the Company's office to grab as much of his wages as he can, but he manages to get a certain amount, and remains drunk till it is over.

With a few who are free men, the Hindu moneylender replaces the master.

It will be easily gathered from this that the number of Suahilis is rapidly falling off. The women are simply prostitutes, and rarely produce children, while the work of carrying loads is so hard, that every expedition means the death of some of the porters. Slave raiding is, moreover, nearly a thing of the past.

Hence the race will be shortly extinct, and African travel on the old lines will be impossible, which will be an excellent thing for all parties. In Chapter XVII. I have pointed out the extreme simplicity and perfection of the porter system as it has been developed by Europeans, alone from a labour supply not much tainted by half-caste Arabs. I recommend those who are obliged to use the old system never to allow any one to be engaged without the most careful personal inspection by a doctor in the presence of the European who is leading the caravan. My experience with the weakly and sick members of my caravan was the greatest trial I had. Many should never have been engaged at all. I refused to take four, in spite of their having received and spent their three months' pay; if I had been wise, I should have refused at least fifteen others. It is also a good thing only to take mature men for actual porter's work, though young boys are very useful as servants.

I think that this book differs from every book of African travel that I know, in one respect. It has no chapter on either missions or the slave question. I cannot, however, resist the temptation of pointing out the obvious fundamental reason of slavery, which, though extremely simple, seems to be quite overlooked in this country.*

Slavery is a necessity of Mohammedan Arab life. The Zanzibar Arabs of Muscat, as well as the Egyptians and Turks, cannot exist without

* Except, perhaps, by Captain Lugard.

slaves. Family and social life is impossible without it in all Arabian countries.

Now, both slave boys and girls are hopelessly depraved. The immorality is such that probably not one quarter of those who die are replaced by slaves brought up in the household. Hence a perpetual supply of slaves is necessary, and that is the root of the slave trade.

We in England are attempting an impossibility. On the one hand, we uphold the state of Zanzibar, which is based on slavery. On the other, we attempt to put slavery down by our cruisers, and by perfectly futile legislation at Zanzibar and along the coast.

Slavery, in fact, is a minor department of the Arab question.

Missionary work is more difficult to speak of. I have known missionaries of every denomination, and of every shade of character and utility. Many would probably be of more use in teaching Sunday schools in England, and some are so dangerous and turbulent that they ought to be promptly removed.

On the other hand, I should not be alive were it not for the kindness of missionaries; and of the good that is done by those who are of the right temper and spirit it is impossible to speak too highly.

The Roman Catholics, were it not for their disingenuous political methods, always perform a valuable work. They have no interests outside it; they understand that manual, mental, and spiritual training go together; they have perfect organisation and discipline; and what is more important, they really love their flock, and strive to be their real friends in every possible way.

On the other hand, the best type of Protestant missionary is incalculably superior, because a really good man has free play for his individuality;

Fig. 45.—WAWAMBA.

while the inferior type is utterly useless, if not positively dangerous.

The ordinary mission boy (as a layman understands him) is an unmitigated scoundrel. This, however, one must expect, as no mission gets rid of any boy that affords the least promise.

Moreover, one must not expect so much from the Christian native in Africa as people habitually do. A boy who is usually not removed by a single generation from savagery cannot be expected to show the truthfulness, honesty, unselfishness, and purity which, as we know, always and invariably characterise European youths who have been brought up in Christian teaching, and represent in their instincts about twenty centuries of hereditary civilisation.

No human being can estimate or criticise the spiritual work that is carried on in any mission. The mental and manual work is so obviously good that no sane person can have anything but praise to give.

I do not myself think that such subjects as Latin, Greek, Hebrew, mathematics, moral philosophy, and civilisation, which do (or did) actually form the curriculum at one mission station, should be taught to natives; but I do not pretend to be a judge of these matters.

I have known what really savage life means. I have also had the opportunity of seeing the work of such bodies as the London Missionary Society, the Free and Established Church of Scotland, and the Universities Mission. I cannot speak in a sufficiently calm and reasonable manner of the good that they do.

In some of them there is, perhaps, a tendency to treat the natives too much as the equal of the white man (which they can never be), and, perhaps, not fully to realise the advantage of training in habits of hard work, but in spite of such minor details, one is amazed at the advance made during the last ten years, and which seems to increase in rapidity with time.

At the same time, mission work can only be successful if the natives are thoroughly aware that the white man has overwhelming strength, though that need never be exercised unless on provocation.

Finally, the missions being a necessary factor in the situation, enormous obstacles are thrown in the way alike of the Government and the mission, if they do not give each other cordial help.

CHAPTER XX.

HINTS ON OUTFIT AND EXPENSES.

IT is almost or quite impossible to give such a list of items as would be complete and sufficient for the outfit of every traveller in every part of East Africa.

The essential point is to know how much time one has at one's disposal, and also exactly what one wishes to do.

I think the most important general advice that I can give is to have all arrangements worked out down to the smallest detail, even to the number of bootlaces and penknives that one intends to take, before starting.

When you have thus worked out your expenses to a round sum, then add half as much again for contingencies, and you will probably find it near your expenditure.

It is particularly in regard to stores of all kinds that this advice applies. If one is about to undertake a journey with porters, everything that you require should be packed before leaving England,

HINTS ON OUTFIT AND EXPENSES.

in such a way that, if the porters are at hand, you can start the day after landing at your destination.

It is, I think, a very great mistake to leave anything in the nature of packing or purchase for such places as Zanzibar or Mombasa. It means, amongst other things, a delay on an unhealthy and feverish coast which may have grave consequences to health. The price of everything is higher, and any special thing that you want is sure not to exist in the place at that time.

Of course the important thing above all others is the question of health. Unless the Europeans preserve their full vigour of mind and body, the object of the expedition will certainly not be attained and the lives of the porters will probably be sacrificed.

My own experience is that marches should, if possible, be kept to four hours a day. Start in the very early morning as soon as it is light enough to see the road, but, before starting, take as substantial a breakfast as you can possibly manage. That is, if there are no eggs or cold meat at hand, use tinned meats or something that will afford a substantial reserve for the day. Let your special follower always carry a few biscuits and a tin of corned beef or *bully* in case of accidents. Starting, then, at 6 a.m., march at the best speed you can for three hours; then rest for half an hour, if possible near a stream, and then go on to camp. Take a cold bath, and get a good meal ready as soon as possible—that is, about noon. From 12 to 4 there is sure to be plenty to do in the tent. The route has to be plotted, observations taken, native chiefs to be interviewed, while your men have quarrels, punishments, and sores which must be attended to; and, if of a scientific turn, you have a wide variety of occupations, *e.g.*, plants to be pressed and labels written, snakes and toads to be plunged in spirits, rocks to be packed, as well as notes (which should be as full as possible), to be written.

From 4 to 6 p.m., if you have time and strength, a close and minute observation of the country about is always of advantage, or if there is any game, then is the time to try for it. I did not like leaving my caravan on the march to shoot, partly because one never knew what might not occur, and partly because of the fatigue.

At sunset have your dinner, and after it, or with it, a small glass of whiskey. I think it not at all advisable to touch alcohol until this time of the day when one is sure to be exhausted and in a low state of mind and body; it is, I think, best not to march on Sunday.

Travelling in this way one can keep one's health for months, even in a dangerous climate; and though for a short period of two or three months it is possible to travel straight on or even 20 or 30 miles on one day (which has to be done pretty

HINTS ON OUTFIT AND EXPENSES.

frequently under any circumstances), it is always dangerous and very often fatal.

The general conduct of the caravan depends so much on the number of the porters, and on whether you are alone or not, that it is difficult to give much advice of any use. I had no information before starting, and was obliged to find out by bitter and painful experience much that was extremely simple.

The most important clue is to organise everything. Every man should have his special work to do on arriving in camp. Certain men have to pitch your tent, others to pile the loads, which should be counted by a European. One man

Fig. 46.—CAMP AT MKUYUNI.

should bring wood and water for your cook, and sets of men should take it in turn to fetch wood for the camp fires. It is, I find, a very good plan to have every ten porters under a special headman or askari; this makes the giving out of food and the general camp work easier to the men themselves, as otherwise the weaker may be obliged to do everything for days together.

As to treating the men, I do not think I ever got as much out of them as other travellers seem to have done, so perhaps my advice is not of much value. The leading hint is to treat them exactly as a schoolmaster in the olden time used to treat his boys. Never be familiar, or partial, or overlook impertinence or neglect of duty. At the same time, I used to do everything I could to make them comfortable *without appearing to do so.*

I found that this answered very well, as I never had any serious difficulty with them.

It is also important never to believe or trust in any particular man above the others, and to remember that truth is a very hazy notion amongst them. For personal attendants I have always found young boys the most willing and intelligent, and I think this is a general experience.

Fig. 47.—An Askari.

HINTS ON OUTFIT AND EXPENSES.

With regard to medicines, I found the majority of human diseases can be roughly divided, for travelling purposes, as follows:

Sores, bruises, and accidents	Elliman (horses), sticking-plaster, iodoform, carbolic oil.
Dysentery, diarrhœa ...	... Ipecac.; chlorodyne.
Constipation ...	... Cockle's pills.
Fevers	... Quinine; antifebrin.

I think these remedies are the most useful for a non-medical person who has to treat a caravan. There are, however, many small medicine boxes which are highly recommended by others, *e.g.*, the Congo chest. The fault of these is that they are too varied, and there is, as a rule, too little of the most useful things.

Clothes are a part of one's individuality, but most people certainly take out too many. Light tweed and khakee are, perhaps, the best for ordinary walking purposes, while a well-shrunk flannel suit for the camp is a great luxury. Flannel shirts to the amount of six for a year, and as many socks as one can find space for, should be taken. One also requires one suit of fairly respectable appearance if one arrives at a European station. I do not believe in sun-helmets, and have found that an umbrella and double terai-hat is by far the most generally useful head-gear. Solar topees are a nuisance in rain and in forest or scrub, but perhaps one should be taken.

Boots are a very important point. If I were

going on another expedition I should take two pairs of strong walking boots and about ten pairs of leather-soled deck or tennis shoes. I find these latter are the most comfortable wear for ordinary native paths. A pair of patent leather shoes sometimes exhibit the most wonderful wearing qualities. I have walked about 300 miles in one pair, but this is not a usual experience.

Food is a matter which deserves very careful examination. It is hopeless to attempt to carry sufficient meat or vegetables for every day. Therefore goats, sheep, and fowls should be bought where possible, and a month's supply kept in hand. I think a cow giving milk is certainly to be recommended wherever it is possible to obtain one. Cattle travel as well as men; sheep are not quite so good, and goats are the worst of all. The usual supply of what is known as "chock boxes" for stations in East Africa, is one per month; and this is as much as one can manage on the march.

The following would be what I should consider a fair allowance of necessaries for one man for a month:

				Weight.
1 tin	Tea	giving 100 cups		$\frac{3}{4}$ lbs.
4 ,,	Cocoa and milk	,, 40 ,, (if not stolen)		5 ,,
1 jar	Meat extract	,, 10 plates soup		$\frac{1}{2}$,,
2 bottles	Bovril	,, 20 ,, ,,		$\frac{3}{4}$,,
1 dozen	Soup squares	,, 24 ,, ,,		$1\frac{3}{4}$,,
2 tins	Biscuits	,,		5 ,,
4 ,,	Flour	,, 4 lbs. or 30 scones		5 ,,
3 ,,	Lard	,, 3 ,,		$3\frac{3}{4}$,,
1 ,,	Salt	,, 1 ,,		$1\frac{1}{4}$,,
1 bottle	Curry powder	$\frac{1}{4}$,,		$\frac{1}{4}$,,

HINTS ON OUTFIT AND EXPENSES.

							Weight.	
1	tin	Pepper	⎫					
1	,,	Cream of tartar	⎬	¼ lbs.			¼ lbs.	
1	,,	Carbonate of soda	⎭					
2	,,	Corned beef	giving	4 days' supply			2½	,,
2	,,	Salmon	,,	4	,,	,,	2½	,,
2	,,	Sausages	,,	4	,,	,,	2½	,,
4	,,	Jam	,,	30	,,		5	,,
1	,,	Sugar	,,	30	,,		1¼	
2½	boxes	Ozokerit candles	,,	15 candles			3¼	,,
3	bottles	Whiskey (pint)	,,	30 glasses			3	,,
1	tin	Kola chocolate	,,	2 lbs.			2¼	,,
1	bottle	Limejuice					1¼	,,
2	tablets	Carbolic soap					½	,,
1	,,	Sunlight soap					1	,,
1	bottle	Quinine	2 oz.	⎫				
2	,,	Chlorodyne		⎬			1	,,
1	,,	Carbolic oil	4 oz.	⎭				
1	,,	Rangoon oil		⎫				
1	,,	Elliman (horses)		⎬				
1	box	Tooth-powder		⎪				
2	,,	Cockle's pills		⎬			1	,,
1	ball	Twine		⎪				
2		notebooks		⎭				
1		Penknife						
3	tins	Tobacco	¾ lb.				1	,,
1		Pipe						
4	boxes	Matches						
					About	..	53 lbs.	

It will be seen that, though this does not include such things as milk, butter, or vegetables, the weight mounts up to 53 lbs., which is more than a man's load, as the weight of the box is not included.

Every person would, of course, prefer some different arrangement of these articles of food. I drew out this list simply as a guide.

The Kola chocolate may be obtained from Mr. T. Christy, 27, Lime Street, E.C. It must be repacked in proper tins, and in spite of its insidious pleasantness, should be reserved for occasions on which a great physical effort has to be undergone. It is, in fact, a powerful stimulant with the inevitable reaction.

I took my supplies from Messrs. Lazenby and Sons, both on this last journey and on a former one. The quality of the provisions was most excellent, and in the packing and general arrangement they spared no trouble, with entirely satisfactory results.

Most of these goods are sold in tins, and, in cases where they are not, I think it is advisable to put them in tins before starting. The kind I have found most satisfactory is cylindrical with a circular lid at the top, which is pressed up by a key (self-opening Noakes' tin), like that of Lambert and Butler's tobacco tins.

This form is perfectly water-tight, and one can even carry spirits of wine in those that are emptied without any perceptible evaporation.

The remarks apply especially to Kola chocolate and tobacco, which are usually sold in boxes, quite unsuitable for rough work. In fact, if a box is packed in this manner it may be immersed in a river or exposed to a tropical shower without any bad consequences. The contents are also protected from insects of all kinds.

In packing clothes, instruments, and one's belongings generally, my experience is that ordinary tin trunks, such as one gets in London at

HINTS ON OUTFIT AND EXPENSES. 365

from 5s. to 10s. each, are the most satisfactory. The African trunks, largely advertised, are absurdly expensive and heavy for ordinary purposes. The main advantages of tin trunks are the following: if properly made, nothing short of absolute immersion can wet the contents. They can scarcely, under ordinary circumstances, be cracked, burst or torn, and no insects can, as a rule, enter.

Leather and wood are quite unsuitable, and should never be taken unless the contents are enclosed in small tins as mentioned above.

Strong American cloth and tarpaulins sometimes resist rain wonderfully, but they cannot be completely trusted to do so, and I could not recommend them.

During this last expedition I devised a form of bed which I found in my own case eminently satisfactory. It resisted every possible ill-treatment, and I found it extremely comfortable to sleep in. It is composed of three tin boxes (or four if required) placed against one another. The lids of each box are double; one is composed of an ordinary tin cover, and is lifted off at night to be utilised as a bath or table; the other lid is a board, on which is a cushion with sofa springs like an ottoman, and can be reversed as shown in the figures, so that the stuffed portions of the three form a fairly comfortable couch. These boxes are scarcely heavier than ordinary packing cases, and can be used to carry clothes and bedding, or anything that is required. I devised this as I found stretchers always liable to break and extremely uncomfortable to sleep upon. In fact, they save certainly one, and probably two, porters. I had the lid of one made rather deeper, and used it throughout my journey as a bath. The other two lids formed a table, as shown in the figure, but I recommend regular legs, as shown in

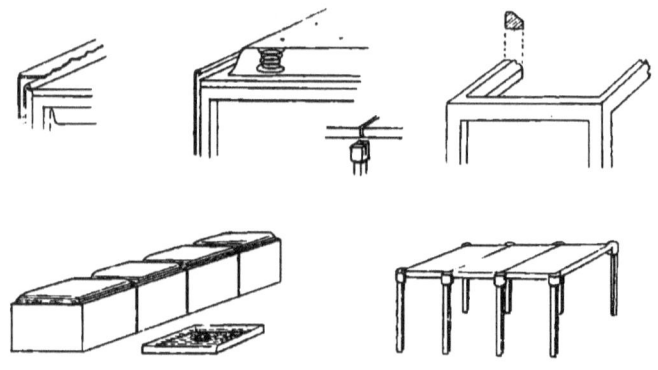

Fig. 48.—A Patent Bed.

Fig. 48, instead of the eight plain sticks driven into the ground which I used myself. Being short in stature only three were required for *me*, but in the figure I have shown four.

The shape of the tin box adopted above is an eminently useful one. I possess one made on this principle, which has been many expeditions and is still as good as ever.

Before I started, I made many attempts to find out what would be advisable to take, but I never

HINTS ON OUTFIT AND EXPENSES.

discovered a full list which appeared to me at all satisfactory. Some are too complete, *e.g.*, a certain missionary recommends *a gross of clothes-pegs*. I did not know that these were of special utility for missionary work, and cannot make out what they were used for. My clothes were hung on any convenient bush! The important thing is to take as little as possible. Most travellers take far too much, and, in consequence, things hide themselves and involve loss of time and temper.

The consumables are given above, pp. 362, 363, and the following permanences, mainly extracted from my own list, may be of use in drawing out one to suit other particular tastes.

	£	s.	d.	£	s.	d.
Water bottle	0	4	9			
Kettle (seamless steel)	0	4	1			
Saucepans (3, seamless steel)	0	9	10			
4 Enamelled iron plates...	0	2	11½			
2 Cups and saucers (enamelled iron) ...	0	1	9			
1 Enamelled iron tumbler	0	0	7			
,, ,, teapot	0	2	8			
,, ,, milk jug ...	0	1	9			
,, omelette pan	0	0	10½			
Scotch girdle	0	2	3			
2 Large forks, 2 small do.	0	2	6			
2 Table spoons, 2 dessert, 2 tea do.	0	3	1			
3 Table knives, 1 cook's, 1 hunting ...	0	10	0			
Carvers	0	4	6			
2 White umbrellas	0	10	0			
2 Pairs strong walking boots	3	10	0			
10 Pairs shoes (cheap deck or tennis)...	2	10	0			
Terai hat	0	18	0			
Carried forward				9	19	7

	£	s.	d.	£	s.	d.
Brought forward				9	19	7
Cloth cap	0	1	0			
Solar topee (?)						
2 Tweed suits	6	0	0			
2 Khakee ,,	4	4	0			
1 Flannel ,,	1	1	0			
6 Flannel shirts	3	0	0			
2 Sleeping suits	1	15	6			
1 Merino vest, 1 pants	0	14	0			
12 Pairs socks	0	14	0			
2 Pairs braces	0	3	8			
12 Handkerchiefs	0	12	0			
1 Housewife (needles, pins, thread)	0	5	6			
1 Rough towel	0	2	0			
Sponge and bag	0	7				
Handglass	0	2	2			
Toothbrushes	0	3	0			
1 Tin Keating	0	0	8			
Groundsheet for tent	0	12	6			
Tent	8	0	0			
Deck chair	0	8	6			
Bed (3 tin boxes)	6	0	0			
2 Blankets (sheets ?)	0	8	4			
Pillow (air)	0	5	3			
Mosquito netting (7 yards)	0	10	6			
Ulster	3	0	0			
Waterproof	2	0	0			
Small folding chair	0	7	6			
Legs for table	0	10	0			
File	0	0	10			
Oilstone	0	2	3			
Hammer and nails	0	1	8			
Axe	0	1	6			
Corkscrew	0	1	3			
Screwdriver and screws	0	1	7			
Saw (?)						
Clinical thermometer	0	15	0			
1 Box Antifebrin	0	0	8			
Carried forward				52	12	11

HINTS ON OUTFIT AND EXPENSES. 369

	£	s.	d.	£	s.	d.
Brought forward ...				52	12	11
1 Bottle Ipecac. pills ...	0	1	6			
Sticking-plaster and lint ...	0	2	0			
1 Bottle Iodoform	0	2	0			
2 Ransome's Patent ink bottles	0	15	0			
Ink pellets (2 boxes)	0	1	2			
Writing paper (5 quires and envelopes)	0	2	0			
Pencils (3 H.B. and 1 or 2 graphite) ...	0	1	0			
3 Penholders and nibs	0	0	6			
Writing case	0	7	9			
				1	12	11

Shakespeare, Bible, R. Browning, Kipling, Wolseley ("Soldier's Pocket-book"), Hints to Travellers, &c. Maps, Mapping paper.

*Instruments—
Sextant
Artificial Horizon
Chronometer watches (3)
Prismatic compass
Boiling-point thermometer
Maximum and minimum thermometer
Wet and dry bulb thermometer
Sling thermometer

Photography—

Camera (Meagher's)	10	4	0			
Lens (Ross rapid symmetrical)	5	3	6			
Dark tent	2	0	0			
Slides (glass half-plate) 10 dozen ..	2	0	0			
				19	7	6

Guns—

Martini-Henry Sporting	7	0	0			
200 Cartridges for do. ...	1	15	0			
Winchester carbine ·4590	4	2	6			
200 Cartridges	1	15	0			
				14	12	6
Carried forward				88	5	10

* No price can be easily given for these, as any sum might be spent on them.

	£	s.	d.	£	s.	d.
Brought forward ...				88	5	10
Shot gun ...	5	0	0			
300 Cartridges (No. 5 green)...	1	7	0			
Revolver ...	0	15	0			
100 Cartridges ...	0	4	2			
Gun cases and cartridge bags	1	13	0			
				8	19	2
				£97	5	0

It will be seen that even such an outfit as given here is not far short of £100, of which guns and cartridges came to £23 11s. 8d., and photographic materials £19 7s. 6d. One may fairly allow that these can be disposed of on the return journey for about a third of their value.

It will be noticed that, instead of a fitted canteen, utensils of seamless steel and enamelled iron are put down. It is true that these can be broken, but it requires more trouble to do this than the average servant will take. Ordinary canteens are far too delicate for a Suahili cook. These kitchen utensils are best carried in baskets; it is as well to allow two baskets, one a full load, and the other half a load, and in these items bought on the road and tins actually in use can be carried.

With regard to tents, Edgington is certainly the best man to patronise. Mine was a composite one. Originally it was a *tente d'abri;* to this I added walls about 3 feet high, and subsequently a green rot-proof fly with special light poles. The

HINTS ON OUTFIT AND EXPENSES. 371

total weight was 72 lbs., which was usually carried by one porter who was greatly above the average in strength.

The Salisbury stool is not a success in practice, but something about the same size is very useful. A deck chair is really a necessity.

I have to thank Sir Robert Edgecumbe for the useful tip for mosquitoes shown on the enclosed sketch. It is, I think, best to wait till one arrives

Fig. 49.—MOSQUITO CURTAIN.

at the coast before sewing the netting together in such a form as will be most convenient.

Map-making is a subject which would require a chapter to itself. I am neither qualified nor disposed to write about it. I only give the following hint. Do not do too much, and do not make it on a large scale unless you have great experience and are thoroughly trained. I personally found the plane-table a nuisance, as it takes too long to set up, and as one has seldom sufficient time to visit the salient points necessary for working it. I think the best method would be to practise in the country before starting, with some one of experience.

It is, I think, necessary to take a camera. Captain Hill, R.E., has quite recently invented a photographic method of taking longitudes, and General Stewart's panoramic camera may replace the plane-table in future work, but both these instruments are scarcely in current use. Of course a Kodak or its varieties is very convenient and useful, but I do not think the results are ever, except under special circumstances, so good as those produced by a regular camera, and I fancy this is more pronounced when the photographer is a beginner like myself. The experience of others seems to be that developing and printing on the journey is a mistake. My slides were brought out and carried home in special tin boxes with lids fitting over the sides, and holding two dozen plates. They were exposed to about 18 months' carriage, and I think that the system is the right one, for the failures which I experienced were, I think, due to my own inexperience and carelessness. A dark tent of some kind would have been an enormous advantage, or perhaps a changing box.

Of sporting matters I know even less, but I have noticed that most of the best sportsmen I saw used chiefly a light rifle, such as the Martini-Henry recommended. This is quite safe with any animal except the rhinoceros, elephant and buffalo, and for these I think even a ·577 Express (which I carried) is scarcely heavy enough. Probably an 8-bore would be best for such game. Of course there are combination guns in existence which profess to be equal to a rifle and shot gun combined, but I do not believe they can be as good, and they cost more than double the price of the two separate weapons.

I found a Winchester very useful for game, but it is specially adapted for accidents with the natives, and if there is little chance of trouble of this kind it is scarcely necessary to take it.

With regard to scientific outfit, one can do a very great deal, but the collection and preparation usually requires special training, which few possess. Those who do understand thoroughly one branch of science require no hints of mine on the subject. The following may, however, be of use to a pure layman.

First, with regard to botany; everything depends on the scale on which you propose to collect. I know of one instance in which about 700 numbers, or nearly that number, of species has been collected and dried in a week. I have never managed to obtain more than 2,000 numbers in 6 months, but the difficulty increases enormously with time. In a week a very fair knowledge of the flora of a district can be obtained, particularly if one remembers that the best plan of action is to keep a careful eye on the general features of a country, and especially examine any place which seems to be *different from the general aspect* of the district. Thus, in a country covered usually with grassy plains or scrub, examine any projecting hill where there are rocks, or which may be specially dry and exposed. Also it is well to look out carefully for ravines and the banks of streams, though in the tropics these are usually so dry in summer, and so rapid and swollen in the rains, that the results are often disappointing. Walking along the outside fringe of a wood or forest is usually more productive than proceeding inside, for the conditions within it are usually the same over a wide area, and a very short walk will enable one to pick up all the commoner forms.

It is a mistake to force one's way through thick jungle, as, if it is at all dense, half an hour may be spent in penetrating 100 yards. During that time one may search a mile and a half on a native path with far less exertion.

Of course, if settled permanently in a district, these remarks do not apply, as, even supposing only one day in the week is free, every wood and every cranny and hill within ten miles can be explored in the course of a year's stay.

If the plant is a herb or shrublet under a foot in height, it should be pulled up bodily; a twig of

HINTS ON OUTFIT AND EXPENSES.

a tree or shrub should be about a foot to eighteen inches long. Every specimen should have flowers and leaves, and if possible fruit as well. I think one should take specimens of everything that one sees. The common tropical weeds are usually found on waste ground and on cultivated plots, but if one does not examine such places carefully many plants of great interest are sure to be missed. The following would be a fair and not too extensive outfit :—

	£	s.	d.
Botanical paper (West, Newman & Co.), half a ream*	0	15	0
4 Wire frames on German model	1	0	0
2 Pruning shears	0	8	0
1 Knife	0	2	6
1 Vasculum or indiarubber bag	0	7	6
1 Lens	0	7	6
1,000 Labels	0	5	6
Naphthaline, 2 lbs.	0	2	0
	£3	8	0

The wire frames alluded to are not, so far as I know, kept in stock in England, but they can be easily made by a village blacksmith. The outline is of hoop iron, about one-sixth to one-fourth of an inch thick and half an inch wide, and the wires are best arranged to cross at right angles. Four small chains are attached to one of each pair, and

* The brown paper and frames which are recommended at Kew I find entirely unsuitable.

hooks are put on the other to correspond. It is a matter of the greatest importance that every plant should have a number attached to it, and this is most easily done by small tied-on labels like a minute luggage label. On this should be written the place, district, altitude, date, and notes as to whether it is in an exposed or sheltered, wet or dry place, as well as colour of flower, &c. These points are usually not attended to, and their importance is not diminished by the fact that most herbarium botanists pay no attention to them.

The actual drying of the specimens is a matter of extreme simplicity.

A sheet of paper is laid on the chain half of the frame; this is covered by a layer of specimens, not touching one another; another sheet of paper is laid on, and then another of specimens until about twelve layers are in the pile; then a sheet of paper and the hook half of the frame is laid on; stand or kneel on the top of the pile and slip the chains over the hooks. The elasticity of the frame keeps a gentle pressure on the plants within. Of course almost any number of specimens can be put in a frame, but they dry very much more quickly if there are only a few in each. These frames should be put in the sun at 9 a.m., and taken in and packed in a tin box at 5 p.m. The plants within dry rapidly under these circumstances. Fresh paper should be put in the frames at any rate twenty-four hours after the specimens are first put in and at about two to three days' interval afterwards. In a sunny climate they will dry in about seven days; this will be known by their being brittle to the touch. They should then be removed, with their labels attached, and packed in alternate sheets of newspaper, or any kind of paper available, with a small pinch of the white powder naphthaline scattered on every sheet. They should then be tied up in bundles and packed away in a tin box.

If one is collecting in great quantities, it is advisable either to have numerous frames (say twenty) or to devise some method of rapidly drying them.

I had on this last expedition a large roll of paper, and used to stretch about five sheets between strips of mosquito netting. This answered very well, as I could prepare three hundred specimens a week, but I found it of advantage always to press them first in the wire frames. It is very difficult to get the rolls of paper referred to, however.

Unless one is very specially devoted to birds, reptiles, or amphibia, my experience is that it is not likely that your collections are of very much scientific use. Lessons in skinning and preparation of bird-skins are necessary before starting, and plenty of arsenical soap is a necessity. Spirit is extremely difficult to carry and keep unstolen,

I think the easiest method is to carry all that is required in tins such as those recommended for foods. The amounts may be slightly reduced by wrapping smaller animals in saturated blotting-paper.

For mammalia, traps are a necessity, and I think thirty of different sizes could be profitably set every night. This involves that one man should be set apart to set and examine and collect the traps, and by a system of rewards and punishments a certain amount of assistance can usually be obtained. Suahilis are quite useless at any work of this kind, and natives of the country should be employed wherever possible.

It is very important to take notes of sex, locality, including altitude and date, for every specimen on labels (in pencil) attached to the specimens.

The following hints, drawn out, I believe, by Mr. Oldfield Thomas, may be of use to those who wish to collect mammals:—

1. With the freshly-killed carcase before you, write the label. This should be a number, locality, altitude above sea, sex, date, and the following measurements in millimetres, taken in the flesh: (1) Length of head and body; (2) of tail without end hairs; and (3) hind-foot without claws. In the case of the first two measurements, the body should be straightened out as much as possible, and the tail bent upwards at a sharp angle; and the measurements should then be taken from a point in the angle. The label should also have on its back any notes that may strike you about the place where the specimen was caught.

2. Open the skin by cutting down the belly from the breast-bone to the anus; first push one and then the other knee through the opening, and cut through the legs at the knee joints; clear off the chief muscles of the leg-bones and separate away the skin from the body all round the tail; then holding the skin at the base of the tail firmly between the finger and thumb nails, or in the fork of a cleft stick, pull out the vertebræ from inside with the forceps; then gradually turning the skin inside out, skin it up over the body, shoulders, and head, separating the fore limbs at the elbow joint, and taking great care not to cut it in passing over the eyes; skin it entirely off over the mouth, cutting carefully round the lips. Throughout the operation plenty of fine sawdust will be found of great assistance in keeping the hands, and consequently the fur, dry and unsoiled.

3. Clean the inside of the skin from blood, fat, &c., and then brush it all over with arsenical soap,* being especially careful that the insides of the limbs get some put on them.

4. Turn the skin back right side out and fill the cavity of the body with cotton-wool, putting it in as far as possible in one piece (in tropical climates a few drops of carbolic acid or other disinfectant should be put on the wool to keep off insects). Take care just to fill out the skin without overstretching it, and try to get all your skins filled out to about the same degree. Take a piece of straight wire long enough to extend from the front end of the belly opening to the tip of the tail; shapen, if necessary, one end of it, and wind round it enough cotton-wool to fill out the skin of the tail; then brush it with arsenical soap and push the pointed end down to the extreme tip of the tail-skin, and fit the near end into the belly, packing it round with the wool of the body. Put a small piece of wool into the empty skin of the arms and legs. Then stitch or pin up the opening down the belly.

5. If at all oily or greasy, the fur may be cleaned by being wiped with a rag dipped in benzine, and then having fine saw-

---

* In damp climates powdered oxide of arsenic should be used, as it helps to dry the skin, but caution should be exercised that it is not inhaled during the operation, or allowed to get under the nails.

dust gently rubbed into it, this being afterwards brushed on when dry.

6. Lay the skin on a board or piece of cork, draw out the fore-paws forwards and pin them down to the board by a pin passed boldly through the middle of the paw. Take care that they are pinned as close in to the sides of the neck or head as they possibly can be, in order to prevent their claws catching in other skins when all are packed together in boxes. Similarly pin back, soles downwards, the hind feet close by the sides of the tail. It is of considerable importance that neither fore nor hind feet should project laterally outwards nor should curl up in drying.

7. As the skin dries, try to get the face to assume as natural a shape as possible, and the ears to stand up in their natural position. Tie the label on to the ankle before pinning the skin down.

8. Disarticulate skull from trunk, *roughly* clean it, but do not boil it or separate the lower jaw, and then let it dry. Be very careful not to cut or injure it in *any* way; if there is not time enough to get the brain out through the natural hole at the back, it must be left in to dry up. Label the skull with a corresponding number to that of the skin, and afterwards, when both are quite dry, it may be tied on to the leg of the skin, or the skulls may be packed and sent home separately if so labelled as to prevent any possible confusion.

9. Pack the skins up carefully in small boxes when they are dry, with enough paper or, better still, wool, to prevent them shaking about; but if possible do not roll them up separately in paper *before they are dry*, as drying in paper gives the fur an unnaturally sleek appearance.

10. Bats should have their wings closely folded up on each side of the body, but in such a way as not to hide the fur of the belly. The thumbs should be made to point inwards or downwards, not outwards.

The skinning of larger animals must necessarily be somewhat different to the above, but the make-up of skins should be as described except that when the combined lengths of body and tail exceed 30 inches the tail should be bent up underneath the belly, while the fore as well as the hind feet should be directed backwards. The total length over all of

HINTS ON OUTFIT AND EXPENSES.

middle-sized, such as foxes, &c., should not, if possible, exceed 30 inches, any excess over this length being reduced by directing the hind feet forwards, or even by folding the skin up across the belly.

Suitable traps may be obtained from Mr. Spong, 106, Fulham Road, London, S.W. Pitfall traps, made out of a glass or metal jar sunk in flush with the ground, are also very successful.

Insects are usually collected by travellers, but it is difficult to obtain any information about them in this country. Miss E. Bowdler Sharpe[*] has kindly furnished me with the following outfit :—

	£	s.	d.
Cane net... ...	0	4	0
3 Spare nets	0	6	0
3 Packets chip boxes for moths in nests ...	0	3	0
2 Pairs Forceps	0	5	0
2 lbs. Naphthaline	0	1	0
3 Killing bottles, various sizes ...	0	6	6
	£1	5	6

I do not think it is possible for any one except a German ever to make the time spent on scientific collecting reproductive, pecuniarily speaking; nor without strong private influence and money can any ordinary collector hope to obtain the careful and elaborate descriptions, with the traveller's name rendered immortal by terminations in "ii," which are the most valuable feature of German

[*] I understand that Miss Sharpe, 345, Fulham Road, undertakes to name, or sell on commission if required, any entomological collections.

books of travel. This means that in the future Great Britain will be greatly behind all other nations in all scientific work. People inspired with a quite irrepressible love of nature may not be influenced by such considerations, but that is not a common characteristic in any country.

In regard to such goods as are required for paying one's way, it is not possible to advise, for savage fashions change more rapidly than those of civilised nations. I can only suggest "Amerikani" as the most generally useful cloth. In Uganda cheap made-up clothes, stationery, and small fancy articles are much better than any kind of cloth or beads. These latter are best obtained in London, while the "Amerikani" should be obtained in Zanzibar.

I found a yard of "Amerikani" usually enough to buy food for one man for twelve days, but the proportion has probably greatly changed even during this last year. It is best to ask the most recent traveller from the country one proposes to visit. In the Shiré highlands or any locality reached from them it would probably be best to wait until arriving at Mandala before bying anything of this kind. I was able to buy goods for English sovereigns in Ujiji or Tanganyika, and probably they would be current all over West and South Africa as well as British Central Africa, the Mediterranean coast, and East Africa as far inland as Uganda.

APPENDICES.

APPENDIX A.

NAMES OF NATIVE CHIEFS ABOUT RUWENZORI.

Kasagama	Sultan of Toru.
Makwenda	Msonje head.
A Son of the Queen	Butindi.
Sabeido	Butanuka.
Sons of the Queen	Wimi left bank and head.
,,	Lower Wimi and Butanuka.
Virungo...	Hima and right bank Mubuku.
Korohoro	Sebwe and left Mubuku.
Bakoran	Nyamwamba valley.
Kuliafiri	Island, Albert Edward.
Ambambe	Hill one day N.W. Salt lake.
Kalisa ...	} Near the Salt lake.
Kasuiri ...	
Kaihura	East side Albert Edward (1½ hours from Salt lake).

APPENDIX B.

ALTITUDES.

(Taken by two boiling-point thermometers.)

I took as the given altitude from which to reckon, according to the method advocated in the "Hints to Travellers," the level of the Victoria Nyanza. The test observations were taken at Purkiss' Station, Berkeley Bay, at 6 p.m., the 12th of January, 1894 (temperature 82°). They were 204·7 and 204·8, which, allowing instrumental corrections, gave a mean of 205, corresponding to 3,652 feet. I assumed the level of the Victoria Nyanza to be 3,900 feet.

The following series taken at Matschakos on the 5th and 6th of December at a (mean) temperature of 66°.

	A	B
6 p.m.	202·3	202·5
7 a.m.	202·4	202·6
10 a.m.	202·2	202·4
1 p.m.	202·2	202·4

gave a mean, after correcting diurnal variation and instrumental errors, of 202·55, corresponding to 5,043 feet.

From this one proceeds thus: 5,043 feet
 3,652 ,,
 ———
 1,391 ,,

This corrected for temperature is 1,521 ,,
To which add true altitude 3,900 ,,
 ———
 5,421 ,,

This should be the true altitude of Matschakos, if 3,900 feet is that of the Victoria Nyanza.

The Railway Survey gives for Matschakos, 5,400 feet and for the Victoria Nyanza 3,820 feet, which makes a difference between the results of 59 feet.

I also tested my results with Kinani, for which I obtained, taking the Victoria as 3,900 feet, an altitude of 2,109 feet. That of the Railway Survey is 2,200 feet—that is, 3,820 —2,200, or 1,620 feet below the Nyanza; my result was 3,900—2,109=1,791 feet, so that, in this case, the result

APPENDICES. 385

is not so near, but I am not sure if their observations were on the same spot.

My level of Tanganyika is undoubtedly also very near the true one, as seen by the summary below.

LEVEL OF THE VICTORIA NYANZA AS GIVEN BY VARIOUS OBSERVERS.

Speke (1862)	3,308 feet	Baumann	3,903 feet
Stanley *	3,450 ,,	Emin	4,000 ,,
J. Thomson	3,705 ,,	Pearson	4,002 ,,
Smith	3,734 ,,	Stanley (as computed Zöppritz)	4,058 ,,
Speke (1857)	3,740 ,,		
Stanley (1894)	3,808 ,,	Stanley (1878)	4,168 ,,
Railway Survey	3,820 ,,	Wilson	4,244 ,,

LEVEL OF TANGANYIKA.

Reichard	2,559 feet	Cameron	2,710 feet
J. Thomson	2,610 ,,	Scott Elliot	2,722 ,,
,,	2,618 ,,	Baumann	2,723 ,,
Livingstone	2,624 ,,	Hore	2,740 ,,
Popelin	2,665 ,,	,,	2,750 ,,
Wissmann	2,670 ,,	Stanley	2,756 ,,
Stairs	2,690 ,,	,,	2,770 ,,

LEVEL OF THE ALBERT NYANZA.

Emin	1,800 feet	Mason	2,296 ,,
Lugard	2,150 ,,	Stanley (1894)	2,400 ,,
Mason	2,198 ,,	,, (1878)	2,720 ,,

LEVEL OF THE ALBERT EDWARD NYANZA.

Stuhlmann	2,870 feet	Stanley	3,307 feet
Lugard	3,240 ,,		

* This figure was mentioned by Mr. Stanley in a discussion at the Royal Geographical Society. It will be observed that it differs by 718 feet from the figure given in his book in 1878.

APPENDICES.

List of Altitudes taken by the Author.

Mombasa—Victoria.

Taru	1,044 feet	Languru	5,683 feet
Buchuma	1,155 ,,	Naivasha	6,744 ,,
Marugu effundi	1,333 ,,	Gilgit	6,295 ,,
Maungu	2,232 ,,	Karia Ndouss	6,251 ,,
Mkuyuni	1,806 ,,	Camp Mbaruki	6,197 ,,
Ndi	2,419 ,,	Nakuru Camp	6,742 ,,
Mbuyuni	1,727 ,,	Maji moto	6,083 ,,
Tsavo	1,407 ,,	Mau 1st Camp	6,825 ,,
Ngomeni	1,717 ,,	Raomi	6,965 ,,
Masongoleni	2,871 ,,	Jackson's Camp	8,161 ,,
Nzowi	3,555 ,,	Kampi Aboit	7,788 ,,
Kiboko	2,775 ,,	Mtomweupe	5,969 ,,
Mto Andei	2,298 ,,	Kilelwa	4,772 ,,
Ngurugani	3,206 ,,	Mumia	4,436 ,,
Kilungu	3,922 ,,	Kampala	4,122 ,,
Kwasomi	4,587 ,,		

Ruwenzori.

Mubuku Camp	5,095 feet	Wimi Camp	6,126 feet
Kasagama's	5,296 ,,	,, ridge	7,828 ,,
Kivata Camp	6,615 ,,	Kaleha Camp	5,531 ,,
,, (forest)	7,461 ,,	Butagu (peat)	9,442 ,,
,, (bamboos)	8,694 ,,	,, hill	12,637 ,,
,, summit	10,057 ,,	NyamwambaC'mp	6,990 ,,
Yeria Camp	6,822 ,,	,, ,,	9,603 ,,
,, summit	10,644 ,,	,, rocks	11,141 ,,

Mpororo and Karagwe.

Kanye	5,158 feet	Karaingy Lake	4,303 feet
Bugara (plateau of Karagwe)	5,275 ,,	Kangennyi Lake	4,448 ,,
		Kakaruka	4,361 ,,

APPENDICES.

Urundi and Across to Tanganyika.

Branch Kagera	5,050 feet	Kiriba summit	7,896 feet
General average of		Maboko's	5,664 ,,
Urundi plateau	5,990 ,,	Tanganyika	2,722 ,,
Kiriba Camp	7,093 ,,		

Stevenson Road.

Tanganyika	2,722 feet	Nimbo	4,468 feet
Cherasia	5,030 ,,	Chitepa	4,075 ,,
Mambwe	5,575 ,,	Chambo	3,465 ,,
Pikombo	5,210 ,,	Kamissi	3,256 ,,
Movo	5,013 ,,	Village on Nyassa	
Muenso	5,036 ,,	alluvium	1,715 ,,
Tuliguu	4,679 ,,		

APPENDIX C.

SCIENTIFIC COLLECTIONS.

MAMMALS.—These have been handed to Mr. Oldfield Thomas.

BIRDS.—No satisfactory list has as yet been received, but the number was very small.

The following Reptiles and Batrachians were brought home by me and are described by Dr. Günther in " Annals and Magazine of Natural History," vol. xv., June, 1895.

Agama Gregorii, *Günth.* Buddu, 3,800–4,500 feet.
Mabouia striata, *Ptrs.* Uganda.
Chamæsaura tenuior, *Günth.* New species. Kampala Uganda.
Chamæleon senegalensis var. lævigata *Gray*, Kavirondo and Ruwenzori.
Chamæleon Elliotii, *Günth.* New species.
Grayia Smythii, *Leach* (?) Uganda.
Leptodira rufescens, *Gm.* Ruwenzori.
Boodon lineatus var. bipræocularis, *Gthr.* Uganda.

Elapsoidea Guentheri, *Bocage*. Ruwenzori.
Rana mascaraniensis, *Dum. Bibr.*
Pyxicephalus adspersus var. Shiré highlands.
Bufo regularis, *Reuss*. Buddu and Shiré.
Rappia viridiflava, *Dum. Bibr.* Uganda.
Rappia marmorata, *Rapp.* Shiré highlands.

A crab which I found common on Ruwenzori is, according to Professor Geoffrey Bell, Thelphusa berardi, *Savigny*.

This form also occurs in Dr. Gregory's collection from Leikipia. I found it in the small mountain streams.

INSECTS.

I brought home with me a large collection of all kinds.

Dr. Butler, of the Natural History Museum, has kindly supplied me with the following list of Lepidoptera.

Amauris damocles.
,, albimaculata.
,, Elliotii sp. nov.
Limnas chrysippus.
Mycalesis technalis.
,, vulgaris.
,, aurivillii sp. nov.
Enotesia sp.
Neocaenyra Gregorii.
Ypthrina itonia.
,, albida.
Charaxis candiope.
Hypolimnas mysippus.
Euralia anthedon.
,, dubius.
Junonia calescens.
,, galami.
,, Kowara.
pyriformis sp. nov.
,, infracta.
,, cebrene.
,, Gregorii sp. nov.

Hypanartia schœneia.
,, Hippomene.
Pyrameis abyssinica.
,, cardui.
Aterica cupavia.
Diestogyna ribensis.
Pseudargynnis duodecim-punctata.
Neptis melicerta.
Ergolis enotrea.
Eurytela dryope.
Cyrestis camillus.
Argynnis excelsior, n. sp.
Acræa sotikensis.
,, planesium.
,, eponina.
,, lycia.
,, iturina.
,, quirina.
,, pseudegina.
,, zetes.
,, egina.

APPENDICES.

Planema lycoa.
Polyommatus bœticus.
Catochrysops parsimon.
Everes jobatus.
Tarucus pulcher.
Catalinus margaritaceus.
Zizera Knysna.
„ gaika.
Allotinus zymna.
Hyreus lingenis.
„ falkensteinii.
„ palemon.
„ equatorialis.
Mylothris croceus sp. nov.
Nychitoma sylvicola.
Terias zoe.
„ regularis.
„ desjardinsii.
„ senegalensis.
Callonine hildebrandtii.
Teracolus lucullus.
„ bifasciatus.
Belenois mesentina var. aurigenii.
„ severina var. infida.
„ instabilis.
Nepheronia thalasmia.
Papilio demoleus.
„ Mackinnoni.
„ bromius.
Papilio erinus.
„ Jacksoni.
Serangera djœtala.
Pyrgus dromus.
Cyclopides midas.
Heteropterus Lepelletieri.
Padraona zeno.
Rhopalocampta unicolor.
Macroglossa trochilus.
Xanthospilopteryx deficiens.
„ incongruens.
„ hypercompoides n. sp.
Charilina amabilis.
Syntomis fantasia.
Epitaxis sp. nov.
Callarcha Elliotii sp. nov.
Pterotis tigrus.
Canopus bubo.
Argina amanda.
Eligma duplicata.
Malacosoma thoracica sp. nov.
Nonagria sp.
Remigia repanda.
Hypena velatipennis.
Zebronia podaliralis.
Coptobasis ovialis.
Acropteris erycinaria.
Abraxas rosea, sp. nov.
Aciptilus.

Some of these forms are very curiously related.

Dr. Butler ("Proc. Zool. Soc.") remarks that the Cyrestis and two species of Hypanartia referred to are connected, or may be expected to connect, with Madagascar species by transitional varieties.

The new species of Argynnis I found to fertilise the Viola Abyssinica on Ruwenzori. Dr. Butler says of this species: "There can be no doubt that this mountain form and that of Kilimandjaro had a common origin, but they are now too widely separated geographically to be regarded as one species, seeing that the differences of form and colouring between them are unquestionably constant."

BOTANICAL COLLECTIONS.

A large number of living plants were given to Kew Gardens, but no list of these has been received.

Herbarium specimens to the amount of 2,700 numbers have been brought home, but the naming of these is, I am sorry to say, delayed.

Fungi.—A number are in process of description by Miss Smith.

DIATOMS.

I have to thank Mr. Murray for the following list of diatoms observed in slides from Fuambo, East Africa, which were given to me by Mr. Carson, L. M. S.

Cymbella amphicephala var. hercynica, *Grun.*
Gomphonema gracile, *E.*
,, lanceolatum, *E.*
,, parvulum, *K.*
Navicula elliptica.
,, mutica, *K.*
,, Pupula, *K.*
,, rhomboides, *Bieb.*
,, radiosa var. tenella, *Bieb.*
,, viridula, *K.* (form approaching the var. rostellata).
Neidium affine, *E.*
,, amplirhynchus, *E.*
,, Hitchcockii, *E.*
Nitzschia Amphionys, *E.*
,, Brebisonii, *N.S.*, very scarce.
Nitzschia linearis, *W. S.*
,, Palea, *K.*
,, serians, *Rabh.*, very scarce.
,, Signoidea, *W. Sm.*
,, Scalaris, *W. Sm.*, a fragment seen.
Purnularia hemiptera, *K.*
,, instabilis, *A.*, *Sch.*, scarce.
,, microstauron, *E.*
,, stauroptera, *E.*, scarce.
,, subcapitata, *Greg.*
Stouroneis anceps, *E.*
,, Phœnicenteron, *E.*
Synedia Ulna var. Longissima, *W. Sm.*

APPENDICES. 391

APPENDIX D.

ARTICLES OF EXPORT.

It is important in dealing with the commercial side of articles of export to work out the freight and miscellaneous charges, as any article which does not reach the value so obtained may be at once disregarded.

The cost of freight, customs, charges, petties, interest, landing, warehouse, insurance and commission, will probably amount to at least £2 per ton, from either Mombasa or Chinde to London.

Now by the suggested railway from Mombasa to Uganda I have shown (in Chap. XVIII.) that the cost of freight cannot be taken as less than 5s. per train mile, that is to say, £165 per train for 657 miles, or assuming 50 tons to the train, £3 6s. per ton.

No article worth less than £5 6s. per ton can therefore be exported from Uganda. This must be carefully borne in mind, if one is to realise the relative importance of the articles mentioned below.

It is obvious that most food products must be at once left out.

BANANA.—The banana certainly yields very valuable products for local use (see p. chap. iii.), and may be grown anywhere up to 6,600 feet, but for the reason given above, there seems no chance of export.

IVORY.—The number of elephants now existing in British territory is not by any means a large one. I have attempted in the following to show where they are to be expected at present. They still exist not very far from Kikuyu to the north-east, and apparently extend all round Kenia, and from thence to Mount Elgon. I came across numerous traces of them in the Mau forest, between Raomi and the Guaso Masai. There are also probably some left in Sotik and Lumbwa. From Elgon they appear to be found along the Somerset Nile to Unyoro and the Albert

Nyanza (in Chagwe, occasionally, coming within four days' journey of Kampala). There appear to be plenty in the forest district round Kivari, between the Mpango river and Ruwenzori, and, as I have mentioned, they are always to be found somewhere between Chukarongo and Kasagama's on the east side of the mountain. A few probably still exist on the Nyamgassa river, a little north of the Salt lake. There are also a few on the eastern shore of the Albert Edward Nyanza, north-west of Makowalli's, and a little south-east of my route. This probably exhausts the localities for the East African sphere, unless some are still left on Kilimandjaro.

In the German sphere of influence there may be some on Kilimandjaro, but they are probably completely absent now from Karagwe, Urundi, and the whole eastern shore of Tanganyika.

The number remaining in the Congo country I cannot estimate, but there is a very rich ivory country lying between 2 and 6 degrees S. latitude, close to the border of the German sphere, and which is most easily reached from the north end of Tanganyika.

In British Central Africa elephants probably exist along the western border, from Lake Moero through the Angoni country, and possibly down to the Zambesi. The few remaining on Mlanje, and along the Lower Shiré river, will almost certainly be soon exterminated.

This southern ivory is said to be worth a third more than the hard "gendi" ivory of Unyoro.

The value varies very greatly from 120 to 180 dollars per frasila of 35 lbs. One tusk is said to have scaled 215 lbs., but usually they are from 50 to 70 lbs. weight.

Now, in estimating the amount of ivory to be expected in the future, one must carefully distinguish between the annual supply due to elephants shot, and the much larger amount which is obtained by buying the accumulations, often of many generations, of native chiefs. These stores may still yield a certain supply for perhaps ten years longer, but after that period they will almost certainly be exhausted.

Hence after that time ivory will only be obtained by shooting elephants. The elephant is so slow a breeder that the diminution of the ivory supply will proceed with extraordinary rapidity after this point is reached.

Now it is at the present time that Government will have the greatest difficulty in obtaining any revenue. Hence, obviously, the whole trade in ivory should be made a monopoly of Government. It is absurd for private traders to obtain the whole benefit of the work done by Government. Yet it is by no means easy to see how this is best arranged.

It is doubtful whether a European could obtain much more than his expenses in shooting elephants, as the places where this is possible are usually so very much out of the way (Toru, Unyoro, and round Kenia).

Unless this is done by Government servants, no sort of control can be kept over the destruction of young and female elephants, and even a very heavy tax on exported ivory will have no effect on this evil.

Of course, civilians with experience in trading should be immediately sent to obtain as much as possible for Government, in such places as the Salt lake, Unyoro, Sotik and Kikuyu. They could be paid by commission, with probably a very profitable result for the Government exchequer.

COFFEE.—This has been frequently commented on in the letterpress. M. L. Decle gave me a sample on which Messrs. Patry and Pasteur, 38, Mincing Lane, report as follows :—

"The Coffee is similar in appearance to that usually shipped from the West African Coast, but is of better quality, and, if properly prepared, would, no doubt, realise better prices. The present sample is exceptionally even, *i.e.*, all the berries are of equal size, and unless it has been picked shows extremely good quality.

"The value of 75s. to 77s. per cwt. we give you is for a quantity of, say, about 20 to 100 bags, a shipment of anything under 20 bags would not realise full value. Your samples contain a few beans which appear to have fermented on the way, and were evidently damp when gathered. This would, of course, greatly interfere with the sale of the Coffee, as it gives it a peculiar smell. There have been a few consignments of Uganda Coffee to our market, but of such small quantities that it is difficult to say if a steady demand would be established for same. We have no doubt, however, that fair prices would be realised, as our market is good, and likely to remain so for some time, owing to the comparatively small supplies. With regard to Banana meal, dried Bananas, Wimbi meal and maize, these articles are unknown to us, but we shall be very pleased to inquire for you of the best firm to go to, and we will write again later. We note you wish us to send the Coffee sample to the Imperial Institute; with your permission we will keep it a few days before doing so, so as to be able to show it to our friends who are interested and deal in coffee.

"The present value of fair Casengo (African) Coffee is about 73s. to 75s. per cwt."

Coffee is now grown by the natives in Uganda in a most haphazard and untaught way. It is of excellent quality, and would certainly repay export. So far as I could gather it occurs now only in Uganda, and chiefly in Buddu and the islands of the Victoria. I could not distinguish any great differences in climate or average soil between Kavirondo and Buddu, and it is, I think, almost certain that all the country bordering the Victoria Nyanza, within say 20 miles, is capable of growing good coffee. It is probable, to my mind, that the area suitable for coffee is enormous; but, as with all such products, one can only say with certainty that coffee plantations would pay in any spot when one has seen plants at least four years old in a thriving condition. That coffee-growing about the

APPENDICES. 395

Victoria Nyanza would pay is, however, I think, pretty certain.

PEAS AND BEANS.—I sent a collection of all the most usual kinds to Messrs. Roffy and Son, 41, Seething Lane, who report as follows: "It is very difficult to say with certainty what price these articles would realise, as they are all practically unknown, and it is possible that some of them might contain a percentage of poisonous oils; this would have to be ascertained before they would be marketable, and the only means of doing this would be to send over 100 sacks of each specimen to try the market with.

"For the coloured beans there would only be a limited sale at any time, and the present relative value is 16s. to 20s. per 480 lbs.

"The small white beans would make a better price (say about 25s. to 30s.), and the large brown bean 20s. to 25s. Of course they would have to be thrashed before they were shipped; if sent in the pods they would be almost useless. The small seed we do not know the value of, and cannot tell what it is. It probably would have no value in this country.

"Any other information you should require we shall be happy to supply you with.

"We should imagine that the soil and climate which produced these specimens would be capable of growing other articles to perfection, far more suitable for the London market, and we may mention that we had large quantities of African Mealies sent to us for sale, and these would always command a much better market than any of your specimens, and could be relied upon to sell readily at from 17s. to 23s. per 480 lbs."

It is, therefore, fairly obvious that, except under the most favourable conditions of transport, no export of these can pay.

TOBACCO.—The native tobacco is grown everywhere that there are natives, and seems to require the very slightest care in cultivation. It is strong and rank, and the natives have no idea naturally of curing it.

The French fathers have manufactured cigars from it; they also say that it is liable to the attacks of an insect, but I do not think from what I have seen that this is the case in most parts. I think the climate should make curing a matter of no difficulty, and the prospects of raising good tobacco seemed extremely probable.

Food Products.—*Vine.*— The trials by the French fathers have so far proved unsuccessful; but it seems to me probable that there are large areas in which vines would bear extremely well.

Wheat.—Wheat has been successfully grown in Uganda, both by Europeans and natives; and the ground on which I have seen it is a kind of soil and climate in no way differing from that found over enormous areas of the British sphere of influence. It is specially in Uganda, Unyoro, Usoga, Kavirondo, and parts of Toru that I have noticed the sort of soil and position in which it is grown in Uganda. It seems to me, therefore, that East Africa might in time become one of the great wheat-producing countries of the world; and even at present a European might find it profitable to cultivate wheat on a large scale for local demand. This demand would, however, be solely confined to Europeans, as the natives do not care for it.

Rice.—One of the things which appeared to me most astonishing in the whole district was the absence of rice. The enormous swamps of Uganda, Unyoro, Ankole, &c., where, in fact, almost every valley is filled by a broad morass, seemed to me to be natural rice fields of a most easily cultivated kind. In the interior of Madagascar rice is grown in similar swamps, at an altitude higher than that of most parts of Uganda, or more frequently about the same (4,000 to 5,000 feet). The cause seems simply to be the presence of the universal banana. It is true that rice cultivated at Kampala has proved a complete failure, but in the patch which I saw it had been suffered to get entirely dry, and had not been grown in a swamp at all. It seems to me that if the natives could be induced to take the trouble of cultivating it, a very large amount could be produced. Moreover, on the mountains Ruwenzori, Elgon, &c., in the forest region, a very large amount of rice could possibly be grown in the rainy season, though it is equally possible that the climate is too cold.

Millet is extremely common everywhere, and could be raised in enormous quantities.

Bulo, or Wimbi (Hungry Rice).—This is another cereal yielding a very excellent flour, which, in fact, forms a porridge superior to oatmeal. It is utterly unknown, so far as I am aware, in England, and there is, therefore, no prospect of export at present.

Indian Corn.—The cultivation is usually rather local. I have seen it chiefly in Uganda, Usoga, Kavirondo, and the Semliki valley. There is, however, little doubt that it could be produced over large areas in East Africa.

Sugar.—This plant is grown very successfully both in Uganda and Ukambane. Probably there is an enormous area suitable for its cultivation.

Tea.—This has never been tried in East Africa, to my knowledge. Certain spots, *e.g.*, Ruwenzori, seem well adapted to it, but the machinery required will be a very great difficulty.

Dyes.—The cheapness and enormous supply of Aniline dyes make it almost impossible to obtain any new article which is of commercial importance.

Indigo.—At any rate, two species of Indigofera, yielding Indigo, grow wild in Uganda, and there are many districts apparently suitable, but machinery is also required for this

Kula Wood.—The sample obtained at Niamkoria, Tanganyika, was submitted to Dr. Cooke, Imperial Institute, and by him to Professor Hümmel, at Leeds. From their report I extract the following remarks: " Its general behaviour is extremely like that of Camwood (*Baphia nitida*), Barwood (*Pterocarpus Soyanxii*), and Sanderswood (*Pterocarpus santalinus*). It dyes, however, with much greater difficulty, and the shades are yellower.

"These woods have been much employed in the past, but they are now doomed to disappear sooner or later, since they yield colours which are fugitive to light."

My specimen probably came from another species of Pterocarpus. It is possible it may be of use for French polishing, but it can scarcely be a matter of great importance. It is much used about Tanganyika, to give the faces of warriors and dancers a bold and ferocious appearance.

Ndawa.—The leaves are stripped and boiled, or steeped for two hours in hot water. The bark-cloth make in Usoga is dipped in this and assumes a dark blue colour.

Niwa.—The bark of a tree found in Ukambane. Mr. Christy says of this: "Oak-bark would give as good a colour. It is very bitter and heavy, and has much resin in it."

Dyeroot.—Root used in dyeing cloth at Kituta. This is probably a mordant and of no importance.

OILSEEDS.—*Palm oil.*—The tree is very common at the north-eastern extremity of Tanganyika, and extends along the east shore southwards nearly to Ujiji. I have no doubt that it could be produced easily about Lake Nyassa, where it is now found, *e.g.*, on the North-western shore, and also along the Zambesi river. It is possible that it might pay for export from these places, but I do not care to say so definitely in view of the heavy freight.

Sesame, Beniseed (*Sesamum Indicum*).—This plant is abundant though local in East Africa. It is probably capable of cultivation on an extended scale, but it is only in very favoured localities that the value would be large enough to make it a profitable article of export.

Castor oil, cottonseed oil, &c., could also be produced in many places.

GUMS.—A specimen of gum from Kampala, which is obtained from a very common tree in Uganda, "Mwafu," has a certain interest, as it was used by the Arabs as frankincense in their mosques.

Messrs. G. N. Souratty and Co., 38, Fenchurch Street, report as follows : "The one, the darker of the two wrapped in a leaf, appears to be a species of Gum Elemi, but from so small a sample it is almost impossible to judge of its quality or properties. Gum Elemi is imported from Manila in a softish viscid mass of strong pine flavour, white and yellowish in colour, and the value is now about 40s. per cwt.; consumption is not large. Your sample is very dark in colour, has somewhat the flavour of Elemi, but is much harder than that gum usually is."

The following were received from T. Watson, Esq., East African Scottish Mission, Kibwezi, January 6, 1894, and were reported on by Mr. T. Christy:—

"*Gum Mastic.*—Called Mkuyuni or Kurpini, 'a very common tree.' The juice of this tree if not allowed to congeal, and if then mixed with spirit, makes a delicious beverage. This sample is very dirty, but even in this state it is worth 2½d. to 3d. per lb.; if sorted and cleaned, much more. This is made from a species of fig.

"*Gutta or Euphorbia Gum.*—No. 1.—This sample is clean and has been well preserved. It shows good elastic properties.

"Nos. 2 and 3.—Two samples in tins are very fermented; difficult to report on.

"No. 4.—No. 4 tin looks like almadina, which comes here from Portugal and sells at 2d. to 3d. per lb. It greatly improves rubber and gutta when mixed with it. It is sometimes called 'Potato gum.'"

Of course, if this Euphorbia gum is really of any commercial value, it opens up very large commercial possibilities. The tree from which it is produced is extremely common throughout the whole of the thorn-tree desert as far as Kibwezi, and even Nzowi. I hear, however, from Mr. Jackson, at Kew, that these Euphorbia gums frequently contain a very large amount of resin, which makes them extremely brittle. The one imported to Liverpool is derived from a Morocco species, and appears to be chiefly used for adulteration.

The same, or a closely allied species of Euphorbia, appears again in the Victoria region, and is particularly common about the Albert Edward Nyanza.

FIBRES.—The markets for fibre are at present very fully supplied, and it is of course not to be expected that business men will take the trouble to reorganise their methods of supply unless there is a very marked superiority shown by a new product. Under these circumstances, I am afraid that none of those which I brought back can be expected to yield a large return. None appear to have a very marked superiority over well-known kinds, and the cost of transport would probably overbalance the greater cheapness of collection and preparation.

The banana fibres (Migomba of Suahili, Biei, Biamatoka of Waganda) may be at once dismissed from all consideration, as with the enormous supply available in the West Indies and the Canary Islands, no export from East Africa can possibly compete, even where the preparation, as it is not, in a thoroughly satisfactory state.

Dr. Cooke reports as follows :—

"*New Fibre from Niamkoria, Tanganyika.*— This is somewhat the same class as jute, and worth about £10 per ton in London."

The fibre is four to five feet long, and, according to my information, is produced from the bark of a tree and is probably easily prepared. I understand that the tree is not very common. There will scarcely be a sufficient margin of profit at present to export this fibre, as the cost of transport will not be far off this figure. Still a substance like this can be utilised to fill up trucks and steamers on the return journey when, as at present, cargo is not available.

Sanseviera cylindrica.*—This fibre seems to be very similar to that produced from the closely allied *Sanseviera guineensis.*

---

* I have not as yet heard whether this plant is *Sanseviera cylindrica*. Mr. Rendle is working out the plants of this order in my collection.

APPENDICES. 401

Dr. Cooke reports on it as follows (from Uganda specimens) : " No. 11—This is a strong fibre and worth about £16 per ton. No. 12—This might be worth about £20 per ton."

Mr. T. Christy reports as follows on specimens kindly sent to the coast for me by Mr. T. Watson, of Kibwezi : " This is a fairly well cleaned fibre, but might be much brighter and better ; it is worth £17 to £18 per ton."

The plant is extremely common in the thorn-tree desert, about Toru and as far as Kibwezi and Ukambani. It is there called "Makongo," or "M'bwau." It is also common throughout the Victoria region and Albert Edward, where it is called " Ngongwe."

The difficulty lies in preparation. Probably a suitable machine composed of a series of toothed rollers revolving in a stream of water, would enable it to be more rapidly and cheaply prepared than it is at present. I regard this as opening up a legitimate prospect of success. The plant could be cultivated in enormous quantities, without any difficulty, and the price is quite high enough to cover all expenses. It would be advisable for the Government official in Ukambane to be instructed to make careful experiments in preparation, and send home a trial shipment of some 20 tons.

Hyphaene fibre.—Mr. T. Christy reports as follows:—"If it is required for paper, every end where it is joined on to the stem must be cut off, because it has a formation of wax that crops up all through a paper when made with it. For hats and bags it is not well liked because it is found to be so short, and has so many ends and joins."

The plant is found commonly in East Africa.

Makonge madogo.—Mr. T. Christy says :—" This bundle arrived in bad order, not well cleaned, and was not strong, so no price could be fixed for it over £9 a ton."

The Ukambane name is " Kiongwa." The plant is, I think, common and, probably, should be tried again, as export might be possible.

Cotton.—A small specimen brought from South-East Victoria Nyanza, by M. L. Decle, is said to be worth about 1d. per lb., or, if better cleaned and free of seed, it might be worth 4d. a lb. This comes to £9 8s., or £37 12s. per ton, which should be well worth export if the latter price can be obtained.

The whole of the Victoria region should be capable of producing cotton.

In British Central Africa the alluvial of the Zambesi, Shiré, and Lake Nyassa appear to be well suited to this plant. There is an enormous area of these lands, but I have not had any definite accounts of the plant. A plantation at Mandala has been an utter failure, but I do not think it was either in a suitable place or well planted.

Kagogwa fibre.—Dr. Cooke reports that this is worth £13 per ton. The plant is very common in Uganda.

Kitogo or Papyrus fibre.—Dr. Cooke suggests that this might be useful if exported in the flat state. Of course if a price to pay very little more than the cost of import were obtainable, any quantity could be produced, as the numerous swamp-rivers of Uganda are composed of it. I doubt if this is possible however.

The following kinds brought back by myself are unfavourably reported on :—

Grass ropes, used in Kavirondo for cattle halters, and made from a species of Andropogon.

Tissiamena, used in making baskets in Kavirondo, and made from a species of Indigofera.

Bangi or Hemp (Cannabis sativa).—The plant is very commonly cultivated in the Victoria region and about the Albert Edward, and probably could be produced in any quantity.

Kafumbo.—Made from the bark of a species of Gomphocarpus. It is found in Uganda but is not very common.

Lusambia.—A common tree in Uganda *(Tecoma sp.),* which yields excellent timber. The fibre of the bark is much employed by the natives.

INDIARUBBER *(Landolphia sp.).*—I found this on Sotchi Blantyre. In 1893 about £250 worth was exported from Chiromo; there is said to be plenty in Southern Angoniland.

COCOANUT-PALM.—This is said to occur on Lake Nyassa, Lower Shore, &c. The tree in six or seven years yields something like £8 to £10 per acre (64 trees).

European vegetables seem to thrive everywhere in British Central Africa.

Fruits.—Strawberries and other small fruit can also be easily grown, but so far as I can gather, apples, peaches, and stone fruits generally do not succeed.

Cattle.—Seem at one time to have been abundant, specially on the Stevenson Road, and even on the plains about Karonga, but now have been much reduced in numbers by the disease. One of the most hopeful signs in the Shiré highlands is the manner in which they are beginning to replace porters for transport.

Horses.—It seems now proved that horses, if properly treated, can be used. This is an exceedingly important point for the future of the country.

Sheep, Goats, and Poultry.—Appear to exist everywhere and do well.

TIMBERS.—The following seem to be the more important timbers in British Central Africa:—

Katope (Eugenia sp.?).—A long and straight trunk with wavy grain, which is, unfortunately, liable to warp and to be attacked by insects.

Msuku (Uapaca Kirkii).—A good wood exceedingly common, but seldom more than 12 inches in diameter.

Cedar (Widdringtonia Whytei).—Apparently a very useful wood, but there is not a large amount left, as it seems only to grow above 3,000 feet on Mlanje, and is there chiefly confined to the ravines.

Mula, mpembu, Parinarium mobala.
Mpindimbi (Vitex umbrosa).
Mbawa (Khaya senegalensis).

INDEX.

Aborigines, rights of, 159
Abyssinia, 216
Acokantherin, 30
African Lakes Railway and Route, 318, 319, 321–329, 332–335, 398
African politics, 228, 229, 240, 241, 253, 269
Ainsworth, Mr., 15–17
Akenjaru, 253, 256, 262
Albert Nyanza, 336, 385
Albert Edward Nyanza, 227–231, 385
Alexandra Nyanza, 256
Alluvial plains, Kagera, 40, 41, 237
,, Nyassa, 289, 295, 296
,, Ruisamba, 84, 85, 123, 124
,, Semliki, 126
,, Tanganyika, 280, 281
,, Zambesi, 332
Altitudes, 383–387
, datum, 384

Altitudes, Albert Nyanza, 385
,, Albert Edward, 385
,, Kagera river, 325
,, Mombasa to Victoria, 386
,, Mpororo - Karagwe, 386
,, Ruwenzori, 386
,, Stevenson Road, 387
,, Tanganyika, 385
,, Urundi - Tanganyika, 387
,, Victoria Nyanza, 385
Ambambe, 133
America, Floral divisions of, 225, 266
Angola, 216, 218
Angoniland, 294
Ankole, 67, 69, 73, 198, 218, 229
Antari, 67, 70, 228
Antelope, *see* " Game "
Antelope-shapes, 17
Arabs, 69, 241, 275, 276, 277, 282, 283, 284, 285, 286, 287, 301, 302, 349

INDEX.

Archean rocks, 162
Articles of export, 391-403
Arum, 152
Athi, 14, 15, 17, 20
Attacks on men, 7, 156, 265

BABOONS, 112
Baker, Mr., 193
Bamboo, 31-32, 95-98, 100-137, 195, 270
Bamboo grass, see "Elephant grass"
Banana, 17, 47, 48, 111, 112, 140, 391
„ fibre, 400
Banghi, 402
Bark-cloth, 149, 150
Basalt, 169
Baumann, Dr., 322, 325
Bee (carpenter), 143
Beniseed, 398
Birds, 126, 127, 230
Bird-skins, 377
Bikira, 61, 68
Black ibis, 85, 89
Blindness, 288
Botanical collecting, 373-377
Botany, 90, 207-226, 271
„ see "Plant," &c.
Breaks of bulk, 336
British Central Africa, 181, 200-220, 288-304, 329
Buchanan, 292
Buchuma, 186
Buddu, 39, 60
Bugufu, 255-261
Buhimba, 244, 252
Bulo, 397
Bushbuck, 17
Busikosa, 265

Butagu, 134, 140, 154, 160, 168
Butanuka, 85, 122, 164, 168, 169, 171
Butenga, 244, 245
Butterflies, 63

CAMERON, Commander, 279
Canoes, 236
Carson, Mr., 289
Castor oil, 98
Cattle, 50, 233, 260, 264, 289, 297
Cattle ranching, 17, 21, 24, 85, 121, 198, 233, 403
Cedar, 403
Central Watershed, 70, 73, 176, 181, 197, 216, 217, 219, 231, 239, 243, 262
Changamvi, 5
Chiromo, 205, 206
Chukarongo, 127, 169
Climate, 20, 27, 44, 131, 133, 139, 197, 199, 200
„ Cocoanut-palm zone, 179
„ Coffee zone, 180
„ Colony zone, 180
Cloud, 96, 97, 190, 195, 196
Cloud-belt, 179, 220, 221
Coal, 177
Cocoanut-palm zone, 5, 21, 179, 186, 187, 201, 290, 296, 330, 333, 403
Coffee, 48, 49, 292, 293, 296, 393, 394
Coffee zone, 21, 36, 180, 183, 200, 293-295, 296
Collections, Appendix C., 387
„ botanical, 390
„ Crustacean, 388

INDEX.

Collections, diatoms, 390
" insects, 388-389
" reptiles and batrachian, 387
Colonisation prospects, 51, 115, 116, 131, 180-182, 187, 198, 237, 245, 257, 282, 293-296
Colony zone, 20, 21, 180, 187, 189, 197, 200, 289, 296, 331
Congo, 279, 309
Congo-Zambesi watershed, 181, 332
Cotton, 49, 297, 402
" seed, 398
Cow, 275
Crocodiles, 238
Currency, 54

Dances, 152, 259
Dengue fever, 188
Desert plants, 6
Dhow, 275, 278, 279
Donkeys, 20, 23, 28, 29
Ducks, 27
Dyes, 397, 398

Edwards, Captain, 302
Egypt (geology), 161
Eldoma, 30, 31
Elephants, 83, 84, 230, 391, 392, 393
Elephant grass, 65
Elgon, 15, 220
Elmenteita, 23
Emin, 190
English vegetables, 20, 50, 297, 403
Euphorbia, 6, 33, 179

Euphorbia gum, 399-400
Expenses of Expedition, 291
Export (see " Articles of "), 391

Fever, 78, 89, 139, 145, 182, 189, 197, 199, 201, 205, 212, 215, 235, 277
Fibres, 17, 400, 401, 402
Fires (grass), 33, 44, 124
Firesticks, 31
Fletcher, Mr., 302
Floral Regions, 210, 211
" Central Ridge, 216, 224
" Easterly Wet, 215, 220, 224
" Westerly Wet, 211, 212, 220, 224, 274
Flowering season, 208, 209, 210
Forest, 13, 14, 15, 31, 42, 43, 44, 63, 94, 96, 125, 137, 195, 212, 215, 217, 264
Fort Abercorn, 205
Fort Johnston, 205
French policy, 335
Frogs, 80
Fruits, 403
Fungi, 99, 100

Game, 9, 15, 17, 27, 34, 126, 248
Gazelle, 9
Geese, 27
Geology, 36, 42, 161-171, 231, 232, 234, 280
German Line, 318, 330
" methods, 69, 76, 157, 158, 160, 234, 235, 265, 339, 340

Gibb, Captain, 68
Giraffe, 9
Glaciation, 172, 175
Gneiss, 163-166, 169, 170
Goats, 403
Gordon Bennett Mountain, 196
Götzen, Baron von, 272
Grant, Mr., 66
Guaso masai, 28, 29
Guinea-fowl, 248
Gum, 398, 399
Gum-mastic, 399
Gutta, 399

HALL, Mr., 19
Hartebeest, 34, 248, &c.
Heather region, 97, 98, 138, 143, 195
Hindu moneylender, 343, 344, 350
Hippopotami, 236, 237, 238, 254
Horses, 403
Hot-spring, 102 (see "Winni")
Hungry rice, 397
Hyphaene fibre, 401

IBANDA, 168, 230
I. B. E. A. Co., 4, 11, 348
Indian corn, 397 (see "Maize") 397
Indigo, 397
Insect collecting, 381
   ,,   visitors, 98, 143
Iron, 38, 39, 165, 245
Ivory, 117, 287, 329, 391, 392, 393

JACKSON'S Hartebeest, 17, 27
Jigger, 188, 232, 238

KABBAREGA, 66, 152, 159
Kabogo, 278
Kafumbo, 402
Kagera, 40, 41, 61, 67-70, 163, 176, 235-239, 245, 248, 251, 253, 322-326
Kogogwa, 402
Kaihura, 164, 168-171, 228
Kajeti, 241, 242, 248, 251
Kakaruka, 244, 245, 251
Kakitombo, 236
Kampala, 67, 68
Karagwe, 41, 69, 70, 177, 198, 234, 239-254
Karaingy, 242
Karagwanzi, 134, 152, 159
Karemi, 278
Karimi, 133, 168, 170, 171
Karonga, 205
Kasagama, 85, 86, 104, 105, 107, 152, 159
Kasiliwamba, 234
Kasuiri, 10
Katanga, 333
Katara, 77
Katonga, 61, 165, 337
Katope, 403
Katwe, 169, 170 (see "Salt Lake")
Kavirondo, 23
Kenia, 220, 224
Kiarutanga, 164, 176
Kibona, 230
Kibwera, 251
Kibwezi, 13, 21, 205
Kidong, 24
Kikuyu, 17, 19, 21, 22
Kilimandjaro, 220, 224
Kilimanyambi, 273
Kirk, Sir J., 21

INDEX. 409

Kiriba, 194, 220, 257, 261, 262, 264, 267, 270, 272, 273
Kiromanyi, 60
Kishakka, 241, 256, 262
Kisozzi, 242
Kissigali, 133, 176, 239
Kitangule, 69, 70, 176, 285
Kitoboko, 70, 176, 323
Kitogo, 402
Kituta, 199, 205, 278, 288
Kivari, 92, 168
Kivata, 89, 91
Kola chocolate, 363
Kongoni, 1
Korohoro, 81
Kula wood, 397
Kuliafiri, 80, 106
Kungwe, 278
Kurumbutu, 61
Kyojia, 165

Labour, 53, 117, 299, 300
Langheld, 76, 234
Languages, 149
Languru, 14, 17
Laterite, 164, 263
Latoma, 176, 239, 323
Lawson Mountain, 194
Leopards, 82, 83
Levels of Tanganyika, 280, 281
Likumbuliyu, 290
Lions, 17, 86, 89
Livingstone Mountains, 282, 294
Locusts, 32, 100, 258, 300, 301
Long-necked animals, 10
Lubwas, 205
Lugard, Captain, 130
Lukala, 70, 75, 76

Lukojia, 81
Lusambia, 402

Maboko, 273
Machakos, 15, 22
Mackinnon Peak, 194
Maize, 48, 152, 397
Majimoto, 29
Makowalli, 228, 229, 233, 235
Makonge fibre, 401
Makwenda, 89
Malagarazi, 217, 261, 282
Malarial germs, 203-205
Mammalia, collection of, 378-381
Mandala, 290
Manson, 203
Marching, 2, 12, 61, 357, 358
Marshes, danger of, 205, 206
Masai Highlands, 14, 20, 23, 27, 35, 217, 219
Masongoleni, 13
Matope, 205
Mau, 15, 31, 33
Mazera, 5, 14
Mbawa, 103
Mean temperature, 183
Medicines, 359, 361
Meteorology, 178, 196, 197
Meronyi, 160
Mfumbiro, 176, 220, 261, 272
Mgaira, 244
Mill, Dr., 195, 202
Millet, 48, 152
Minerals of value, 171
Miocene, 221
Missions, 56, 199, 299, 343 353-355
Mkuyuni, 10
Mlanje, 217, 220, 224, 290

Moir, Mr., 290
Mombasa, 2, 3, 180, 185
,,   products of, 4, 5
,,   railway, 314, 318, 326, 327, 331, 335, 340
,,   tramway, 4
Monkeys, 146, 147
Monsoons, 184, 185
Mosquitoes, 80, 128, 132, 203-205
Mpango, 110, 169
Mpembu, 403
Mpindimbi, 403
Mpororo, 227, 229, 235
Msonje, 89, 91, 116
Msuku, 403
Mtagata, 239
Mubuku, 81, 82, 83, 145
Muhokia, 169
Mula, 403
Mumia, 36, 37, 164
Music, 276, 348
Musical instruments, 51
Mutilation, 232
Mwesi, 257, 258, 261-269, 273

Nabajisu, 61
Naivasha, 23
Nakuru, 23, 28
Nando, 20, 34, 36, 188
Native races —
    Angoni, 300, 301, 303
    Atonga, 298, 300, 303
    Awemba, 300, 302
    Makua, 303
    Masai, 16, 18, 20, 23-26
    Waankoli, 73, 74, 75, 232, 233
    Waganda, 37, 130

Native Races (continued)—
    Wagufu, 255-261
    Wahima, 55, 56, 74, 92, 93, 104, 105, 108, 109, 129, 252, 253, 259
    Wakamba, 16, 17, 24
    Wakaragwe, 73, 74, 240-242
    Wakavirondo, 36
    Wakikuyu, 15, 18, 19, 24, 37
    Wakondja, 104, 108, 111, 116, 121, 143
    Waleikipia, 26
    Wanandi, 26
    Wandarobbo, 30, 31
    Wanjuema, 106, 107, 129, 148
    Wanyamwesi, 306, 341
    Wanyoro, 116
    Waruanda, 228
    Warundi, 261-269
    Wateita, 10, 11
    Watoru (see " Wahima "), 132
    Watussi, 74, 75
    Wasuk, 26
    Wawamba, 129, 143, 148, 149-154
    Yao, 198, 199
Native rotation of crops, 37, 17, 112
    ,,   villages, 37
Naturalists' work, 146
Ndawa, 398
Nile watershed, 32
Niwa, 398
Ntsora, 124
Nyamgassa, 133, 170
Nyamsigira, 230

INDEX. 411

Nyamwamba, 82, 112, 166, 172
Nyankulu, 262
Nzowi, 13, 15, 20

OBSERVATIONS of living animals, 147
Oil-palm region (*see* "Cocoa-nut"), 181
Oil-seeds, 398
Orographic block, 166
Ostrich farms, 10, 17
Outfit, 356-382
,, bath, 366
,, bed, 365
,, boots, 361-362
,, canteen, 370
,, clothes, 361
,, Food, 362, 363, 364
,, guns, 369, 373
,, hats, 361
,, mapping, 369, 371
,, month's supply, 362
,, mosquito net, 371
,, packing, 357, 364, 365
,, photography, 369, 371
,, requisites list, 367-369
,, Salisbury stool, 371
,, table, 366
,, tent, 370

PACK animals, 309, 313, 316, 317
Palm-oil, 398
Papyrus fibre, 402
,, swamps, 40-42
Peas and beans, 395
Plant evolution, 6, 32, 35, 91, 93, 94, 95, 97, 99, 102, 103, 207, 208, 209, 222
,, distribution, 97, 98, 101, 207-226

Porters, 2, 11, 12, 305, 341, 359, 360
Poultry, 403
Premolar, 82, 145
Python, 238

RAIDS, 116, 152, 160, 228, 229, 259, 285
Railways, 303, 310-315
Rainfall, 101, 117, 183, 184, 189, 197
Rent, 54
Rhinoceros, 17, 246-248
Rovuma, 215
Royal Society application, 1
Ruamiga, 230
Ruampala, 70, 78, 235
Ruansindi, 168, 230
Rubata, 229, 231, 232
Rubber, 5, 179, 298
Rufue, 236
Rufui, 176
Ruisamba, 79, 84, 92
Ruizi, 77, 165, 176
Rumaliza, 284
Rumanika, 240, 241, 324
Rumonge, 285
Rusanga, 165
Ru-Vuvu, 253, 255, 256, 312, 327
Ruwenzori, administration of, 121, 122
,, climate of, 90, 93, 94, 188-190
,, cost of, 121
,, discovery of, 190 193
,, first sight of, 78
,, formation, 170
,, geology, 166, 167

INDEX.

Ruwenzori, native chiefs on, 382
    North-east valleys, 81
    ,, value of, 116–118
    ,, view of, 70

SABAKHI, 187, 215
Sahara Sea, 222, 223
Salt Lake, 122, 127, 128, 131, 169, 236
Salt stream, 124
Salutations, 268
Samia, 164
Sand grouse, 17
Sangwe, 241, 243
Sanseviera fibre, 400–401
Scholl, 166
Sebwe, 81
Seeds, distribution of, 91
Sefu bin Raschid, 277
Semliki, 122, 133, 134
Scribombo, 229, 234–236
Sesame, 398
Sheep, 403
Shiré, 215, 290
Shiré Highlands, 32, 181, 332
Sikhs, 302
Slavery, 107, 109, 122, 284–287, 351, 352
Snow, 175
Somaliland, 219
Somerset Nile, 337, 338
South African geology, 162
Speke, 240
Stairs, Captain, 166
Stevenson Road Plateau, 200, 218, 288, 289, 294, 332
Stokes, Mr., 233
Stuhlmann, Dr., 140

Suahili, 77, 107, 139, 228, 305–341
Sugar, 397
Sunbirds, 98, 99
Sunstroke, 251, 252
Superstitions, 76, 155, 260
Swamps, 62, 63, 263, 336, 337

TANGANYIKA, 181, 198, 199, 215, 217, 264, 270–287, 333
Tea, 49, 397
Temperature and health, 202, 203
Teneriffe, 224
Tengetenge, 154, 157–159
Thefts, 12, 155, 267
Thermometer observations, 178, 179
Thorn-tree Desert, 5, 6, 186, 219, 330
Tiasimbe, 61
Timber, 27, 31, 64, 289, 403
Tin boxes, 364, 365
Tissiamena, 402
Tobacco, 21, 49, 232, 395
Trade goods, 382
Transport, 41, 117, 118, 121, 236, 245, 305–319
Transvaal, 217
Tree forms, 202
Trees and fever, 206
Tsavo, 11, 22
Tutschila, 291

UGANDA, 50
Uhha, 257, 262
Ujiji, 285
Ukambani, 13
Umbrella, 78
Uriji, 245, 246, 251

INDEX. 413

Urundi, 198, 258, 261-269, 322
Usige, 275
Usoga, 38, 39, 50
Usongora, 104

VALLEY-SHAPES, 172
Victoria Region, climate of, 44, 181, 188
,, cultivation in, 42, 43, 49
,, elevation of, 165
,, extent of, 35
,, flora of, 35, 219
,, forests of, 43
,, formation of, 40
,, geology, 163-165
,, imports, 59
,, Nyanza, 39
,, plateau of, 78, 231
,, products, 43
,, prospects, 59, 60
,, rainfall, 47
,, sinking of Nyanza in, 40
,, transport, 41
,, valleys, 33
Vijongo, 89, 164, 168, 176

Villa Maria, 61, 68
Vine, 396
Virungo, 109
Visanganwi, 256, 262, 263, 265
Visegwe, 170, 229
Volcanic craters, 124, 127, 128, 133, 167-170, 230

WAGGON transport, 310-313, 317
Wamaganga, 77
Water, 10
Waterbuck, 84
Water carriage, 306-308, 321
Watt, Mr., 17, 19
Weapons, 30, 260
Weissmann, Herr, 209
Werowangi, 241, 242
West African geology, 161
Wheat, 20, 21, 48, 289, 297, 396
Wimbi, 397
Wimi, 93, 100, 101, 112, 117, 190, 212
Windermere, 248
Wind on plants, 95
Winds, prevalent, 185, 195, 196
Woman, status of, 113, 114

YERIA, 93, 100, 110

ZAMBESI, 215
Zebra, 17, 27, 248

www.ingramcontent.com/pod-product-compliance
Lightning Source LLC
Chambersburg PA
CBHW051735300426
44115CB00007B/571